Deryck Beyleveld, Marcus Düwell
The Sole Fact of Pure Reason

Kantstudien-Ergänzungshefte

Im Auftrag der Kant-Gesellschaft
herausgegeben von
Manfred Baum, Bernd Dörflinger,
Heiner F. Klemme und Konstantin Pollok

Band 210

Deryck Beyleveld, Marcus Düwell

The Sole Fact of Pure Reason

Kant's Quasi-Ontological Argument for the Categorical Imperative

DE GRUYTER

ISBN 978-3-11-099679-1
e-ISBN (PDF) 978-3-11-069134-4
e-ISBN (EPUB) 978-3-11-069142-9
ISSN 0340-6059

Library of Congress Control Number: 2020945680

Bibliographic information published by the Deutsche Nationalbibliothek
The Deutsche Nationalbibliothek lists this publication in the Deutsche Nationalbibliografie; detailed bibliographic data are available on the Internet at http://dnb.dnb.de.

© 2022 Walter de Gruyter GmbH, Berlin/Boston
This volume is text- and page-identical with the hardback published in 2020.
Typesetting: Integra Software Services Pvt. Ltd.
Printing and binding: CPI books GmbH, Leck

www.degruyter.com

Preface

For a long time we have been convinced that the methodology of Kant's transcendental philosophy is that of eliciting the strict requirements of human agential self-understanding and subjecting them to critique. Thus, when Kant says that the categorical imperative is an a priori synthetic proposition, we maintain that he considers acceptance of it to be a strict requirement of human agential self-understanding. However, until relatively recently, we have been puzzled as to what exactly Kant's argument for this contention is. This said, we have never seen good reason not to take him at his word that the argument he presents and relies on for the categorical imperative in *Critique of Practical Reason* (*CPrR*) is the same argument he presents in *Groundwork of the Metaphysics of Morals* (*GMM*) (see *CPrR* AK 5:8). For reasons we will make clear in this volume, we have always found implausible and founded on very shaky grounds the widely accepted view that *CPrR*, by reasoning from the moral law to free will, abandons *GMM*'s claim that the categorical imperative is established by a transcendental deduction. However, we struggled to provide a convincing portrayal of what Kant does in *GMM* and *CPrR* that verifies his concordance claim until we connected his claims about the *sensus communis* to his argument for the categorical imperative while reading *Critique of the Power of Judgment* (*CPoJ*) with students on the Research Masters Course in Philosophy in Utrecht in 2012. Once this connection is made, what Kant says about the *sensus communis* provides strong support for the view that the categorical imperative is the maxim of human agential self-understanding (the maxim to render thinking from the viewpoint of the particular agent that one is consistent with thinking of oneself from the viewpoint of an agent *per se*). It also prompts re-evaluation of what Kant is designating when he refers to common human understanding or common human reason in *GMM* and *CPrR*. As soon as we hypothesized that he was, thereby, referring to the *sensus communis* of *CPoJ*, a completely different picture of the commonly accepted structure of the argument of *GMM* emerged. We had assumed along with almost everyone else that, in the first section of *GMM* (*GMM* I), by claiming that the categorical imperative is found in common human understanding, Kant merely claims that

(1) people very generally think that there is a categorical imperative;
(2) *GMM* II reveals (by analysis of the concept of a categorical imperative) what those who believe that there is a categorical imperative must accept about it; and
(3) *GMM* III attempts to show that all human agents must believe that there is a categorical imperative.

But thinking of the common human understanding of *GMM* I as the *sensus communis* of *CPoJ* suggests a different view. When, e.g., Kant says that the categorical imperative is found entirely a priori in common human understanding (*GMM* AK 4:406), he means that it is found in exercising the a priori powers of mind of the *sensus communis* (which he says are powers all who possess humanity in their persons must be thought to have [*CPoJ* AK 5:293–294]). And this gives rise to the thought that he thinks that the categorical imperative is given to human agents as something they must accept by understanding the concept of the *sensus communis* viewed as the concept of human agential self-understanding; indeed, that the categorical imperative is the imperative to act in accord with the strict requirements of agential self-understanding. On this basis, because he maintains that understanding the concept of a categorical imperative requires human agents to think that they are governed both by the universal law of mechanism and that they have free will (which they cannot be in the same aspect), the task for *GMM* III is merely to show that such a conception of what it is to be a human agent is coherent. We then found that thinking about the structure of *GMM* in this way makes sense of some other things that Kant says in *GMM* and *CPrR* that are otherwise very puzzling. Chief amongst these are two things. The first is why Kant thinks that he can establish as undeniable the actual, as against the merely possible, existence of the categorical imperative simply by showing that it is rationally possible (coherent) to consider that one has free will. The second is how he can ground the categorical imperative in pure practical reason (the law of which is the moral law *as such*) by reasoning that is not viciously circular, given that he views the categorical imperative as the moral law as such *in its application to finite heteronomously affected agents*. Above all, thinking about the structure of *GMM* in this way enables us to see that the argument for the categorical imperative in *CPrR* has, as Kant claims, the same logical structure as the argument in *GMM*.

We do not claim that our interpretation of Kant's argument is entirely novel. Indeed, there are many of its distinctive elements in writings, most notably, of Lewis White Beck, Pauline Kleingeld, Onora O'Neill, Klaus Steigleder, Kenneth Westphal, and Michael Wolff. What we think we achieve in this volume is to put these elements together in a more complete and consistent way than other commentators have done by the way in which we link Kant's claims about the common human understanding to his claims about the *sensus communis* of *CPoJ* and the degree of importance we attach to understanding his argument for the categorical imperative in relation to the role it plays in his moral argument for the existence of God.

Numerous colleagues and friends have commented on aspects of this book in earlier drafts and presentations in colloquia and conferences. We owe particular thanks to Joel Anderson, Patrick Capps, Rutger Claassen, Dascha Düring, Liesbeth Feikema, Joshua Jowitt, Pauline Kleingeld, Cheryl Lancaster, William Lucy, Sem de Maagt, Tim Meijers, Shaun D. Pattinson, Klaus Steigleder, Stuart Toddington, Kenneth Westphal, and Paul Ziche. Henk van Gils helped us in getting an overview over the literature. We have to thank Charlie Blunden, Bram Galenkamp, and Sjaroes Salimian for preparing the index and Nikè van Wijck for proofreading the files. A particular thanks we owe to Jan van Ophuijsen for his enormous work in carefully correcting the files.

Deryck Beyleveld
Marcus Düwell
November 2019

Contents

Preface —— V

Chapter One
Introduction – Setting the Scene —— 1

Chapter Two
Kant's Argument for the Categorical Imperative Constructed —— 35

Chapter Three
A Priori Synthetic Practical Propositions as Strict Requirements of Human Agential Self-Understanding —— 57

Chapter Four
Kant's Justification in the Context of His Critical Philosophy as a Whole —— 71

Chapter Five
The Moral Law as the Sole Fact of Pure Reason in *CPrR* —— 85

Chapter Six
The Moral Law as the Sole Fact of Pure Reason in *GMM* —— 111

Chapter Seven
Klaus Steigleder and Michael Wolff —— 141

Chapter Eight
Owen Ware —— 175

Chapter Nine
How Valid is Kant's Argument? —— 187

Bibliography —— 199

Subject Index —— 205

Persons Index —— 211

Chapter One
Introduction – Setting the Scene

Preliminary Remarks

According to Immanuel Kant, the *Groundwork of the Metaphysics of Morals* (*GMM*)[1] is 'nothing more than the search for and establishment of the supreme principle of morality' (AK 4:392). He refers to this principle as 'the moral law', 'the categorical imperative', or as 'the fundamental law of pure practical reason',[2] for which he provides several formulae, including that which is widely known as the Formula of Universal Law (FUL):

> [A]ct only in accordance with that maxim through which you can at the same time will that it become a universal law.[3] (*GMM* AK 4:421)

---

1 Apart from *Critique of Pure Reason*, where we employ the customary A:B citation, *Blomberg Logic* (Kant 1777) and 'What Does It Mean to Orient Oneself in Thinking?' (Kant 1786), our citations employ the numbering of the German Academy edition (AK volume number: page number). We refer to Kant's works by title rather than date, and use the following abbreviations: *Anthropology* for *Anthropology from a Pragmatic Point of View*; *GMM* for *Groundwork of the Metaphysics of Morals*; *CPuR* for *Critique of Pure Reason*; *CPrR* for *Critique of Practical Reason*; *CPoJ* for *Critique of the Power of Judgment*; *Religion* for *Religion Within the Bounds of Mere Reason*; and *MoM* for *Metaphysics of Morals*. In the Bibliography, Kant's texts are listed according to the dates of their original publication.
2 Kant often treats the terms 'the moral law' and 'the categorical imperative' as synonyms. But, as we understand him, the moral law *as such* (vs the moral law *as the categorical imperative*) is the fundamental law of pure practical reason (which governs a purely rational will as a law of its nature), and the categorical imperative is the fundamental law of pure practical reason as it governs finite incompletely rational embodied beings (which human beings are). This is very important, so we will try to draw attention to it whenever it matters, even at the expense of some inelegant phrasing. When we refer to the 'moral law' without qualification we imply that it does not matter whether it is the moral law as such or the categorical imperative that we are referring to. Kant is less transparent. Michael Wolff (2009), who also insists on the importance of correctly understanding the relationship between the fundamental law of pure practical reason, the moral law, and the categorical imperative, expresses it rather differently. (See Chapter Seven.)
3 Much has been written about what the FUL permits or requires an agent to do. We think that the FUL permits an agent to guide his, her, or its actions by a practical precept (a maxim) that prescribes what it is permissible, impermissible, or required for the agent to do as a matter of principle only if the agent is rationally able, at the same time, to think that all other agents are rationally able to accept guidance of their actions by the same maxim.

Kant's moral theory deals with the following main questions:
A. If a categorical imperative exists, what is its nature and content?
B. Is it possible for a categorical imperative to exist?
C. Does a categorical imperative exist?
D. Given an affirmative answer to C, what must human agents believe about the nature of the world and their own existence?
E. What rules does the categorical imperative (the FUL) require and permit human agents to adopt in the circumstances and conditions of real life?

A, B, and C are the main concerns of *GMM* and Chapter I of Book One of *CPrR* (with *CPuR* and *CPoJ* also contributing to Kant's answers to B and C). Aspects of D are involved in his answers to A, B and C, from which further implications are drawn mainly in the rest of *CPrR*, the final sections of *CPoJ*, *Religion*, and *Anthropology*. E is the primary concern of *MoM* (although some illustrations are provided in *GMM*, *CPrR*, and elsewhere).

This book is about Kant's views on C, which derive from his answers to A and B. Its concern is not with their validity, but with what they are, about which there is considerable scholarly disagreement, much of which revolves around whether or not he holds the same views in *GMM* and *CPrR*. We maintain that Kant gives or presupposes the same answers to A and B, and the same affirmative answer to C and justification for it in both *GMM* and *CPrR*. Furthermore, we contend that, in order to appreciate this and understand how he justifies his answer to C, it is necessary to place his justification of the categorical imperative in the context of his

---

However, when stating the FUL, Kant's depicts a maxim in a footnote in a way that does not straightforwardly fit this understanding of what a maxim is, for he tells us there that a maxim is 'the subjective principle of acting', and that a subjective principle is one that

> contains the practical rule determined by reason conformably with the conditions of the subject (often his ignorance or also his inclinations), and is therefore the principle in accordance with which the subject acts. (*GMM* AK 4:421 fn)

Furthermore, a maxim 'must be distinguished from the *objective* principle, namely the practical law', which is universal, in that it is 'valid for every rational being, and the principle in accordance with which he *ought to act*, i.e., an imperative' *(GMM* AK 4:421 fn).

This cannot be taken to be a definition of a maxim (despite the fact that Kant describes it as such at, e.g., *CPrR* AK 5:19) because it employs two senses in which a principle can be subjective. In one sense, it is what the subject (agent) adopts *vs* what the subject ought to adopt. In the other, it is what the subject ought to adopt *vs* what all subjects ought to adopt. Furthermore, if a maxim is necessarily distinct from a universal law it is impossible for a permissible maxim to be willed at the same time (as the FUL requires) as a universal law. We discuss these matters further in Chapter Seven.

critical philosophy as a whole, in which it is particularly important to understand what his methodology for justifying an a priori synthetic practical proposition is, for that is how Kant consistently describes the categorical imperative. In relation to this, we maintain two things. First, interpretations of Kant's justification of the categorical imperative that view it as an argument from human agential self-understanding in both *GMM* and *CPrR* are on the right lines, but only the constructions of Onora O'Neill (esp. 1989) and that of Kenneth Westphal (e.g., 2016) – which largely follows O'Neill – interpret human agential self-understanding in terms of what Kant designates as the three maxims of the '*sensus communis*' in *CPoJ* (AK 5:293–294), which is vital. Secondly, the relation between Kant's answer to C and those aspects of his views on D that concern the existence of God and human immortality reveals what he means when he says that 'the moral law' is given to human agents as the sole fact of pure reason in *CPrR* (AK 5:31), and also explains why he does not also designate 'the moral law' 'the sole fact of pure reason' in *GMM*. However, only one other commentator who views Kant's justification as an argument from human agential self-understanding makes this connection – Michael Wolff (2015).

In this chapter, we first provide a brief overview of extant interpretations of Kant's views on the status and justification of the categorical imperative to identify the range of questions that these interpretations raise. Secondly, we introduce some features of our account that must be understood to locate our construction in relation to its competitors. Thirdly, we state *what* we consider Kant does in order to justify the categorical imperative, which is preliminary to our presentation of *how* we think he does this in Chapter Two. Fourthly, we reveal how we intend to defend our construction. In the process, we spell out in some detail the most widely accepted set of constructions, which we call 'the widely accepted view' (the *WAV*), which we will have already introduced; provide reasons for operating on a defeasible default presumption that the *WAV* is mistaken; and use this as a basis for identifying a select group of rival interpretations that also reject the *WAV* that will require various degrees of special attention in defending our construction. Finally, we outline what we will do in the remaining chapters of this book.

A Brief Overview of Interpretations

Dieter Henrich (1960) and Karl Ameriks (1981) provide the most influential versions of the *WAV*.[4] Briefly stated, according to all versions of the *WAV*, in *GMM*,

---

[4] Other commentators who espouse versions of the *WAV* include: H. J. Paton (2000); W. D. Ross (1954); T. C. Williams (1968); Dieter Henrich (1975); Christine Korsgaard (1989); Henry E.

Kant argues that the existence of the categorical imperative is shown to be rationally undeniable by a 'transcendental deduction'. However, by the time he writes *CPrR* three years later, he has decided that this argument is unsound. Instead, *CPrR* portrays the categorical imperative as 'the fact of reason',[5] thereby
(1) rejecting both the possibility of, and the necessity for, a transcendental deduction of the categorical imperative; and
(2) reversing the cognitive relation between being bound by the moral law/categorical imperative and having free will that he argued for in *GMM*.

Regarding (2): *GMM* contends that human agents necessarily presuppose that they have free will; that having free will and being bound by the moral law are reciprocal concepts; thus, that human agents necessarily presuppose that they are bound by the moral law as the categorical imperative (AK 4:446–448). On the other hand, *CPrR* states that the moral law is the *ratio cognoscendi* of free will (AK 5:4 fn), which is to say that agents know that they have free will only because they already know that they are bound by the moral law, not the other way around.

As for the moral law, it is given to human agents as the fact of reason (AK 5:31). Commentators who accept the *WAV* provide different accounts of what Kant means when he says this and of the consequent cognitive status that he thinks any belief that there is a categorical imperative possesses. They also differ in their assessment of the success of what they take to be this new justification of the categorical imperative, most holding that, while the argument of *GMM* is very problematic, the argument of *CPrR* is worse. One exception to this is Henry E. Allison (1990), who considers that *CPrR* not only improves on *GMM* but is reasonably successful, and we will consider his construction in Chapter Five.

We think that the *WAV* is mistaken; and we are not alone in opposing it. Early gainsayers include Lewis White Beck (1960a and 1960b), Michael H. McCarthy (1982), and Onora O'Neill (1989, 2002), and there are signs that the tide of opinion is beginning to turn against it. This is indicated (in different ways) by the contributions of Klaus Steigleder (2002, 2006), Michael Wolff (2009, 2015), Pauline Kleingeld (2010), Heiko Puls (2014), Owen Ware (2017), and Jochen Bojanowski

---

Allison (1990); Andrews Reath (1997, 2011); Dieter Schönecker (1999, 2006, 2013, 2014); John Rawls (2000); Stephen Darwall (2006); Paul Guyer (2007); David Sussman (2008); Allen W. Wood (2008); and Jens Timmermann (2010).

5 While most commentators depict Kant as holding that the moral law is a/the fact of reason, Kant never refers to the moral law itself as 'a/the fact of reason'. He only ever refers to it (and free will itself) as 'the fact of pure reason' or as 'the sole fact of pure reason'. It is moral *consciousness* (consciousness of the fundamental law of pure practical reason) that he refers to as a fact of reason. We consider this nuance to be significant, for reasons we will explain later.

(2017).⁶ All of the latter six scholars, with the exception of Kleingeld, hold that Kant argues, in *both GMM* and *CPrR,* that the moral law is the *ratio cognoscendi* of free will, free will the *ratio essendi* of the moral law.⁷ All bar Bojanowski, including Kleingeld, hold that there is justificatory methodological continuity between the two works, but not all agree on what Kant's justificatory methodology is. Puls and Ware claim that Kant does not attempt to establish that acceptance of the categorical imperative is rationally necessary for all agents in either work, merely (on different grounds) that it is rationally necessary only for those agents who are already morally committed in both works. Against this, Steigleder, Wolff, and Kleingeld maintain that Kant persistently employs a transcendental deduction to establish the rational necessity of acceptance of the categorical imperative for all human agents. On the other hand, although Bojanowski considers that Kant persistently holds that acceptance of the categorical imperative is rationally necessary for all human agents, he claims that *CPrR* dispenses with a transcendental deduction to demonstrate this.

If this is a bit difficult to take in, more detail will be provided about all nine of these *non-WAV* constructions and the *WAV* later. We draw attention to these views now merely to show that various questions raised by Kant's views on the justification of a categorical imperative are still open to debate. These questions include the following:

1 What does Kant understand by a transcendental deduction/justification of a categorical imperative?
2 Does he think that a deduction/justification is possible/necessary?
3 What cognitive status does he assign to the FUL?
4 Does he provide substantially different answers to these questions in *GMM* and *CPrR*?

---

6 See also, e.g., Deryck Beyleveld 2017, in which an early version of the construction of the present book is suggested, but not fully argued for, being presented as a Gewirthian interpretation of Kant for the purposes of explaining Alan Gewirth's methodology of dialectical necessity for justifying a categorical imperative (see Gewirth 1978) and the way in which Gewirth differs from Kant on the content of the categorical imperative. Kenneth R. Westphal (e.g., 2016) is also worth noting. He largely follows Onora O'Neill's account, which he uses to argue that Hegel reconstructed and developed Kant's views on the justification of the categorical imperative rather than rejecting them.

7 The *ratio cognoscendi* of free will is the basis on which the existence of free will is known or justified. The *ratio essendi* of the moral law is the ontological property that agents must have in order to be able to 'encounter' the moral law in themselves (*CPrR* AK 5:4 fn); it is the property that enables them to act, not only in accord with the moral law, but for the sake of the moral law and nothing else (e.g., *CPrR* AK 5:81); it is the causality of pure practical reason (e.g., *GMM* AK 4:461; *CPrR* AK 5:48, 55–56).

Implicated in these questions (as we have already intimated) is another question, which is particularly relevant for this book: namely, 'What does Kant think is the relationship between the categorical imperative being established as an a priori synthetic practical proposition and its being given as the sole fact of pure reason'?

Some Explanatory Briefing for Our Construction

Later in this chapter, we position our own construction in relation to those we have indicated. However, it rests on some theses about Kant's views on these questions that we need to give some indication of in order to be able to state clearly, even for mere positioning purposes, what it is.

First, we hold that Kant's view on justification in philosophy *generally* is based on the claim that all statements that take an object (i.e., which have a referent) are made by a thinking subject.[8] Philosophy consists of critical self-reflection on judgments and the possibility of making them, and the questions that Kant poses for his critical project are derived from his view that there are essentially three different types of judgments (theoretical, practical, and aesthetic). This claim is not uncontroversial; but it is not novel, because it is shared by a number of contemporary scholars including David Bell (1987), Onora O'Neill (1989, 1992), Beatrice Longuenesse (1998), Klaus Steigleder (2002), Michael Wolff (2009, 2015), Wayne Waxman (2014, 2019), Rudolf Makkreel (2015), and Kenneth Westphal (esp. 2016). In a transcendental deduction, Kant is not interested exclusively in the semantic content of concepts *in vacuo,* and his claim that transcendental deductions validate a priori synthetic propositions is at odds with the doctrine (which informs much current analytic philosophy) that what can be known a priori can be ascertained only by understanding the semantic content of concepts *in vacuo* (see, e.g., Steigleder 2002, xiii). Kant *is* interested in the semantic content of concepts in a transcendental deduction; but his distinctive focus there is on understanding how concepts can/must be understood by beings able to think of themselves as able to make judgments in and about their thinking, believing, acting, and anything else that necessarily involves representation by an 'I'. As such, his critical project does not derive its conclusions from taken for granted basic propositions, but is

---

8 According to Kant, it is by virtue, and only by virtue, of 'the fact that the human being can have the "I" in his representations . . . [that] he is a *person*' (*Anthropology* AK 7:127). To be able to have the concept of 'I' is to have the faculty of thinking, which is that of understanding. Furthermore, before a child starts to refer to 'himself' by means of 'I', 'he merely *felt* himself' and only now '*thinks* himself' (*Anthropology* AK 7:127).

self-reflective in seeking constructions governed by the insistence that a proposition is only tenable if it is one that an embodied being, like a human being, can coherently think of him/her/itself as holding. The constitutive coherence sought in a transcendental deduction is neither the internal coherence of a proposition, nor coherence between propositions, but coherence between judgments made and the conditions of the judging human subject coherently being able to entertain or make, not just these judgments, but *any* judgments.[9] In other words, Kant's critical project, at root, aims to discern the strict requirements and limits of human self-understanding. Put differently, Kant is fundamentally interested in what is contained in the concept of an act of judging, and what this tells us about what we can know or rationally believe. As such, his critical project does not rest on an idealistic metaphysics. Its considerations are presupposed in making any attempt to debate idealism *vs* realism in metaphysics. Whatever metaphysical position one holds, it is contained in judgments, which must be consistent with what one must think if one is to be able to think coherently of oneself as a being capable of making any judgments at all. As Wayne Waxman puts it: '[I]f we cannot think something, the question whether we can know it cannot even arise' (2014, 3). Related to this, in claiming that a transcendental deduction establishes a proposition as an apodictic a priori synthetic proposition, Kant does not assert that such propositions are necessary truths but that they are rationally necessary presuppositions of the ability of human beings to make *any* intelligible claims about objects (synthetic propositions), where for a synthetic proposition to be rationally necessary is for its acceptance to be a strict requirement of human self-understanding, and for it to be intelligible is for it to be rationally possible for a human being to entertain it.

Secondly, and parallel to this, we hold that Kant does not seek to justify universal claims in his *practical* philosophy by reference to generally held normative

---

9 We agree with Westphal that, for Kant

> [t]he self-conscious 'I think' that matters most is the 'I judge' that is central to rational thought and action in any of its forms. Only the strong sense of 'I judge' that involves critical assessment makes possible thought and reasoning, as contrasted with mere vocables, rhetoric, propaganda or the rote following of protocols. . . . [It] is the kind of self-conscious judgment required to understand, to appreciate and to *assess* any substantial piece of reasoning, including moral reasoning. (2012, 16)

Indeed, we think that Kant advances an even stronger claim, holding that possession of the powers of self-conscious judgment required to assess any substantial reasoning is also necessary to engage in mere rhetoric, propaganda or the following of rote protocols. These activities still involve reasoning, only not rationally acceptable reasoning.

commitments, but as strict requirements of human *agential* self-understanding (which is to say, by reference to normative commitments that are not coherently deniable by any human agent – an agent being someone able to think practically, which is to say, someone able to do things for reasons).[10] Kant's claim that there are some normative commitments that are universal is the claim that there are some normative commitments that human agents ought to hold in order to think coherently of themselves as possessing the universal properties that make any human being an agent, despite the fact that there might be, and are, enormous differences between the concrete conditions under which human agents live and between the convictions and other properties they contingently have. Related to this, when he speaks in *CPrR* about a 'fact of pure reason', he is not referring to any sort of 'empirical fact' but to a normative commitment that beings must recognize if they are to understand themselves coherently as capable of making any practical judgments. At the same time, the abstraction from all contingencies that this involves does not imply that a categorical imperative is a true proposition ascertained by a special faculty of insight possessed by a transcendental ego unaffected by any contingencies that attend human existence into normative/evaluative truths that exist in a Platonic realm of ideal forms. Justifying a categorical imperative by showing its acceptance to be a strict requirement of *human* agential self-understanding necessarily requires human agents to be characterized as *also* possessing the contingent physical, psychological, social, historical, and biological characteristics, and being subject to the variable circumstances that make each of them unique individual agents. Although Kant does claim that reason requires human agents to form, and reflect upon, the idea of having a 'purely rational will', this idea only has importance for his idea of moral justification because he considers that *any* judging being must be able to relate *imaginatively* to how a being with a purely rational will (one that operates in a way that is unaffected by any contingencies) would necessarily think in order to understand him/her/itself as an agent.[11]

---

10 We do not think that Kant regards agential self-understanding as a sub-category of self-understanding. Because he maintains that practical reasoning has primacy over theoretical reasoning in that 'all interest is ultimately practical' (*CPrR* AK 5:121), in the final analysis, *for justificatory purposes*, he regards all *self*-understanding as agential self-understanding.

11 Our view that this is Kant's position is also influenced by linking his claim that agents necessarily presuppose that they have free will to Alan Gewirth's contention (e.g., 1978) that morality, understood as a system of rules governed by a categorical imperative, is (and can only be) justified on the basis of its 'dialectical necessity' (which is to say nothing more and nothing less than that morality is, and can only be, justified as a strict requirement of human agential self-understanding). See, e.g., Deryck Beyleveld 1991, 1999, 2013, 2015, 2016, 2017; Deryck Beyleveld and Roger Brownsword 2001, Chapter 5; Deryck Beyleveld and Gerhard Bos 2009;

Thirdly, we maintain that Kant derives rationally necessary acceptance of having free will from being bound by the moral law in both *GMM* and *CPrR*, arguing that acceptance of the moral law as the categorical imperative is directly a strict requirement of human agential self-understanding, and that acting in accord with the strict requirements of human agential self-understanding is itself categorically imperative. Thus, the fact that Kant holds that being bound by the moral law and having free will are reciprocal concepts (*GMM* AK 4:446, *CPrR* AK 5:29) entails that he thinks that it is impossible to have a morally neutral justification of metaphysical free will that is then used to justify the categorical imperative; and he shows his awareness of this when he discusses an apparent vicious circularity in his argument for the categorical imperative in *GMM* (AK 4:449–453). The reason why he thinks that his justification is not viciously circular is that, while he holds that acceptance of the strict requirements of human agential self-understanding is itself a strict requirement of human agential self-understanding, the pursuit of human agential self-understanding cannot be given any external justification and does not need one. This is because having the powers of human agential self-understanding is necessary for human beings to be able to make *any* intelligible statements, and to ask *any* questions, about practical reasoning. In other words, Kant claims that the categorical imperative, which (in the final analysis) is nothing other than the command to act in accord with the strict requirements of human agential self-understanding, has the status of a 'postulate', which is an

> immediately certain proposition [i.e., a proposition the certainty of which is not mediated by (derived from) *any other* proposition], or a principle that determines a possible action, in the case of which it is presupposed that the way of executing it is immediately certain.[12]
> (*Jäsche Logic* AK 9:112)

---

and Marcus Düwell 2017. While our views about some details of the relationship between Gewirth and Kant expressed in these sources have changed over time (as have our views about the details of Kant's justification), the view propounded therein is consistently that what Kant means by an 'a priori synthetic practical proposition' is what Gewirth means by a 'dialectically necessary commitment'. This, we think, is as important for understanding Gewirth as it is for understanding Kant, even though Gewirth himself almost invariably contrasts his views with Kant's with little attention to the similarities between them (though conceding the similarities claimed in Beyleveld 1999 in Gewirth 1999, 213). Gewirth's views, which are routinely mischaracterized by most critics, will not, however, be appealed to as such in our presentation of Kant's justification, though our interpretation of Gewirth does play a part in our assessment of the validity of it.

12 *Jäsche Logic* is a manual of Kant's lectures compiled and edited from Kant's lecture notes and other lecture materials dating from 1765 and later by Gottlob Benjamin Jäsche (at Kant's request, and published in 1800). Questions might be raised about the legitimacy of using

The construction we will provide and defend is not entirely novel, because much of what we have said is shared by other interpretations – most extensively by those of Steigleder 2002, 2006 and Wolff 2009, 2015. However, it is distinguished from both of the latter by viewing human agential self-understanding as constituted by the synthesis of what Kant calls the three maxims of the *sensus communis* in *CPoJ* (AK 5:294). These three maxims are: 'To think for oneself', 'To think in the position of everyone else', and 'Always to think in accord with oneself'. Kant's claims about the maxims of the *sensus communis* – which he says are the fundamental principles of the faculties of mind that are necessarily possessed by any beings able to lay claim to being human (*CPoJ* AK 5:293–294), '[u]niversal rules and conditions for avoiding error in general' (*Jäsche Logic* AK 9:57), and precepts for 'reaching wisdom' (*Anthropology* AK 7:123; also AK 7:178, where they are designated 'unalterable commands' for thinking beings) – are important because they

(a) provide strong support for our contention that his justification of the categorical imperative is that acceptance of it is a strict requirement of human agential self-understanding;

(b) show how having the capacities needed to be capable of human agential self-understanding ground, and (at times) constitute, what he refers to as the 'common human understanding' or 'common human reason';

(c) clarify what he is doing when he begins his examination of the idea of a categorical imperative in *GMM* by claiming to find the categorical imperative entirely a priori in *sound* common human understanding;

(d) render it plausible for him to think that human beings are entitled to treat the moral law as a 'fact of pure reason' as a product of understanding their humanity in everyday life;[13] and

(e) provide important guidance on how he thinks the FUL is to be interpreted, applied, *and* justified.

Jäsche Logic to interpret *GMM* and *CPrR* because it post-dates the latter two. While we accept that caution is required here, we nevertheless hold that an appeal to later works is only of dubious value when there is good specific reason to think that their statements supporting our construction are incompatible with what Kant clearly holds in *GMM/CPrR*. Other later works to which we will make significant appeal are *CPoJ*, *MoM* and *Anthropology*.

13 It is clear from context that, when Kant speaks of human beings, he means members of the species *Homo sapiens* who are agents (beings with a will, i.e., beings who are capable of reasoning practically). He certainly does not identify being human *carte blanche* with being a member of the species *Homo sapiens*. For Kant, the essential capacity that constitutes a member of our species' humanity is the ability to think (possessing the capacity to understand), which he considers to emerge with one's capacity to have self-representation as an 'I' (see, e.g., *Anthropology* AK 7:127).

Kant's claims about the three maxims of the *sensus communis* have, however (like his claims about the relationship between his argument for morality and his argument for the existence of God and immortality), received scant attention in relation to his grounding of the categorical imperative.[14]

Our construction focuses mainly on the three sections of *GMM* (*GMM* I, *GMM* II, and *GMM* III) plus its Preface, and the Preface, Introduction and Chapter I of Book One of *CPrR*. It is a systematic internal reconstruction of Kant's justification of the categorical imperative rather than a commentary that follows the chronology of these texts. This is because our goal is to provide an exegetical account of the *logical* (*inferential*) *structure* of Kant's justification of the categorical imperative. In consequence, we sometimes employ terminology that differs significantly from Kant's own.[15] In addition, in order to be faithful to Kant's methodology of reflecting on rational commitments from the first person perspective of human agents (which follows from his methodology being an analysis of the strict requirements of human *self*-understanding), we often present his reasoning from the perspective of a representative human agent, whom we call 'Agnes' (who could be any human agent) and, when necessary, we refer to another human agent (any other human agent) with whom Agnes interacts in thought or deed as 'Brian'. We employ this device to distinguish, on the one hand, the internal perspective of 'an embodied incompletely rational human agent' *as such* from the contingent perspectives of any particular individual human agents and, on the other hand, from the construction of 'pure practical reason' that Kant considers to be a rationally necessary imagining of any human agent.

We do not expect our readers to be familiar with the secondary literature on Kant's views about the justification of a categorical imperative; and we will indicate the views of other Kant scholars if we discuss them. But we do expect our readers to have read *GMM* and at least the Preface, Introduction and Chapter I of Book One of *CPrR*. We will not attempt to discuss all the arguments for all the

---

14 Onora O'Neill (1989) and Kenneth Westphal (who follows O'Neill in this, see Westphal 2016 especially) are exceptions in recognising their importance both in grounding Kant's claim to establish the categorical imperative as undeniable for human agents, and in revealing what the FUL requires for it to be permissible for an agent to adopt a maxim. With the latter focus, they view the categorical imperative (which they correctly identify with the maxim to always think in accord with oneself) as a 'followability' principle that permits an agent to adopt a maxim only if it *can* be adopted by all other agents. In Chapter Two we comment on their view about the grounding of the followability principle.

15 A case in point is our use of 'human agential self-understanding', since Kant himself never uses this locution. In our opinion, however, this locution (and 'practical self-understanding' or 'human self-understanding', which he also does not employ) accurately describes the framework within which his argument for the categorical imperative is conducted.

views attributed to Kant in the secondary literature. Doing so would require an enormous volume. In any case, we do not think it helpful or necessary to do so. Even attempting to classify all the interpretations available is likely to obscure rather than clarify matters, and we consider that the goals of exegesis are better served by concentrating on presenting what we believe to be the most accurate representation of Kant's views. Nevertheless, we cannot ignore other interpretations altogether, and we certainly need to deal with examples of different interpretations of claims that our construction appeals to. Just how we will deal with interpretations other than our own, and why we consider that we can legitimately sidestep a comprehensive survey and critique of all constructions that have been offered, will be explained in this chapter.

It should also be noted that we rarely offer a complete justification of any of our claims at any one point in this book. In introducing many of our claims, we provide only some evidence or reasoning for them, to which we will add later. In the process, we will often restate what we have said before in slightly different terms because of the different contexts in which Kant makes the claims we are discussing. This is necessary because these claims are interconnected systemically and it is impossible to cover all of their interconnections at once. To see the interconnections requires attention to different aspects of Kant's critical philosophy viewed as a comprehensive system for self-critical thinking, which are sometimes presented in different works with different aims. A degree of reiteration is also an unavoidable consequence of an attempt to articulate and evidence what we think Kant's argument is when, if we are right about its nature, Kant claims that its validity is established simply by understanding the kind of argument that it is when he characterizes it in different terms in different places.

With all this understood, we will now present our view of the *strategy* Kant employs to conclude that the FUL is categorically binding on human agents as an imperative, which derives from what he thinks needs to be done in order to establish that the categorical imperative exists. The *logical structure* of the reasoning by which we think he implements this strategy is presented as an outline argument sequence in Chapter Two.

The Strategic Architecture of Kant's Argument

Our construction is built around what we consider to be a basic insight. This is that, in *both GMM and CPrR*, Kant maintains that, *given* the concept of a categorical imperative *and* the nature of the conceptual connection between *thinking this concept* and *thinking the concept of human agency*, the *only* thing needed to establish the existence of the sole categorical imperative is to show that it is not

incoherent for finite embodied agents to think that they are bound by the moral law (which they can only be if they have free will). More fully, we contend that Kant claims to establish the existence of the categorical imperative by linking
(i) an analysis of the conceptual relationship between thinking the concept of a categorical imperative and thinking the concept of being a human agent (to conclude that human agents are strictly required to think and understand the concept of a categorical imperative) with
(ii) an analysis of what is *contained in the concept* of a categorical imperative, to conclude *not only* that
   (a) if it exists, its content is given by the FUL;
       but also that
   (b) human agents are strictly required to think that the categorical imperative exists;
       but that
   (c) it can only exist if pure reason is capable of being practical in them – which is to say if they have free will[16] – while their wills are also capable of being affected by heteronomous incentives;[17]
with

---

[16] Having free will (Wille) must be distinguished from the capacity to act voluntarily ('Willkür'). Although Kant does not explicitly draw attention to this distinction in these terms until *Religion*, it is implicit in earlier works, including *GMM* (see Steigleder 2006). Kant conceives of human agents as beings who have the capacity to choose means to pursue ends they have chosen, on the basis of which they necessarily view themselves as subject to hypothetical imperatives. The kind of choice that Willkür expresses can be evidenced by feeling that the choice is something that expresses who one is. As such, it is possible that it is caused by factors governed by causal laws of nature. On the other hand, Kant views the spontaneity involved in the exercise of free will as incompatible with governance by causal laws of nature, and as something that no experience can show agents that they have. In *GMM*, Kant only starts using the terms 'free will' or 'freedom of action' at *GMM* AK 4:446. But, as he tells us at *GMM* AK 4:447, free will and autonomy of the will are the same thing, and he connects autonomy of the will with free will directly at *GMM* AK 4:433, and indirectly by his characterization of autonomy of the will already at *GMM* AK 4:394, through the idea of a will that is 'good in itself and, regarded for itself' apart from any further purpose (see also, e.g., *GMM* AK 4:397, 4:400, 4:402) or the idea of a pure will, one governed by pure practical reason (e.g., *GMM* AK 4:409, 4:412, 4:417, 4:419).

[17] Kant thinks that the moral law *as such* (the law of pure practical reason) is a law of nature for a purely rational will. Thus, (ii)(c) states that for a categorical imperative to exist, agents whose wills are capable of being affected by heteronomous influences governed by the universal law of nature must also be capable of being governed by what is a law of nature for a purely rational will. To avoid any confusion, we will refer to the universal 'law of mechanism' and 'mechanistic causality'causality'causality' (which Kant usually refers to as the universal 'law of nature' or 'natural causality') in connection with laws of the sensible world to which heteronomous influences belong.

(iii) a defence of the rationally necessitated idea – established by (i) linked with (ii) – that the categorical imperative exists against any suspicion that this necessitation reveals an antinomy in human reason as a whole, which suspicion (if borne out) would mean that the concept of a categorical imperative is incoherent and the rationally necessitated thought that a categorical imperative exists is a deceit of human reason.

We contend that comprehending that, why, and how Kant puts (i), (ii) and (iii) together, is necessary to understand his justification of the categorical imperative, and that comprehending this requires recognition that he holds that the existence of the categorical imperative is justified in and by comprehending the necessary and sufficient conditions for justifying its existence. In other words, he holds that the categorical imperative is nothing other than the command to judge actions and maxims by the criterion for a possible categorical imperative. And it follows from this that he holds that any justification of the categorical imperative cannot be morally neutral. Furthermore, we contend that the way in which Kant puts (i), (ii) and (iii) together entails that he holds that the comprehension that constitutes the justification as a whole – to be distinguished from (iii), which is only a part of it – is a practical deduction in being an argument from within human agential self-understanding. In Kant's own terminology (see, e.g., *CPrR* AK 5:46–47), his justification that the categorical imperative is an 'apodictic a priori synthetic practical proposition' combines an 'exposition' of the concept of being bound by a categorical imperative – which conjoins (i) and (ii) – with (iii), a defence of the coherence of the concept of a categorical imperative in the face of presuppositions of the possibility of empirical knowledge. That Kant contends in (ii)(b) that, in human agential self-understanding, understanding the concept of a categorical imperative strictly requires acceptance that the categorical imperative exists, is one reason why we suggest that Kant's argument may be called a quasi-ontological one. From a rational construction point of view, (ii)(b) is essential for Kant's argument to succeed. Without (ii)(b), everything else that Kant claims to establish can only show that it is *possible* for a categorical imperative to exist. In showing that it is both possible, which is the achievement of (iii), *and* necessary, which is the achievement of (i) and (ii), for human agents to think that they have free will, the categorical imperative is shown to be not merely presented, but validated, as an apodictic (i.e., rationally undeniable) a priori synthetic practical proposition (*GMM* AK 4:420), one that is connected completely a priori with the concept of the will of a purely rational agent (or, as Kant puts it, 'the concept of the will of a rational being as such') (*GMM* AK 4:426) but not contained in it (*GMM* AK 4:420 fn).

Of course, we must establish that this is what Kant argues, not merely that this is what he needs to argue. Important evidence is provided by what Kant means by 'exposition of a concept'.

> The *expounding* [exposition] of a concept [as against the exposition of intuitions] consists in the connected (successive) representation of its marks, insofar as these are found through analysis. (*Jäsche Logic* AK 9:142–143)

In *CPuR*, he says that by *exposition*

> I mean the clear, though not necessarily exhaustive, representation of that which belongs to a concept: the exposition is *metaphysical* when it contains that which exhibits the concept *as given a priori*. (B38)

Furthermore, he tells us that there is a difference between a definition and an exposition. '[N]either empirical concepts nor concepts given *a priori* allow of definition'. Only concepts that 'I have invented' can I define. Concepts that 'are given to me either by the nature of understanding or by experience' can only be expounded (*CPuR* A729: B757).

On the basis that Kant holds that the concept of a categorical imperative is given (exhibited) a priori in human agential self-understanding, we infer that he holds that exposition of the concept of a categorical imperative includes analysis of what is contained in human agential self-understanding, and we maintain that it is on this basis that he holds that the categorical imperative is not arbitrary, a mere convention, even though it is a legislative creation (invention) of the self-understanding of every human agent. The concept of a categorical imperative is given in human agential self-understanding by human agential self-understanding. It has a seemingly paradoxical quality in being both something 'I' have 'invented' yet is still 'given *to* me' a priori. But this is just another way of saying that human agential self-understanding presents its pursuit and maintenance as an end in itself, which is important because Kant holds that only concepts that agents give to themselves (so can be defined) can ground apodictic principles, and this might seem to suggest that he thinks that the existence of a categorical imperative cannot be shown to be rationally necessary by exposition of its concept. However, the concept of human agential self-understanding is a very special concept. This is because, according to Kant (or so we claim), for any concepts (including the concept of human agential self-understanding) to be given to human agents presupposes that they possess the powers of agential self-understanding. As such, the concept of agential self-understanding is both the invention of each human agent and given a priori to each human agent. In yet other words, it is both legislated to human agents and legislated by human agents in exercising their powers of agential self-understanding. It is, thus, unique in being a concept that can be defined as well as expounded.[18]

Consequently, the analysis involved in Kant's exposition of the concept of a categorical imperative does not merely seek to reveal what is contained in the concept of a categorical imperative, thereby uncovering what anyone who holds that there is a categorical imperative ought to accept (by virtue of understanding the concept of a categorical imperative). It also includes reasoning of a kind that enables the conclusion that having the concept of a categorical imperative is having one that is necessitated by sound use of the powers of thinking that those capable of any kind of practical reasoning must think themselves to have. In other words, in addition to (ii), it includes (i); and (i) and (ii) together constitute an analysis of what is contained in the idea of possessing human agential self-understanding. If this seems to be a stretch, clear support for it is given by what Kant says is shown by 'exposition' of the categorical imperative, which is

> what it [the categorical imperative] contains, *that it stands of itself altogether a priori and independently of empirical principles*, and then what distinguishes it from all other practical principles. [Our emphasis added.]   (*CPrR* AK 5:46)

It must also be appreciated that Kant distinguishes a 'metaphysical exposition' from a 'transcendental exposition'

> I understand by a transcendental exposition the explanation of a concept, as a principle from which the possibility of other *a priori* knowledge can be understood. For this purpose it is required (1) that such knowledge does really flow from the given concept, (2) that this knowledge is possible only on the assumption of a given mode of explaining the concept.   (*CPuR* B40)

As applied to exposition of the concept of a categorical imperative, we understand Kant to be saying that the analysis of (ii)(c) that reveals that human agents must suppose that they have free will (because free will as the *ratio essendi* of the moral law is necessary to explain how human beings can be bound by the moral law) is a transcendental exposition of the concept of a categorical imperative. Thus, the exposition of the concept of a categorical imperative, which is metaphysical in being given a priori by human agential self-understanding, contains a transcendental exposition that reveals (because a categorical imperative

---

18 Unfortunately, Kant does not make this clear in *CPuR*. This is important because we think it is not only crucial for understanding why he thinks that the categorical imperative can serve as the criterion for its own existence without vicious circularity (see further Chapter Two), but is equally important for understanding why he says that the moral law is the sole fact of pure reason (see below).

appears to have two incompatible *rationes essendi*) that establishing the 'reality' of the categorical imperative requires the defence of (iii). By way of contrast, in exposition of a concept (like 'space'), which is given as a necessary presupposition of all outer appearances, a transcendental exposition of it is all that is necessary to establish the

> reality, that is, the objective validity, of space in respect of whatever can be presented to us outwardly as object, but also the *ideality* of space in respect of things when they are considered in themselves through reason. (*CPuR* A28: B44)

In his First Introduction to *CPoJ*, Kant says

> If philosophy is the **system** of rational cognition through concepts, it is thereby already sufficiently distinguished from the critique of pure reason, which, although it contains a philosophical investigation of the possibility of such cognition, does not belong to such a system [i.e., philosophy] as a part, but rather outlines and examines the very idea of it in the first place. (AK 20:195)

In our opinion, in the context of practical philosophy, the activity of philosophy includes the exposition of pure practical concepts as well as the critique of pure practical reason, the latter involving the defence/deduction of (iii), the composite of (i), (ii) and (iii) constituting Kant's justification of the categorical imperative, which regulates what Kant calls 'the metaphysics of morals' (the application and implications of the FUL), thus constituting the 'groundwork' of the metaphysics of morals. That Kant distinguishes 'a groundwork of the metaphysics of morals' from a 'critique of pure practical reason' at *GMM* AK 4:392 is consistent with this, even though his stated reason for doing so in *GMM* is that he considers that a complete critique of pure practical reason involves considerations that go beyond the components of it necessary to ground the categorical imperative. These additional considerations are those of the possibility of human immortality and the existence of God that occupy Book Two of *CPrR*, for which he says *(CPrR* AK 5:3) a critique of practical reasons entire facility is necessary.

We are now able to state what we think Kant is telling us when he says that the moral law is the sole fact of pure reason. First of all, when he says that moral consciousness (consciousness of the fundamental law of pure practical reason) is a fact of reason (*CPrR* AK 5:30–31), he means that having the *concept* of a *categorical* imperative, which implicates the *concept* of pure practical reason, and, thereby, the *concept* of a free will, is a strict requirement of human agential self-understanding. To be conscious of pure practical reason is to be conscious of free will, which Kant says is not and cannot be an object of empirical consciousness; consciousness of it can only be an awareness of it in thought, which is to have the concept of it. Secondly, when he says that '[p]ure reason is practical of itself alone and gives (to the human being) a universal law which we call the *moral law*' (AK 5:31), he means that acceptance of the categorical imperative is a strict requirement of human agential self-understanding. Thirdly, when he says that the moral law *so given* is the sole fact of pure reason (AK 5:31), he signals two things of particular significance: (a) that the categorical imperative/the moral law *as such*/free-will, the concepts of which form a co-ordinate idea, represent the only concepts of practical reason that human agents must accept have regulative authority over all activities involving reason that take an object simply by understanding the concept of this co-ordination; and (b) that free will, in being the *ratio essendi* of the moral law and a *ratio essendi* of the categorical imperative, is the *only* object of speculative theoretical reason that Agnes's agential self-understanding strictly requires her to believe exists that pure reason *as a whole* requires her to believe exists (but only for practical purposes). While Kant holds that there are other objects of speculative theoretical reason, such as God and her immortality that Agnes must accept exist because her acceptance of the categorical imperative is a strict requirement of her agential self-understanding, and might, therefore, be called facts of pure *practical* reason, they are not permissibly also regarded as facts of pure reason *as a whole*. This is because they are not *rationes essendi* of the moral law *as such*/human agential self-understanding. While human agential self-understanding strictly requires Agnes to believe in the existence of God and her immortality as well as her free will, the existence or otherwise of God and her immortality does not affect the possibility of Agnes possessing agential self-understanding. Co-ordinately, while pure practical reason strictly requires Agnes to believe that God, her immortality, and free will exist, pure reason is practical in Agnes independently of the existence or non-existence of God and her immortality. But having free will *constitutes* pure reason being practical in Agnes, so pure reason cannot be practical in Agnes if she does not have free will.

It follows from this that Kant's designation of the moral law as the sole fact of pure reason in *CPrR* does not signal that the moral law as the categorical imperative has a different epistemic status from that for which he argues in *GMM*. This designation also does not signal that his argument for the categorical imperative having this status is different in the two works. His argument for the existence of the moral law as the categorical imperative is that its acceptance is a strict requirement of human agential self-understanding in the same way in both works. *GMM* and *CPrR* are related in the following manner. *CPrR* deploys *GMM's* justification of the categorical imperative to justify the claim that human agents have free will *in order to* justify the claims that *CPrR* makes about God and human immortality. The function that Kant's claim that the moral law-free will is the sole fact of pure reason serves in this endeavour is to specify the epistemic status of belief in free will *as distinct from* the epistemic status of belief in God and immortality. The reason why Kant does not call the moral law-free will couple the sole fact of pure reason in *GMM* is simply because spelling out the implications of his justification of the categorical imperative in this direction is a task he leaves for *CPrR*, because doing so is not necessary to show that the existence of the categorical imperative is validated by its acceptance being a strict requirement of agential self-understanding. This said, we do not doubt that Kant, in *GMM*, thinks of the moral law-free will couple as the sole fact of pure reason, because the epistemic relation between the categorical imperative, God, God and human immortality, is already sketched in *CPuR* (A804–831: B832–859).[19] For this reason, while *GMM* does not *describe* the moral law-free will couple as the sole fact of pure reason, this does not mean that he does not depict this couple in *GMM* in a way that accords it the epistemic status of the sole fact of pure reason, and we contend that he does depict it in this way using different terminology when he says, *inter alia,* that rational nature exists as an end in itself and that it is this fact that grounds the moral law (*GMM* AK 4:428–429) and that the moral law and free will are reciprocal concepts (AK 4:446) (on which see Chapter Six). Conversely, depicting the moral law-free will couple as the sole fact of pure reason in *CPrR* does not mean that Kant does not present his *GMM* justification for the categorical imperative in *CPrR*. What *CPrR* does is present the argument of *GMM* in a way that facilitates linking it to his claims about the existence of God and human immortality, justifying which linkage is the central aim of *CPrR* clearly stated in its Preface.

Positioning and Defending Our Construction

While much of our construction might be thought contentious, it is not controversial that, in both *GMM* and *CPrR*, Kant holds that the concept of a categorical imperative is coherent. Kant says that

> [t]he union of causality as freedom with causality as natural mechanism, the first of which is established by the moral law, the second by the law of nature . . . in one and the same subject, the human being   (*CPrR* AK 5:5 fn)

is possible because representing a human agent as having free will represents 'him . . . as a being in itself . . . in *pure* [consciousness]', while representing him as subject to causality by natural mechanism represents him 'as an appearance . . . in *empirical* consciousness. Otherwise the contradiction of reason with itself is unavoidable' (*CPrR* AK 5:5 fn).[20] (See also, e.g., *GMM* III AK 4:461; *CPrR* AK 5:47.)

---

19 See further Chapter Four.
20 We have rearranged the order of the quote slightly, but in a way that does not alter its sense. The last sentence implies that Kant treats it as axiomatic that pure reason cannot be thought to be in conflict with itself. He does so because he maintains that to think it in conflict with itself is

However, there is considerable disagreement about why, or even whether, Kant contends that human agents *must* think that they have free will; and this disagreement extends to whether he holds the same view about this in *GMM* and *CPrR*. Commentators are also not unanimous on exactly *why* Kant thinks that it is coherent for agents to think that a categorical imperative exists.

We have already introduced the *WAV*. We will now spell it out in slightly more detail.

The widely accepted view (WAV)

According to the *WAV*, *GMM* claims to establish that the categorical imperative exists by showing that finite embodied imperfectly rational agents (such as human agents) necessarily presuppose that they have free will (*GMM* AK 4:447–448). Because having free will and being bound by the moral law are reciprocal concepts (*GMM* AK 4:446), it follows that human agents are strictly required to think that they are bound by the moral law as the categorical imperative *unless* it can be shown to be incoherent for them to think that their wills are governed by the law of a free will yet subject at the same time to the universal law of mechanism – in which case their strictly required thought that the categorical imperative exists would be revealed to be 'a mere phantom of a human imagination overstepping itself' (*GMM* AK 4:407; cf. AK 4:445).[21] However, Kant maintains that the reason why human agents necessarily presuppose that their wills are subject to the universal law of mechanism and the reason why they necessarily presuppose that they have free will are related to each other in such a manner that it is impossible to show that it is incoherent for them to think that they have free will. Thus, human agents must think that they really do have free will and that their rationally necessitated thought that they are bound by the categorical imperative is not a delusion. (*GMM* AK 4:451–457)

Why Kant thinks that human agents necessarily presuppose that they have free will is a matter of dispute amongst proponents of the *WAV*. But, regardless of their differences, they depict him as holding that the necessity for human agents to presuppose free will is the morally neutral *ratio cognoscendi* of the

---

to deny the possibility of thinking it in conflict with itself. When all is said and done, the problem for Kant is not so much to show that the concept of a categorical imperative is coherent, but merely to reveal that it can be coherent and how it must be thought to be coherent.

21 This quote is taken out of context, but it expresses the consequence Kant envisages accurately, and is clearly related to the condition he lays down for morality being 'no phantom' at *GMM* AK 4:445, where the context is clear.

moral law (the morally neutral reason why human agents know that they are bound by the moral law). Consequently, the *ratio cognoscendi* of the *categorical imperative* is that human agents necessarily presuppose that they have free will, hence are bound by the moral law, *given that* it is coherent for them to do so (because pure *theoretical* reason, at the very least, cannot show that it is impossible for them to have free will or even presupposes that they have free will).

But, according to the *WAV*, Kant changes his mind in *CPrR*.[22] He now realizes that it is impossible to establish that human agents necessarily presuppose that they have free will without first establishing that pure reason is practical in them, which is to say, without first establishing that they are bound by the moral law. This is because they cannot know that they have free will on the basis of any empirical experience or any direct a priori intuition (*CPrR* AK 5:31). Indeed, they cannot even form the concept of free will without first having the concept of pure practical reason/morality/a *categorical* imperative (*CPrR* AK 5:29–30). However, the concept of free will necessarily presents itself to those who are aware of and understand the concept of pure practical reason/the moral law/a *categorical* imperative (*CPrR* AK 5:29–30). As Kant puts it, 'the moral law is the *ratio cognoscendi* of freedom', while 'freedom is . . . the *ratio essendi* of the moral law' in their reciprocal relation (*CPrR* AK 5:4 fn). Consequently, the existence of a categorical imperative cannot be established on any morally neutral basis, which means that it cannot be justified by any transcendental deduction because (*according to the WAV*) such a deduction is necessarily theoretical. Instead, the moral law is *'given'* to human agents as a fact of reason (*CPrR* AK 5:31). According to some, by this, Kant claims that the moral law is known to exist by an inherent faculty of moral intuition.[23] Although he continues to maintain that the categorical imperative he identified in *GMM* is an apodictic a priori synthetic practical proposition, he has changed his mind about the nature of such a proposition and the way in which it can be justified as such.[24] According to others, he has

---

22 H. J. Paton (2000) and Dieter Henrich (1975) think that Kant might have realized that his justification failed by the end of *GMM*, but that he did not point to a new view until *CPrR*.
23 E.g., Paul Guyer 2007, 462, who refers to Kant as engaging in 'foot stamping'; and Allen W. Wood 2008, 135 (according to whom Kant engages in 'moralistic bluster'). Dieter Schönecker (1999, 2006, 2013, 2014) and Jens Timmermann (2010) have more favourable views about Kant's 'new' justification.
24 In effect, Kant is held to adopt a moral realist position of a kind that regards the moral law as a necessary truth that holds independently of sense experience, which agents know they ought to comply with by a faculty of insight into necessary truth rather than by a transcendental deduction.

abandoned his *GMM* view that the categorical imperative can be justified as an apodictic proposition for *all* human agents.[25] He now holds that reason cannot require all human agents to accept unconditionally that there is a categorical imperative. However, because the existence of a categorical imperative is generally accepted, and understanding its concept requires recognition that it must take the form of the FUL,[26] the question of the existence of the categorical imperative does not arise in common practical discourse. In other words, Kant's persistent claim that the categorical imperative is apodictic is now confined to discourse between morally committed agents, which commitment is that of common human understanding (understood as popular, i.e., inductively widespread, human agreement). As Andrews Reath puts it:

> Whether it is reasonable to accept the requirements of morality is not in question in ordinary practical contexts. In claiming that the validity of the moral law is given as the 'fact of reason', Kant holds that it cannot and need not be grounded in anything outside of our ordinary moral consciousness, in which we are directly aware of the law-giving activity of reason. (1997, x)

Reasons for a defeasible default presumption against the WAV

As we have already indicated, contrary to the *WAV*, a few commentators contend that the justifications provided in *GMM* and *CPrR* are compatible with each other.

An obvious prompt for the claim of compatibility is Kant's assertion that *CPrR*

> presupposes, indeed, the *Groundwork of the Metaphysics of Morals*, . . . insofar as this constitutes preliminary acquaintance with the principle of duty and provides and justifies a determinate formula of it. (*CPrR* AK 5:8)

Many proponents of the *WAV* pass over this declaration without comment. Perhaps they share Dieter Schöneker's opinion (2013, 8, fn 10) that Kant is not saying that *CPrR* presumes *GMM's* justification of the existence of the categorical imperative. He is saying only that *CPrR* operates on the presumption that *GMM's* analysis of the idea of a categorical imperative has correctly identified

---

[25] E.g., Dieter Henrich 1960; Karl Ameriks 1981; Henry E. Allison 1990, 230–249; John Rawls 2000; Stephen Darwall 2006; Andrews Reath 1997, 2007 and 2012; David Sussman (2008).
[26] In *CPrR*, the FUL is designated the 'Fundamental Law of Pure Practical Reason: So act that the maxim of your will could always hold at the same time as a principle in the giving of universal law' (*CPrR* AK 5:30).

the form and content of any categorical imperative *if it exists*.²⁷ We disagree with this for the following reasons.

(1) As Owen Ware (2017, 140 fn 28) points out, the word that Kant uses for 'justifies' here is 'rechtfertigen', which he never uses in connection with mere specification of the content and form of the categorical imperative revealed by what is contained in its concept.

(2) If Kant thinks that *CPrR* presumes only that *GMM* has correctly identified the content and form of any possible categorical imperative, then it is odd for him to say that *GMM* provides *and* justifies it. Providing it will be all that *CPrR* presumes that *GMM* does.

(3) In *GMM*'s Preface, Kant describes his aim as 'nothing more than the identification [Aufsuchung] and justification [Festsetzung] of the supreme principle of morality' (*GMM* AK 4:392). While Mary Gregor translates 'Festsetzung' as 'justification' here, it is probably better translated as 'establishment' (which is how she translates it at *GMM* AK 4:419–420). But there is no significant difference in meaning between establishing a principle and justifying it. In both cases, enough reason is provided to consider the principle to be valid. So, because providing and justifying a determinate formula of the categorical imperative (*qua CPrR*) matches identification and establishment of the supreme principle of morality (*qua GMM*),²⁸ unless we are to infer that *GMM* also claims to show *only* that *if* a categorical imperative exists *then* it takes a particular form and has a particular content and not that *a commitment to its existence is justified*, we should conclude that *CPrR* presumes that *GMM* has shown that commitment to the existence of the categorical imperative is justified.

(4) In *CPrR*, Kant continues to claim that the categorical imperative is justified as an apodictic a priori synthetic principle (e.g., *CPrR* AK 5:31). Whatever he means by this, he clearly distinguishes establishing a categorical imperative as an apodictic a priori synthetic principle from showing that mere analysis of the concept of a categorical imperative reveals its content and form *if it exists*.

Given this, the *WAVs* claim that, when Kant says (*CPrR* AK 5:4 fn) that the moral law is the *ratio cognoscendi* of free will, he reverses the order of cognition between free will and the moral law that he asserted in *GMM*, is untenable.

---

27 One *WAV* proponent, Kenneth K. H. Chung (2010, 82) even claims that Kant has nothing explicit to say about *GMM* in *CPrR*.
28 This point is also made by Ware (2017, 126).

This is because the claim that *CPrR* presupposes *GMM's* justification of the categorical imperative must, since it is unqualified, be taken to cover not only the epistemic status given to the categorical imperative but the logical structure of its justification as well. Furthermore, Kant's declaration that *CPrR* presupposes *GMM's* justification is made in very close proximity to his assertion that the moral law is the *ratio cognoscendi* of free will. This suggests that we should read Kant's assertion at *CPrR* AK 5:4 fn as an attempt to clarify his position in *GMM,* or to correct a misunderstanding of it, not as a declaration of a mistake made in *GMM*. Indeed, given the importance of the matter at hand and we will argue that what is at stake here is Kant's view of the cognitive status of his entire system of critical philosophy, not merely that of the categorical imperative it is extremely implausible that Kant would have left any room for doubt, which he certainly does, that his assertion at *CPrR* AK 5:4 fn constitutes a reversal/ abandonment of his position in *GMM if that were his intention.*

In any event, that his assertion in *CPrR* that the moral law is the *ratio cognoscendi* of free will does not proclaim a reversal of his *GMM* position has textual support from *GMM* itself. It must be borne in mind that Kant holds that the moral law *as such* is the law of pure practical reason. Immediately before the passage headed 'Freedom Must be Presupposed as a Property of the Will of All Rational Beings' (which is where proponents of the *WAV* claim that Kant contends that the necessary presupposition of free will is the *ratio cognoscendi* of the moral law), he declares that the purpose of what is to follow is preparation for making 'comprehensible'

> the deduction of free will from pure practical reason, and with it the possibility of a categorical imperative as well.   (*GMM* AK 4:447)[29]

This implies not only that Kant holds that the moral law *as such* is the *ratio cognoscendi* of free will; it implies, when read with what he claims to be the task for *GMM* III, that free will is the *ratio essendi* of the moral law *as such* and a

---

[29] See Michael Wolff (2009, 546 fn 64); Heiko Puls (2011, 543 fn 19); Deryck Beyleveld (2017, 148), Owen Ware (2017, 119), Jochen Bojanowski (2006, 275ff, 2017, 63 fn 17). We take Kant to mean that he intends to show that it is not incomprehensible to attribute a capacity for pure practical reason (which is strictly analytically connected to the possession of free will) *to a human agent* (which is accomplished by establishing that it cannot be shown to be impossible for human agents to possess free will). This is because he holds that the concepts of free will and pure practical reason are, *in themselves,* strictly analytically connected and biconditionally so, from which it follows that he cannot think that *their* linkage to each other poses any difficulties of comprehension.

ratio essendi of the categorical imperative (for which subjection to heteronomous influences is also a *ratio essendi*).

Related to this, in *GMM* II, Kant says that the task of *GMM* III is

> to investigate entirely a priori the possibility of a *categorical* imperative, since we do not here have the advantage of its reality being given in experience, in which case ['und also'] the possibility would be necessary not to establish it but merely to explain it. [Our translation]³⁰
> (*GMM* AK 4:419–420)

In Mary Gregor's original translation, 'und also' is translated as 'so that'. But this suggests that Kant is saying that not being necessary to justify a categorical imperative but merely to explain is the consequence of it *not being given* in experience. This cannot be right, for there can be no doubt that Kant thinks that establishing the possibility (coherence) of a categorical imperative is necessary to justify it. To be consistent with this, Kant must be saying here that if a categorical imperative could be given in experience (i.e., established empirically – which is not the case) then showing its possibility would not be necessary to justify it but only to explain it. That this is what he is saying follows from his use of 'wäre' ('would be') in conjunction with 'und also'. Consequently, we consider that the sense of what he is saying here is most clearly expressed as:

> If the existence of a categorical imperative could be established empirically, showing its possibility would be necessary only to explain it, not to justify it. But because the existence of a categorical imperative can only be given a priori, showing its possibility (which is necessary to explain it) is also necessary to justify it.³¹

Given this, Kant now goes on to say that showing that a categorical imperative is possible requires it to be shown how it is possible for it to be 'an a priori synthetic practical proposition' (*GMM* AK 4:420), which 'requires a possible *synthetic use of pure practical reason*' (*GMM* AK 4:443). Then, in *GMM* III, he claims that

---

30 In the German original, the task is:

> die Möglichkeit eines *kategorischen* Imperativs gänzlich *a priori* zu untersuchen haben, da uns hier der Vorteil nicht zustatten kommt, daß die Wirklichkeit desselben in der Erfahrung gegeben, und also die Möglichkeit nicht zur Festsetzung, sondern bloß zur Erklärung nötig wäre.

31 Kant does not here state that explaining the possibility of a categorical imperative is *sufficient* to justify it. However, that he holds that this is so is implied by coupling his claim that what is necessary to explain it is also necessary to justify it with his statement (made earlier at *GMM* AK 4:419) that the objectively represented necessity of a categorical imperative cannot rely on any presupposition and the only question needing a solution is that of how a categorical imperative is possible.

the question, how a categorical imperative is possible, can indeed be answered to the extent that one can furnish the sole presupposition[32] on which it alone is possible, namely the idea of freedom. (GMM AK 4:461)

Since explaining *how* a *categorical* imperative is possible *to this extent* is a matter of showing that free will, which is the *ratio essendi* of pure practical reason/the moral law *as such*, can coherently be thought to be a *ratio essendi* for an imperative (thus for a categorical imperative),[33] all of this implies that, in *GMM* III, Kant is arguing that having free will is the *ratio essendi* for the application of the moral law (the law of pure practical reason) to human agents, not that it is a/the *ratio cognoscendi* for the existence of the categorical imperative.

These considerations seriously challenge the *WAVs* claim that Kant accords a different cognitive status to the categorical imperative in *GMM* and *CPrR and* its claim that *CPrR* reverses *GMM's* view of the cognitive relation between the moral law and free will. and free will. If Kant means what he says at *CPrR* AK 5:8, has not forgotten what he wrote only three years earlier, and is not trying to deceive us, then we ought to come to the following conclusion. He is claiming that he has established that the categorical imperative has the status of an apodictic a priori synthetic practical proposition by the same method and logical structure of reasoning in both *GMM* and *CPrR,* whatever the presentational differences between these two works might be. Furthermore, in establishing the existence of the categorical imperative, free will is the *ratio essendi* of pure practical reason (the moral law *as such*) and pure practical reason is the *ratio cognoscendi* of free will. However, to this we add a *caveat,* which is that he does not elsewhere contradict his claims that support this direction by making equally clear counterclaims.

---

32 On the basis that Kant holds that the moral law applies, and can only apply, as a categorical imperative to heteronomously affected agents, he cannot think that free will is the sole presupposition of the possibility of a categorical imperative. What he must mean is that, unless free will is a coherent presupposition of a categorical imperative, a categorical imperative cannot exist. We do not consider Kant's statement here to be inconsistent with his claim at *GMM* AK 4:419 that a categorical imperative cannot rest on any presupposition. As we elaborate further in Chapter Two, we consider that Kant always holds that a categorical imperative can and need presuppose nothing other than itself (explicitly stated at *CPrR* AK 5:21), by which he means that it does not and cannot rest on any presupposition other than the coherence of the idea of itself, so not on any *external* presupposition, even though he does not always make this explicit.

33 It is important to appreciate, as we will show later on, that Kant adamantly distinguishes showing that/revealing how free will (hence the categorical imperative) is coherently attributable to human agents from explanation of its possibility in terms of mechanistic causality, which he considers to be both unnecessary and impossible, indeed, 'incomprehensible'.

On this basis, and employing a principle of charitable interpretation, our defence of our construction operates on the defeasible default presumption that the *WAV* is a mistaken interpretation of Kant's justificatory position. In treating this presumption as a defeasible default, we acknowledge that it might be falsifiable. We merely maintain that the onus, the burden of proof, is on supporters of the *WAV* (and any other proponents of substantial, as against merely presentational, differences between *GMM* and *CPrR* regarding the justification of a categorical imperative), to prove beyond reasonable doubt that Kant contradicts the claims he makes that otherwise support concordance between *GMM* and *CPrR*. If it is at all reasonable to interpret apparent evidence for discordance as not contradicting concordance, then that is enough to reject such evidence for discordance. An ambivalent denial, one that can be interpreted as not constituting a denial, may not by itself be taken to deny a clear affirmation. So, any purported evidence for discordance must be strong enough to compel the conclusion that, when Kant says that *CPrR* presupposes the justification given in *GMM*, he is being dishonest, astonishingly forgetful, acting wholly out of character, and/or does not understand the relation between *GMM* and *CPrR*. In our opinion, no alleged counter-evidence (which we will consider in later chapters) passes this test, and, given what we have said about free will being the *ratio essendi* of the moral law in both *GMM* and *CPrR*, chief amongst the claims that we will rebut as constituting clear enough counter-evidence is Kant's contention that

> [t]he objective reality of the moral law cannot be proved by any deduction, by any efforts of theoretical reason, speculative or empirically supported. (*CPrR* AK 5:47)

With the exception of Henry E. Allison 1990, we will not consider the construction of any *WAV* proponent in detail. We single out Allison's construction for special attention (in Chapter Five) because his account of Kant's argument in *CPrR* shares a central tenet of our construction (that a requirement to accept the moral law is given by exposition of its concept). This leads him to say that Kant has not abandoned a deduction of the moral law in *CPrR*, merely the kind of deduction he offers in *GMM*. We will argue that our construction differs from Allison's over the reason/s Kant gives for Agnes to have the concept of morality and that this difference derives from the fact that Allison does not view Kant's argument in either *GMM* or *CPrR* as an argument from and within human agential self-understanding in the way that we have explained this methodology.

Rival interpretations requiring special attention

Our default presumption does not merely (defeasibly) rule out all *WAV* interpretations. It also rules out any *non-WAV* interpretations that portray Kant as arguing that free will is the *ratio cognoscendi* of the moral law only in *CPrR* or in *GMM* as well, or those that maintain that the *WAV* is only mistaken in one of its two defining tenets (which are that Kant [1] abandons a transcendental deduction in *CPrR*, and [2] moves from free will being the *ratio cognoscendi* of the moral law in *GMM* to the moral law being the *ratio cognoscendi* of free will in *CPrR*). So, where does this leave the nine *non-WAV* interpretations that we have mentioned?

Pauline Kleingeld's (2010) interpretation runs contrary to our default presumption because, while she rejects tenet (1) of the *WAV*, she accepts tenet (2). However, she has useful things to say about Kant's methodology of human agential self-understanding, and we will return to her construction in Chapter Three.

Jochen Bojanowski's (2017) interpretation opposes our default presumption because, while he rejects tenet (2) of the *WAV* in favour of holding that the moral law is the *ratio cognoscendi* of free will in both *GMM* and *CPrR*, he accepts tenet (1). Regarding (1), he recognizes that (in *CPrR*) Kant holds that the categorical imperative is shown to be given to human agents as an apodictic a priori synthetic practical proposition for all agents by exposition of its concept. But he thinks that Kant considers that this renders unnecessary the transcendental deduction of free will he essayed in *GMM*. Our response to Bojanowski, which we will put together at numerous appropriate points in our defence of our construction in later chapters, is that Kant also maintains that the categorical imperative is given to human agents by exposition of its concept in *GMM* (though he uses different terminology to say so), and that there is no difference between what Bojanowski calls Kant's 'weak transcendental deduction' in *GMM* and the defence of the result of *CPrR's* exposition that Kant provides in *CPrR* (AK 5:46–47), which Bojanowski recognizes that Kant still offers.

Lewis White Beck's (1960a) construction presents us with some difficulties of classification. We think that Beck rejects the *WAV*, and that Ware (2017, 136 fn 1) is wrong when he says that Beck espouses the *WAV*. But we are unsure whether Beck holds that Kant maintains that free will is the *ratio cognoscendi* or the *ratio essendi* of the categorical imperative in both works. Beck says that, when (in *CPrR*) Kant declares that the moral law 'needs no deduction, he apparently stands the argument of the *Foundations [GMM]* on its head' (1960a, 171). But we need to note the word 'apparently', and Beck then goes on to say that, while the moral law is the *ratio cognoscendi* of free will in *CPrR*, free will nevertheless serves as a 'credential' for the moral law because Kant's argument for free will is 'precisely of the form required if the dialectic of theoretical reason is not to be irresolvable' (1960a, 175), and that this reasoning 'is formally like the deduction of any other synthetic a priori principle in the first *Critique*' as well as that of a synthetic a priori principle in *GMM* (1960a, 172). As in *GMM*, the independent warrant for the *categorical imperative* is the idea of free will (1960a, 173), and '[o]nly this independent warrant makes it possible for Kant to break out of the circle of using freedom to establish the moral law and the moral law to establish freedom' (1960a, 174). This last remark suggests that Beck thinks that Kant attempts a morally neutral deduction of the categorical imperative in both works. Yet Beck also says that the independent warrant of the *moral law* is the fact of pure reason (1960a, 174), which suggests that he thinks that the fact of pure reason *together with* the possibility of a free human will is the complete *ratio cognoscendi* of the categorical imperative, the reason why the moral law *as the categorical imperative* is not a vain idea of pure practical reason but is real. If Beck claims that the *possibility of* free will is a *ratio cognoscendi* of the *categorical imperative* in both *GMM* and *CPrR*, while the independent warrant of the *moral law* (as the *ratio cognoscendi* of free will) is that it is the fact of pure reason in both *GMM* and *CPrR*, then his view is not all that different from our own. This is, however, speculation. Therefore, we will not delve further into Beck's view of the relationship between *GMM* and *CPrR*, though we will have occasion to comment further on his view about what the fact of pure reason is in Chapter Five.

Like us, Michael H. McCarthy (1982) considers that the argument offered in *GMM* and the doctrine concerning the fact of reason/pure reason in *CPrR* are compatible with each other, but he holds that this is because they purport to establish different things.[34] The argument offered in *GMM* is a transcendental deduction that purports to establish that the moral law exists in the form of a categorical imperative (a principle of *duty*). The argument of *CPrR* purports to establish only that pure reason is practical and does not rest on a transcendental deduction. As we understand McCarthy, he sees *CPrR* (in its attention to the fact of pure reason) as focussing on the moral law *as such* rather than as a categorical imperative, while presupposing *GMM's* view of the justification of the categorical imperative. The concept of pure practical reason, in being reciprocal to the concept of free will is the concept of a will that is practical of itself alone, showing which does not require a transcendental deduction, and in this relation the moral law (the moral law *as such,* a law of nature for purely rational agents) is

---

34 We, again, disagree with Ware (2017, 136 fn 2) when he says that McCarthy claims that the arguments provided in *GMM* and *CPrR* are identical.

the *ratio cognoscendi* of free will. of free will. But, to demonstrate the existence of the moral law as a law of nature for a human agent, requires a demonstration of the reality of free will by a *theoretical* deduction, which is impossible. However, the existence of the categorical imperative rests only on the rational necessity for all human agents to act under the idea of free will, which *GMM* purports to establish, and *CPrR* accepts. While this account is in line with our own in various ways, we disagree that Kant's discussion of the fact of reason/pure reason is not directed at establishing that the categorical imperative is the principle of duty. As we will argue in Chapter Five, it purports to show that, in being practical of itself alone, pure practical reason gives the moral law to human agents (*CPrR* AK 5:31), which it can only do if the moral law is viewed as a categorical imperative. McCarthy's claim that the existence of the categorical imperative rests only on showing that human agents must act under the idea of free will also suggests that he thinks that, in Kant's justification of the categorical imperative in both works, free will is the *ratio cognoscendi* of the moral law, which is contrary to our default presumption.

Onora O'Neill maintains, against the *WAV*, that Kant never abandoned his view that the categorical imperative can be justified by a transcendental deduction (2002), and that Kant persistently holds that a priori synthetic practical principles are strict requirements of human agential self-understanding. Furthermore, she holds (as we do) that Kant persistently depicts the categorical imperative as the supreme principle, not merely of all human practical reason, but of all human reason (see, e.g., 1989, 3; 52), which implies that she holds that Kant derives free will from pure practical reason in *GMM* as well as in *CPrR*. And we have already noted that (like us) she depicts the categorical imperative as the supreme principle of the *sensus communis* of *CPoJ*. We will say more about her view of Kant's justificatory methodology, with which we very broadly agree, in Chapter Two. However, she maintains (2002) that Kant's *CPrR* statements concerning moral consciousness being a fact of reason are not part of his argument for the existence of the categorical imperative at all, but *merely* serve to indicate the way in which the categorical imperative, as justified in *GMM*, can be applied in ordinary social life by those who accept that a categorical imperative exists. We disagree with her on this for reasons that will be provided in Chapter Five.

Heiko Puls (2014) claims that Kant reasons in both works from common moral consciousness, which he connects to the feeling of respect for the moral law that is generally held, and that he does not employ a transcendental deduction in either work. While this is not contrary to our default presumption, it depicts the categorical imperative as a principle of heteronomy rather than one of autonomy, and it runs counter to all the reasons we will give for regarding the categorical imperative as a postulate, which is to say, as the supreme a priori principle of the *sensus communis*. We will not, therefore, apart from a short comment in Chapter Five, pay further attention to Puls's construction.

Klaus Steigleder (2002, 2006) and Michael Wolff (2009, 2015) share our view of concordance between *GMM* and *CPrR* insofar as they also contend that Kant holds that pure practical reason is the *ratio cognoscendi* of free will in both *CPrR* and *GMM;* acceptance of the categorical imperative is rationally necessary for all human agents; this rational necessity is constituted by acceptance of the categorical imperative being a strict requirement of human agential self-understanding and it is, by this means, that the categorical imperative is given to human agents as the sole fact of pure reason. We will devote a chapter to consideration of their constructions.

Like ourselves, Owen Ware (2017) maintains that *GMM* and *CPrR* are compatible, and that Kant justifies the categorical imperative by a transcendental deduction in both works that is not morally neutral. However (unlike us), he maintains that Kant, nevertheless, holds that it is neither necessary nor possible to show that all human agents rationally *must* hold that there is a categorical imperative. It is only necessary and possible to show (by showing that/ explaining why it is not incoherent for human agents to hold that they have free will) that it is rationally *acceptable* for them to hold that there is a categorical imperative. In other words, the categorical imperative only holds with rational necessity on any grounds for a select group of human agents, those who are morally committed, and it is impossible and unnecessary to show that it is rationally necessary for *all* human agents to be morally committed. Kant gives the same justification for the categorical imperative in *CPrR* that he gives in *GMM*, but the justification is weak in being relative to a rationally optional commitment, not strong in only involving rationally necessary commitments. In doing so, Ware implicitly challenges our claim that Kant regards the categorical imperative as undeniable because it is a postulate. We will devote a chapter to what we consider to be Ware's misconstruction.

Outline of Things to Come

With this as background, in further presenting and defending our interpretation of Kant's justification of the categorical imperative, we will proceed as follows.

Chapter Two presents in some detail our view of the logical structure of the justification of the categorical imperative from which Kant never wavers. It has two parts. The first part provides further detail about our view of the *methodology* of Kant's justification, according to which he holds that to show that an imperative is categorically binding is to show that its acceptance is coherent as a strict requirement of human agential self-understanding. It also explains why we think that Kant's use of 'Verstand' rather than 'Verstehen' (which is a post-Kantian philosophical term) for 'understanding' does not render our view implausible. The second part presents the claims that we consider Kant makes (or implies) that together provide his basis for contending that human agents unconditionally must accept that the categorical imperative exists. We present these claims as an outline sequence in three stages. Chapter Two does not seek to defend this construction fully, and, as an argument, it is to an extent elliptical, as it requires additional input from the chapters that follow to constitute a complete sequence.

Chapter Three supports our claim that Kant consistently views a priori synthetic practical propositions as ones that must be accepted because doing so is a strict requirement of human agential self-understanding, first, by examining how he relates what he says in *GMM* about the nature of such propositions to the justification he provides there for the categorical imperative, and, secondly, by examining how the idea that the categorical imperative is given to human agents as the sole fact of pure reason in *CPrR* relates to his claim that the categorical imperative is an a priori synthetic practical proposition .

Chapter Four provides systemic support for our characterization of an a priori synthetic practical proposition as a strict requirement of human agential self-understanding by placing Kant's justification of the categorical imperative in the context of his critical philosophy viewed as a system. Particularly significant are statements that Kant makes about
(a) the basic questions of philosophy and their relations to each other and about the aims of a critique of practical reason; and
(b) the three maxims of the *sensus communis* in *CPoJ*, which he says are the fundamental principles of all critical reasoning.

The first set of statements is appealed to in support of our claim that Kant persistently regards the categorical imperative as a principle that all human agents unconditionally must accept. It is also integral to our understanding of what he intends to convey by calling the moral law the sole fact of pure reason. The second set is appealed to in further support of our claim that Kant persistently views acceptance of the categorical imperative as a strict requirement of human agential self-understanding and provides yet further support for our claim that he persistently holds that the categorical imperative is a principle that all human agents unconditionally must accept.

Chapter Five examines Kant's justification in *CPrR* and argues that it has the logical structure that we attribute to it. We examine *CPrR* before *GMM* because the way in which Kant presents his argument in *CPrR* is easier to relate to the way in which we present our construction in Chapter Two than his argument in *GMM,* and because taking his claim seriously that the argument of *GMM* presupposes the argument of *CPrR* suggests that it will be more helpful to interpret *GMM* in terms of *CPrR* when it is unclear how to interpret *GMM* than the other way around. This is because his claim renders it reasonable to suppose that formulations in *CPrR* that differ from those in *GMM* are intended as clarifications of *GMM*.[35]

Chapter Six examines Kant's justification in *GMM* and offers four possible accounts of its presentational structure that share the logical structure that our default presumption of concordance with *CPrR* requires them to have. We prefer one of these accounts, but (given our defeasible default presumption) all that matters for our purposes is that one of them not be countermanded unequivocally by clear counter claims that Kant himself makes.

Chapter Seven compares our construction with those of Klaus Steigleder (2002, 2006) and Michael Wolff (2009, 2015) and reveals the ways in which we consider that our construction improves on theirs.

Chapter Eight examines and rejects Owen Ware's (2017) construction.

Chapter Nine concludes with some brief comments on the validity of Kant's argument. The purpose of these comments is not to provide a definitive assessment of the strengths and weaknesses of Kant's justification. Its objective is to make our readers aware of our personal views on the validity of Kant's justification that might possibly (against our intentions) have pushed our construction in the direction of a revisionary reconstruction rather than the exegetical reconstruction we consider it to be.

---

[35] This is not to say that *GMM* cannot be used to illuminate *CPrR*. It can and will be so used at any point in our defence of our construction when Kant repeats statements made in *GMM* in *CPrR* that are explained in *GMM* but not in *CPrR*.

Chapter Two
Kant's Argument for the Categorical Imperative Constructed

This chapter has two parts. The first part elaborates our view that Kant construes the categorical imperative as a strict requirement of human agential self-understanding and provides further evidence for this. It also considers a possible objection on the grounds that our view attributes to Kant the idea of understanding signified by 'Verstehen' (which, as a philosophical concept, is associated with post-Kantian philosophy) rather than that signified by 'Verstand' (which is the term Kant generally uses). The second part outlines the rational thought dynamics that we claim Kant appeals to in arguing that human agential self-understanding reveals the FUL to be the categorical imperative. We link some of the claims that make up our construction to Kant's textual assertions. However, we do so primarily in order to identify the linkages that our defence of our construction will need to justify in the chapters that follow.

Kant's Justificatory Criterion

In *GMM* I, Kant says that

> the concept of a will that is to be esteemed in itself and that is good apart from any further purpose . . . already dwells in natural *sound* understanding. [Our emphasis added.]
> (AK 4:397)

Furthermore, he tells us that the law of such a will is *'I ought never to act except in such a way that I could also will that my maxim should become a universal law'* (AK 4:402) (in effect, already telling us that it is the FUL) and that it is arrived at 'within the moral cognition of common human reason' (AK 4:403).

At the very beginning of *GMM* II, he says:

> If we have so far drawn our concept of duty from the common use of our practical reason, *it is by no means to be inferred from this that we have treated it as a concept of experience.* [Our emphasis added.]
> (AK 4:406)

And later in *GMM* II, he says that

> it is clear that all moral concepts have their seat and origin completely *a priori* [our emphasis] in reason, and indeed in the most common reason.
> (AK 4:411)

Kant makes statements of this kind at various points throughout *GMM*, *CPrR*, and in some of his other critical writings, which reveals that his reference to 'common human understanding' or 'common human reason' is not, for *justificatory purposes*, reference to what is imagined or believed by the ordinary man or woman, or the person who exhibits what the cultural understanding of Kant's milieu regards as 'common sense' (see, especially *GMM* AK 4:404–405, *CPoJ* AK 5:293, *Jäsche Logic* AK 9:56, *Anthropology* AK 7:139). This is because what such common sense is can only be ascertained by an empirical examination of agents' beliefs. Instead, it is reference to the *a priori* powers of *thought* (reason/understanding) that any human being necessarily possesses who has the ability to do things for reasons, thus, has a will and so can act. Kant does say that it is an empirical fact that the categorical imperative is believed to exist by many human agents. But he considers that this is because human agents necessarily have the a priori powers of the common human understanding and many of them are capable of sound reasoning.[1] These powers are the powers without which human beings would be unable to conceive or believe anything, and no human cultural milieu could exist at all. So, when he says that the moral law is to be found in the moral *cognition* of common human reason (*GMM* AK 4:403), he is saying that the *sound* exercise of these powers presents human agents with the concept of the moral law and strictly requires them to recognize the moral laws supreme authority.

The reason why Kant holds that human agents necessarily possess the powers of the common human understanding is that he holds that agents do things for reasons, which is to say that they follow practical precepts (*GMM* AK 4:412). As such, questions about what it is rational for a human agent ('Agnes') to do necessarily arise for her. But to think that any claims or questions about what it is rational for Agnes to do *can* arise presupposes that Agnes has the powers of reason/understanding that are necessary to render such questions or claims intelligible to her. And it is the possession/exercise of these powers to which Kant primarily refers when he speaks of the common human understanding. Since having these powers is necessary for Agnes to be an agent, it is unintelligible for Agnes to think that she may adopt or hold any view about what it is rationally permissible or required for her to do on *any criterion* if, by doing so, she implies that she is not an agent. For, if she implies that she is not an agent, she implies that she lacks the powers necessary for her to be able to adopt or hold any view about practical reason. So, *if there is a view* about what

---

[1] That he probably overestimated the extent to which this is so is beside the point from a justificatory point of view.

it is rationally permissible, impermissible, or required for Agnes to do that she cannot reject without implying that she is not an agent, then (on the presumption that she is both able and able not to adopt this view, which will be the case because she is an embodied incompletely rational agent subject to being affected by heteronomous incentives), it is categorically imperative for her to adopt this view, and this entails that she categorically ought to hold that all her practical precepts and actions categorically ought to be consistent with this view.

The idea that a view is one that Agnes must agree that she categorically ought to adopt, or else imply that she is not an agent, is the idea of a view that Agnes must adopt because doing so is a strict requirement of her agential self-understanding (i.e., a strict requirement of the sound exercise of the powers of common human reason/understanding that Agnes necessarily possesses). Thus, we maintain that Kant holds that a categorical imperative is a construction of Agnes's agential self-understanding. *As such,* the idea of a strict requirement of Agnes's agential self-understanding does not *merely set the criterion* that any imperative must satisfy in order to be a categorical imperative. The categorical imperative *is constituted for Agnes* by the fact that her agential self-understanding sets the criterion for being a categorical imperative. This is to say that human agential self-understanding sets the adoption of maxims consistent with human agential self-understanding as the categorical imperative. So understood, Agnes's agential self-understanding sets itself (or, more precisely, conformity with its strict requirements) as an end in itself for Agnes's will. Therefore, when Kant says that the categorical imperative is an apodictic a priori synthetic practical proposition, he means that Agnes's acceptance of the FUL is not merely a strict requirement of Agnes's agential self-understanding as a human agent; her acceptance of the FUL *represents* what it is for her to have sound (i.e., intelligible) human agential self-understanding. Thus, human agential self-understanding is not, and cannot be, morally neutral. The fact that the categorical imperative is a strict requirement of human agential self-understanding makes human agential self-understanding the *ratio cognoscendi* of the categorical imperative, but such a justification of the categorical imperative is not on grounds external to the categorical imperative. As a strict requirement of human agential self-understanding, the categorical imperative justifies itself in human agential self-understanding.

In short, we maintain that Kant's view is that understanding having the concept of a categorical imperative provides the criterion for judging its existence and that understanding the criterion for the existence of a categorical imperative *unconditionally* reveals the sole categorical imperative to be the command to adopt practical precepts only if they are in accord with precepts that satisfy this criterion. The command to adopt the criterion for the categorical imperative is itself the categorical imperative. This is equivalent to saying that human agential self-understanding is the criterion for intelligible action and understanding human agential self-understanding reveals that guiding one's action by human agential self-understanding is the sole categorical imperative. Unpacking this, and understanding its presuppositions and implications, is both the basis for and the essence of Kant's argument for the categorical imperative.

We have already given some reasons in Chapter One for thinking that Kant considers that the existence of the categorical imperative is postulated (presented as undeniable) in and by human agential self-understanding by exposition of its concept. To these should be added the following statement from *CPuR*.

> I assume that there really are pure moral laws, which determine completely a priori . . . the action and omission, i.e., the use of freedom of a rational being in general, and that these laws command absolutely . . . and are necessary in every respect. I can legitimately presuppose this proposition by appealing . . . to the moral judgment of every human being, *if he will distinctly think* such a law. [Our emphasis added.] (*CPuR* A807: B835)

Note that, according to Kant,

> [W]hen I make a concept distinct . . . only the form is altered in that I learn to distinguish better, or to cognise with clearer consciousness, what lay in the given concept already.
> (*Jäsche Logic* AK 9:64)

> Consciousness of one's representations that suffices for the *distinction* of one object from another is **clarity**. But that consciousness by means of which the composition of representations also becomes clear is called **distinctness**. Distinctness alone makes possible that an aggregate of representations becomes knowledge . . . because every conscious combination presupposes unity of consciousness. (*Anthropology* AK 7:137–138)

> Furthermore, the faculty 'to think is understanding.' (*Anthropology* AK 7:127)

So, distinctly thinking a law is different from thinking a law clearly. Distinctly thinking a law elicits what is contained in the concept of understanding having the concept of a law. It is to think the concept of having the concept of a law clearly, rather than to think the concept of the law itself clearly, which is only a part of it. Thus, already in *CPuR*, Kant indicates that common human reason only reveals the moral law (as the categorical imperative) on a condition, which is that the concept of *having* the concept of a moral law be clearly understood. The moral law is not an empirical fact about what all human agents believe but is elicited *and* established by what every human agent ought to believe by virtue of understanding the concept of thinking a moral law. Furthermore, these passages, especially with reference to the phrase 'every conscious combination presupposes unity of consciousness' in relation to 'distinctness', suggest that the activity of 'exposition' that Kant refers to at *CPrR* AK 5:46 (by which the moral law is revealed to exist without any external support) is the activity of distinctly thinking the categorical imperative, *and* that it is a *procedure* of self-understanding, indeed, of human agential self-understanding (on which, see further our discussion of Kant's maxims of the *sensus communis* of *CPoJ* in Chapter Four).[2]

If this seems to be a case of Kant supposing what he sets out to establish, then his response to such a charge is that this *must* be presupposed by any agent for the idea of any practical reason to be intelligible. Kant, we contend, would claim that even if this reasoning is circular, it is not viciously circular, which is to say that it is not a *petitio*. Indeed, we think he would say that it is not even circular because the proposition that the categorical imperative exists is not derived from the assumption that the categorical imperative exists, but from understanding the concept of a categorical imperative as a strict requirement of human agential self-understanding.

To say this is to say that, according to Kant, the activity of exposition of the categorical imperative as analysis of the concept of human agential self-understanding is not deductive on any syllogistic model. Presenting the criterion for a possible categorical imperative as itself the categorical imperative enables him to maintain that rationally required acceptance of the categorical imperative on the basis of exposition of the concept of a categorical imperative is immune to the Pyrrhonian Dilemma of the Criterion. This dilemma is that

> in order to decide the dispute which has arisen about the criterion [of truth], we must possess an accepted criterion by which we shall be able to judge the dispute; and in order to possess an accepted criterion, the dispute about the criterion must first be decided. And when the argument thus reduces itself to a form of circular reasoning the discovery of the criterion becomes impracticable, since we do not allow [those who make knowledge claims] to adopt a criterion by assumption, while if they offer to judge the criterion by a criterion we force them to a regress *ad infinitum*. And furthermore, since demonstration requires a demonstrated criterion, while the criterion requires an approved demonstration, they are forced into circular reasoning.
> (Sextus Empiricus 1934, 2.4.20 as quoted by Kenneth Westphal 2002, 19 fn 14)

David Hume's famous dictum that 'ought' cannot be derived from 'is' is an application of the Pyrrhonian Dilemma, in which form it constitutes a possible objection to Kant's justificatory methodology.

---

2 In *Blomberg Logic* (a manual of Kant's Lectures given around 1777), he says, 'With analytic cognition I make a given concept distinct. Synthetic cognition gives me the concept simultaneously with distinctness. The philosopher makes concepts distinct' (298).

Kenneth Westphal (esp. 2016), building on Onora O'Neill's (1989, 1992) analysis of Kant's transcendental methodology, which is consistent with our construction to at least this extent, maintains that, in being a construction of the dynamics of human agential self-understanding, Kant's justification avoids both horns of the Pyrrhonian Dilemma. We agree. More to the point, we agree that Kant thinks so too.

As we understand Kant's thinking on this, though this might surprise some, he does not disagree with Hume's dictum *whenever it has application*. But he thinks that Hume's dictum does not apply to his justificatory methodology. This is because he holds that action in accord with the categorical imperative *is, and can be nothing other* than, action in accord with human agential self-understanding, and nothing other than action in accord with human agential self-understanding *can coherently be thought* to be a criterion for action in accord with human agential self-understanding *or any alternative position* that Agnes might hold. For it to be possible to be anything other, it must be intelligible for Agnes to ask, 'Why ought I to act in accord with my agential self-understanding as a human agent?' But it is only intelligible for Agnes to ask this if Agnes can coherently think that she can adopt some position about *her actions* while implying that she is not an agent, which is not the case.

This is also O'Neill's take on the matter. As she says, according to Kant,

> The principles of reason [the a priori maxims of the *sensus communis*] vindicate their authority by their stamina when applied to themselves. (1989, 38)

> Reason's authority, like other human authorities, is humanly instituted. But it is not on that account arbitrary, or in any sense merely a convention. On the contrary, it cannot be questioned, because intelligible questioning presumes the very authority [reason] it presumes to question. (1989, 42)

Furthermore, we agree with O'Neill and Westphal that the thrust of this response to the Pyrrhonian Dilemma/Hume's dictum is that Kant's critical philosophy is neither 'foundationalist' nor 'coherentist', but only *if* these terms are understood in the following ways. Foundationalism is a view that seeks to justify its claims by *deduction* from *independent* premises alleged to be necessarily true or undeniable in themselves. Coherentism is a view that justifies its claims by locating them in a coherent system of statements governed by a basic statement or statements that are neither true nor false, nor rationally necessary, but ones to which the adherent is simply staunchly committed.

However, though it is customary to conceive of foundationalism and coherentism in these ways, they need not be so understood on the supposition that it is possible for there to be propositions that *necessarily* presuppose themselves.

Given such a supposition, we think that Kant's view may be characterized, without contradiction, as a 'foundationalist coherentism'. It is appropriately designated as a 'coherentism' in requiring all legitimate claims that take any object to be consistent with putative axiomatic claims. It is appropriately designated as 'foundationalist' in that (and only in that) these claims (the strict requirements of agential self-understanding) are held to be presuppositions of the possibility of intelligibly *making any* claims that take an object. The categorical imperative is not self-evident, but self-evidencing for Agnes, not in itself, but *in* Agnes's understanding what it is for her to possess agential self-understanding.[3] Thinking of Kant's position in this way is completely at odds with the view that he thinks that, because there cannot be a morally neutral deduction of pure practical reason from a kind of practical reason that can

> be cited as its basis . . . the most natural characterization [of such practical reason] is simply to specify the basic principles of morality . . . that underlie ordinary moral judgments, and show how they express values, attitudes towards persons and conceptions of agency that are firmly rooted in ordinary thought and experience.
> (Andrews Reath 1997, xxvii)

Nothing can be clearer than that Reath's view has Kant believing (contrary to his express denial) that the moral law/categorical imperative is a principle of heteronomy, located in empirical facts, *unless* we are to believe that Kant holds the view of W. V. O. Quine (1951) that what *we* think of as a priori truths (including the logical principle of contradiction) are nothing other than those commitments *we* (the 'royal we' so beloved of modern analytical philosophers) are least willing to give up. But, of this we can be certain: Kant holds no such view, as (apart from the fact that we are sure that he would claim this to be self-contradictory, on the grounds that one cannot even understand what it is to give up the principle of contradiction without employing it) this makes the categorical imperative applicable only to those who are not willing to give up their commitment to it, and makes its bindingness conditional on their continued willingness not to give it up, which contradicts his claim that the very concept of a categorical imperative is of a practical precept *unconditionally* binding on *all* human agents.

---

[3] We comment further in Chapter Eight on the difference between non-foundationalist and foundationalist coherentism by contrasting Kant's justificatory methodology with R. G. Collingwoods (1940) doctrine that philosophies are grounded in what he calls 'absolute presuppositions', when we discuss Owen Ware's (2017) view on what Kant means when he says that the justification of the categorical imperative can only begin from principles.

The evidence we have so far provided that Kant's position is a 'foundationalist coherentism' must be read in conjunction with the logical structure of his argument for the categorical imperative and the further defences of it that we will present. It is, therefore, worth stating now and for later reference or elaboration some of the claims that Kant makes that bear directly on the response to the Pyrrhonian Dilemma/Hume's/Hume's dictum that we attribute to him. For example, he claims that:
- the categorical imperative can have and needs no external justification, as it would then not be a categorical imperative (*GMM* AK 4:463);
- a critique of practical reason cannot 'be censured for beginning with pure practical laws and their reality, and it must begin there' (*CPrR* AK 5:46);
- a philosopher cannot have any principle other than that of common understanding (*GMM* AK 4:404);
- all human comprehension is relative and we can comprehend nothing absolutely (*Jäsche Logic* AK 9:65) (ditto *Blomberg Logic*, 106);
- 'pure reason, once it is shown to exist, needs no critique . . . [for] it is pure reason that itself contains the standard for the critical examination of every use of it' (*CPrR* AK 5:15–16);
- if there is a categorical imperative then it can and need presuppose nothing other than itself (*CPrR* AK 5:21);
- rational nature exists as an end in itself and is the ground of the categorical imperative (*GMM* AK 4:428–429);
- there is nothing that is absolutely good except a good will (*GMM* AK 4:393);
- there is a 'paradox of method' in a critique of practical reason, *'namely, that the concept of good and evil must not be determined before the moral law . . . but only . . . after it and by means of it'* (*CPrR* 5:63);
- 'the ground of obligation' lies 'a priori simply in concepts of pure reason', and 'all moral philosophy is based entirely on its pure part . . . [which] when it is applied to the human being . . . gives to him, as a rational being, laws a priori' (*GMM* 4:389); and
- the categorical imperative is given to human agents as the sole fact of pure reason (*CPrR* 5:31).

We maintain that all of these are analytically connected to each other and elucidate each other.

However, since we claim that our position on these matters is also O'Neill's (and Westphal's), we need to say something about O'Neill's claim that Kant's first-person methodology is inherently social, operating with a public rather than a private conception of personal reason. According to O'Neill, operating with 'public' reason means that Agnes can only intelligibly make judgments that other agents *can* intelligibly accept. 'Private judgments' are not self-interested ones and 'public judgments' are not communally agreed ones (e.g., O'Neill 1989, 28–50). According to Westphal, this entails that the FUL (being the principle of public reason) specifies that universal communicability is a necessary condition for rational justification in all non-formal domains (2016, Chapter One) – non-formal domains being constituted by synthetic judgments (ones that are about an object), formal domains being constituted by purely logical propositions (in which only logical constants occur essentially) – which means that Kant holds that

> [d]ue to our fallibility and limited knowledge, both factual and inferential, any particular judgment anyone makes is justified only to the extent that one does one's utmost to exercise informed judgment on that occasion, and to the extent that one's judgment survives critical scrutiny by all concerned parties (including oneself). . . . Because informed judgment is socially based, so is rational justification [which is, thus, inherently fallible].
> (2016, 28.1)

But how, then, can O'Neill and Westphal claim that Kant thinks that it is nothing less than unintelligible to question the authority of the FUL as the principle of human agential self-understanding? Kant holds that the categorical imperative is an apodictic a priori *synthetic* practical proposition . So, if Kant holds that all synthetic judgments are fallible, and all propositions are judgments, should he not hold that the existence of a categorical imperative is inherently rationally questionable?

We think that there is a problem here. However, we think that it arises only if one thinks that this characterization, which applies to the application of the FUL to judge the legitimacy of actions and practical precepts according to its tests, and the reasoning that leads to identifying the FUL as the principle of human agential self-understanding, also applies to the judgment that human agential self-understanding is the basis of all human judgment. We do not think that O'Neill or Westphal are here contradicting O'Neill's claim that Kant thinks that the authority of human agential self-understanding is intelligibly unquestionable. The problem is that the way in which Westphal describes the social character of the categorical imperative focusses on the way in which the categorical imperative is applied (which does require the kind of social scrutiny Westphal identifies) rather than on the way in which it is justified (which does not) and so encourages the thought that Kant is not being consistent and does not believe that he can refute a sceptic who refuses to believe that there is a categorical imperative.

But this is not to say that we think that Kant holds that the categorical imperative *itself* does not have a social character. There is a way in which Kant thinks that the inherently personal human agential self-understanding that constitutes the categorical imperative is an inherently social understanding which characterizes the categorical imperative's character in its justification that does not invite a relativistic interpretation. This character lies in the bi-conditional relation that Kant says exists between the first maxim of the *sensus communis* (the maxim of understanding) and the second maxim of the *sensus communis* (the maxim of the power of judgment), and we will explain what this is after we have had a closer look at the three maxims of the *sensus communis* in Chapter Four. The point for now is that we understand Westphal and O'Neill to agree that Kant thinks that he has refuted the moral sceptic, and for this reason we think that they should accept that his justification of the categorical imperative is foundationalist in the following way. The answer to the question, 'How can the categorical imperative be the basis of all judgments without presupposing another judgment as its basis?' is 'Because its acceptance is a strict requirement of human agential self-understanding'. This answer, of course, presupposes that acceptance of the strict requirements of human agential self-understanding is an end in itself; and, in our construction, showing that it has this status is not achieved by showing that it presupposes the proposition that acceptance of the strict requirements of human agential self-understanding is an end in itself. Instead, it is secured by showing that acceptance of this *proposition* is strictly required by exposition of the *concept* of *possessing* human agential self-understanding. It is Kant's derivation of a necessitated proposition by exposition of the necessitated concept of having the concept of a categorical imperative that puts the Pyrrhonian Dilemma out of play. The reason why the categorical imperative is postulated by pure reason as a whole is that it is the only a priori synthetic judgment that has a concept given by understanding as its basis. It achieves its unquestionable status by being postulated, not by presupposition of another proposition, but by human agential self-understanding of the concept of possessing agential self-understanding. Indeed, this is what we take Kant to be saying when he opens *GMM* by declaring that there is nothing that is absolutely good ('good without limitation') except a good will (AK 4:393), once it is appreciated that a good will is a will that reasons in accord with itself (per the third maxim of the *sensus communis* of *CPoJ*, the maxim of reason). It is ultimately on this basis, we maintain, that Kant claims and is able to claim that acceptance of the authority of human agential self-understanding achieves its rational necessity by its mere rational possibility, and that it is altogether unique in this (which we take him to be doing at *CPrR* AK 5:31).

Reading 'Verstand' as 'Verstehen'

However, before we go into details about the thought dynamics of Kant's justification of the categorical imperative, we need to consider a possible objection to the account we have just given of his criterion for the existence of a categorical imperative. This objection is that the term Kant generally uses for 'understanding' is 'Verstand'; but the way in which we depict human agential self-understanding treats 'understanding' as having connotations of 'Verstehen'. As a concept in philosophical theory, 'Verstehen' is a post-Kantian concept and cannot be attributed to Kant's view of what the common human understanding involves. Consequently, our construction is more revisionary and less exegetical than we claim it to be.

Our response to this is as follows.

It is true that Kant generally uses 'Verstand' as a critical construct, and uses 'Verstehen' mainly as a colloquial expression – as in 'Do you know the meaning of this word?' or 'Do you understand what I have just said?' But he uses 'Verstand' in two senses: narrowly, as a specific faculty of cognition involving sense perception, and broadly, as a term that covers comprehension ('Begreifen') and orientation in thinking generally. This broad sense is the primary focus of his short essay 'What Does It Mean to Orient Oneself in Thinking?' (Kant 1786). It is also the sense in which he regards the combined powers of the *sensus communis* as a comprehensive faculty of understanding, in contrast with which the maxim of understanding is a maxim of a sub-faculty of the *sensus communis* as a comprehensive faculty that involves sense perception.

It is also true that 'Verstehen' became the central concept of the hermeneutic movement, which became an important philosophical enterprise only after Friedrich Schleiermacher (1978) and Wilhelm Dilthey (1989). But it is also true that Schleiermacher and Dilthey were heavily influenced by Kant, particularly by *CPoJ*, as Rudolf Makkreel (1990, 1992, 2015) has shown in some detail. The hermeneutic tradition built around 'Verstehen' developed from a discipline that was primarily interested in the interpretation of texts (especially the Bible) as a paradigm for the humanities (seen to be concerned with interpretation of texts, pieces of art, history, and tradition). What Dilthey, especially, did was to use the broad Kantian idea of understanding to institute hermeneutic understanding (understood in terms of 'Verstehen') as a methodology for the humanities distinct from the methodology of the natural sciences (concerned with mechanistic causal explanations). Such a hermeneutic approach was later proposed as a methodology for the social sciences, especially by Max Weber (1997), and for the idea that knowledge and reality are socially constructed by, e.g., Peter L. Berger and Thomas Luckmann (1966). And related ideas became a philosophical paradigm in the Twentieth Century in the philosophies of Martin Heidegger (2010) and Hans-Georg Gadamer (2013).

However, because of these later developments, it is important to be clear about what elements of the idea of Verstehen they employ that are shared by

Kant's broad concept of understanding, which we maintain is the idea of human agential self-understanding in terms of the three maxims of the *sensus communis*. This is because the hermeneutic tradition emphasizes that Verstehen is always historically and culturally embedded, meaning that it is understanding focussed on insights about the object of understanding with awareness of the 'horizon' in which those objects are understood. Hermeneutic understanding does not try to abstract from the subject of understanding but emphasizes a primacy of this subject and the necessity to see the categories and modes of understanding as bound to this subject of understanding, which is the cultural horizon within which the categories and modes of understandings are formed. Without going into the details of the hermeneutic tradition, it is important to appreciate that this historically embedded 'Verstehen' is often seen to be opposed to Kant's use of 'Verstand', which is generally understood only in the narrow sense of *one* faculty of cognition. Furthermore it is often assumed that Kant's concept of 'Verstand' refers to the thinking of an immutable transcendental ego that exists outside of space and time, and thus of history, which is odd because Kant's narrow sense is tied to thinking that involves sense perception, which is embedded in space and time. While Kant might be said at times to employ a different narrow sense of 'Verstand' in relation to the maxim of the power of judgment to generate universal understanding, this maxim (as we will elaborate on in later chapters) is an abstraction from the binding maxim of understanding that involves sense perception that Kant's broad sense of understanding requires to be consistent with the maxim of understanding that involves sense perception. To complicate matters further, the maxim of the power of judgment is directly associated with the faculty of feeling.

We cannot go into the details here, and we certainly do not claim that Kant was already operating with the full awareness of historicity that later research has emphasized. But, for the purposes of this book, three points must be stressed.

First, as should be clear by now, when we speak about 'human agential self-understanding', we are using the term 'understanding' in a generic sense and not only as a term for the activity of the 'faculty of understanding' as the distinct cognitive capacity involving sense perception. Reflecting on the conditions for 'agential self-understanding' involves revealing the presuppositions that are absolutely necessary for Agnes to render it intelligible for her to think that she is an agent.

Secondly, for Kant, human agential self-understanding is the self-understanding of an embodied agent, an agent who is not only governed by rational insights but driven by various feelings and desires. As Kant insists, only an embodied agent, and not a purely rational being, is under the authority of the categorical imperative. Consequently, hermeneutic discussion about the historicity of understanding applies to Kant's human agents.

Thirdly, Kant does not consider knowledge and insights to be attained independently of judgments; correct or justified judgments cannot be understood as direct acquisitions of truths. The central question for him is to understand how knowledge and insights are embedded in basic forms of human orientation. This is made absolutely clear in *Jasche Logic* (AK 9:65), where Kant embeds 'understanding' (in the primary narrow sense) in seven steps of comprehension, starting with unclear forms of representation. It is also implicit in the 'Transcendental Doctrine of Method' in *CPuR* (A730–731; B758–759), where he reflects on the necessity to grasp in one's mind a provisional outline of an object prior to its complete exposition (its definition) in order to be able to form beliefs and attain knowledge. *All* forms of 'understanding' are based on activities of judging agents.

At least some of these features of Kant's 'Verstand' (in the broad sense) are shared with historicized ideas of 'Verstehen'. In our opinion, properly focussed, where these differ is essentially over whether there is any understanding that is necessarily trans-historical (to be distinguished from understanding that is ahistorical). That there is such understanding is implicit in Kant's view that there are presuppositions that are absolutely necessary for Agnes (as an embodied agent) on the presumption that it is intelligible for her to think that she is an agent at all. We claim that it is only with this being understood that Kant's broad notion of 'Verstand' has connotations of 'Verstehen' in the later hermeneutic tradition.

Kant's Justificatory Argument

We have said that Kant's argument for the existence of the categorical imperative in the form of the FUL has three stages.

The first two stages constitute his 'exposition' of the categorical imperative. This exposition *presents* (or 'gives') the FUL to Agnes as an a priori synthetic practical proposition. The third stage constitutes the transcendental deduction by which he *validates* this presentation by defending it against the claim that it reveals an antinomy in pure reason as a whole.

The reasoning involved in these stages (*SI*, *SII* and *SIII*) may be broken into several propositions (*Pr1–Pr10*). We do not claim that Kant presents his justification in this sequential way, nor that he makes all the claims we attribute to him explicitly. We claim only that he would agree to all of them.

SI

Pr1: Agnes, by virtue of *understanding* what is involved in employing means to achieve her chosen ends necessarily reasons in terms of hypothetical imperatives.

Pr2: This is because to act (thus to be an agent) is to employ means to ends voluntarily, a hypothetical imperative for Agnes being constituted by her *understanding* the implication of there being means that are necessary to achieve her chosen ends.

Pr3: It follows that, if Agnes is to understand what it is for her to be an agent, she must understand the concept of a hypothetical imperative.

Pr4: Agnes *clearly* understands the concept of a hypothetical *imperative* only if she understands the concept of a *categorical* imperative (if only negatively, as an imperative that is not hypothetical – which is to say, as an imperative that she must obey, regardless of any incentive or inclination she has either to obey it or not to obey it, or even on account of anything that makes her the particular agent that she is as against another agent). And this is to say that she can only clearly understand the concept of a hypothetical imperative by understanding the concept of a categorical imperative as an imperative that all rationally permissible hypothetical imperatives of any agent must be consistent with.

Pr5: It follows that Agnes's agential self-understanding strictly requires her to understand the concept of a categorical imperative.[4]

In Chapter Five, we will argue that when Kant says that *consciousness* of the moral law is a fact of reason (*CPrR* AK 5:29–31) – which is not to be confused with his claim that the moral law is given as the (sole) fact of pure reason – he means that Agnes's agential self-understanding strictly requires her to be aware of and understand the concept of a categorical imperative. And the reasoning process by which he explains how consciousness of the moral law as the FUL is arrived at is inferentially that involved in *Pr2* to *Pr5*, coupled with *Pr6*.

---

4 *SI* can be presented in a slightly different but compatible way. By virtue of possessing the a priori powers of the common human understanding, the question of the rational permissibility of Agnes's actions necessarily arises for her, because the a priori powers of the common human understanding, by their nature, give rise to concepts of rational permissibility and impermissibility. Whether or not Agnes considers that all claims to permissibility are governed by hypothetical imperatives, considers that they are governed by a categorical imperative, or does not recognize any norms of rational permissibility/impermissibility, her agential self-understanding strictly requires her to understand the concept of a categorical imperative. This is because she cannot *meaningfully* claim that there are no norms of rational permissibility without having and understanding the concept of a categorical imperative. The claim that nothing is categorically required or prohibited is empty unless made about the idea of something that is categorically required or prohibited.

SII

Pr6: If Agnes understands the concept of a categorical imperative, then she must accept that *if* it exists *then* there can be only one categorical imperative (*GMM* AK 4:421)[5] and that it has the content of the FUL and Kant's other formulae for the moral law (all of which formulae Kant holds – see *GMM* AK 4:436 – are formulae for one and the same law, which he must do on the understanding that there can be only one categorical imperative).

Pr7: Furthermore, by understanding that the concept of a categorical imperative is the concept of an imperative that all practical precepts, thus all hypothetical imperatives,imperatives, must be consistent with (see *Pr4*), Agnes must think that if there is a categorical imperative then all her actions and practical precepts, and views about what it is rationally permissible for her to do or accept, must be consistent with the FUL. In other words, she must think that conformity with the FUL is the unconditionally necessary *criterion for* practical rational permissibility. But *understanding this* means that she must think that it is categorically imperative for her to adopt practical precepts/maxims only if they are consistent with the FUL.[6]

---

[5] Kant does not explain this; but the reason is obvious. Given that a categorical imperative is, by its concept, one that all Agnes's practical precepts must be consistent with, if there is more than one apparent categorical imperative then it must be combinable with all other apparent categorical imperatives into a single imperative, otherwise all apparent categorical imperatives cancel each other out and there is no categorical imperative.

[6] When practical precepts are in the form of principles (which they are if they prescribe what the agent unconditionally may or ought to do), the agent must be able to take them to be practical laws if it is to be permissible for the agent to adopt them. Other practical precepts need only be consistent with what the agent must take to be practical laws. Because the FUL prescribes a formal test that Agnes's practical precepts must be subjected to, it does not, by itself, prescribe the material content that her maxims must have. Of course, Kant claims that understanding the concept of a categorical imperative also requires acceptance of the FoH, which requires agents to consider their existence to be an end in itself. But deciding what is necessary to treat the existence of agents as an end in itself requires empirical knowledge. For example, if as Kant thinks, it is ascertainable a priori that human agents must treat human life as an end in itself (*GMM* 4:429), it is not ascertainable a priori what is needed to defend a human life. To arrive at this content requires input from practical (not a priori) 'anthropology for its *application* to human beings' (*GMM* AK 4:412), which is to say that what the FUL will justify can and does depend on biological, social, and psychological factors that affect Agnes's constitutive and contingent abilities to comply with the FUL. In this sense, the FUL, by itself, is empty. But it is not, if Kant's argument for it is sound, empty in the sense that the thought of its binding nature is illusory, or that Kant's methodology for generating categorically binding material rules from it is not categorically binding.

Pr8: Since there can be only one categorical imperative, it follows that Agnes's agential self-understanding strictly requires her to think that the categorical imperative exists and is the FUL.

Note that it is not the mere fact that *if* Agnes understands the concept of a categorical imperative *then* she must think that it exists that strictly requires her to think that she is bound to act in accord with the FUL. It is this fact *coupled with* the fact that Agnes's agential self-understanding strictly requires her to engage with and understand the concept of a categorical imperative. *SII* only effects *Pr8* on the back of *SI*. *Without this link to Agnes's agential self-understanding, a sceptical Agnes may question whether what she must think by virtue of understanding a concept has any relevance for how she may or must act.*

When Kant says (*CPrR* AK 5:31) that *the moral law* is *given* to human agents as the sole fact of pure reason, what he means is that Agnes's agential self-understanding strictly requires her to think that the FUL is the categorical imperative.[7] As such, the moral law as the categorical imperative may be said to be the deed *and* product of Agnes's agential self-understanding. It is the deed of Agnes's agential self-understanding to produce the moral law as the categorical imperative for Agnes. Indeed, *so contextualized*, the categorical imperative might be said to be the product of itself. So viewed, Kant's claim that 'pure reason is practical of itself alone' (*CPrR* AK 5:31) means no more and no less than that *'rational nature exists as an end itself'* (*GMM* AK 4: 428–429), which is equivalent to 'action in accord with the strict requirements of pure agential self-understanding is an end in itself'.[8] That 'pure reason' and 'rational nature' here refer to 'pure agential self-understanding' is dictated by the fact that pure reason, and 'rational nature', cannot by themselves generate a requirement for Agnes to do something. They can only generate

---

[7] What he means (see below) by saying that the moral law/free will *is* the sole fact of pure reason is that free will, as the *ratio essendi* of the moral law, is the only object of theoretical speculative reason that Agnes is strictly required to accept exists that is acceptable to pure reason as a whole, not merely to pure practical reason.

Strictly speaking, per our construction, saying that the categorical imperative is the product of human agential self-understanding only makes the moral law/free will the sole fact of pure reason (for human agents) on the presumption that this does not reveal an antinomy in human agential self-understanding. Prior to reassurance that there is no antinomy, the categorical imperative should be described as the fact of pure practical reason presumptively purporting to be the sole fact of pure reason as a whole. Kant is not always as clear about this as he ought to be.

[8] Justifying this is essential to vindicate our version of the claim that Kant presents the same argument in *GMM* and *CPrR*. This is an important task for Chapter Six.

such a requirement by Agnes's exercise of her self-reflective powers of reason/understanding, and this underpins and elucidates Kant's claim that the moral law is to be regarded as legislated by Agnes's will to itself (*GMM* AK 4:431).[9] Furthermore, it is the claim in *Pr7* that – by understanding the concept of a categorical imperative – Agnes must accept that it exists, that leads us to designate his argument as 'quasi-ontological'. The way that Kant reasons here shares the idea that something exists the nature of which is such that understanding its nature requires acceptance that it exists with Anselm's ontological argument for the existence of God (according to which, understanding that the idea of God is the idea of a Being containing all perfections requires acceptance that God exists). However, we are not suggesting that Kant accepts Anselm's ontological argument for the existence of God (as he certainly does not) (see *CPuR* A592–602: B620–630). Nor are we suggesting that Kant thinks that his argument for the categorical imperative (on the basis of which he offers his own argument for the existence of God) can be used to prove the *noumenal* reality of God (i.e., to establish the reality of God as a fact of *pure reason*), even though he maintains that the rationally necessary status of the moral law renders belief in the existence of God a strict requirement of Agnes's agential self-understanding (*CPrR* AK 5:124–132, esp. 125). According to Kant, the reciprocal existence of the moral law and free will is the *only* fact of *pure reason as a whole,* free will the only thing of which we can have noumenal knowledge (e.g., *CPrR* AK 5:4, 5:103), even though the existence of free will, God and human immortality are all postulates of the moral law (*CPrR* AK 5:132–134), which is to say, facts of *pure practical reason*.[10] Subtle (and, indeed, problematic) as this doctrine is, understanding that Kant holds it to be entailed by his argument for the moral law as the categorical imperative is essential for understanding what his argument for the categorical imperative is. Indeed, it is essential to understand why Kant chooses to describe what he considers to be a strict requirement of human agential self-understanding as the sole fact of pure reason. It is the way that Kant distinguishes the existence of free will, which he depicts as both a postulate of pure reason as a whole *and* a practical postulate, from the existence of God and the existence of human immortality,

---

9 Kant's argument rests heavily on the claim that human agential self-understanding necessarily implicates pure agential self-understanding. It is only on this basis that the requirements of pure agential self-understanding can be thought to generate strict requirements for Agnes's agential self-understanding.

10 In *CPrR*, Kant defines a *practical* postulate as 'a *theoretical* proposition, though one not demonstrable as such, insofar as it is attached inseparably to an a priori unconditionally valid *practical* law' (AK 5:122).

which he depicts as only practical postulates, that we contend reveals what he *intends to convey* by calling the moral law, given to human agents by their agential self-understanding, the *sole* fact of pure reason.

SIII

Pr9: However, understanding the concept of a categorical imperative also strictly requires Agnes to recognize that a categorical imperative has two *rationes essendi*. As *categorical*, its *ratio essendi* is free will. As an *imperative*, its *ratio essendi* is *also* a will subject to the universal law of mechanism (*because and to the extent that* for her reason to generate an *imperative* for Agnes's will, Agnes's will must be subject to influence by heteronomous incentives). Since a will cannot at the same time *be* free and subject to the universal law of mechanism, it needs to be shown that the reason why her agential self-understanding strictly requires Agnes to consider that her will is subject to the universal law of mechanism cannot show that her will cannot be free.

Pr10: Just how Kant purports (see *GMM* AK 4:451–457; *CPrR* AK 5:91–106) to establish that Agnes can coherently hold that she has free will, yet is subject to the universal law of mechanism, is complex. However, for the purpose of this book, which is not to judge the validity of Kant's argument, but merely to establish its logical structure, we do not need to comprehend all the details of his argument. In relation to what is essential, we maintain, first, that Kant thinks that it is Agnes's agential self-understanding that strictly requires her to hold both that she has free will and that she is subject to the universal law of mechanism in the realm of practical reason as a whole. Secondly, we maintain that Kant holds that the way in which Agnes's agential self-understanding requires her to hold that she is subject to the universal law of mechanism is so related to the way in which her agential self-understanding requires her to hold that she has free will that the former can provide no grounds for her to hold that she cannot have free will, even though *her existence* as an agent (her *being* an agent) cannot be constituted by having a will that is free yet subject to the universal law of mechanism. Whatever the details of this, we maintain that *Pr10* is to establish (validate) that the FUL is an apodictic a priori synthetic practical proposition by establishing that there are no grounds in theoretical reason, empirical or pure, that can undermine the claim that governance of Agnes's will by the FUL is rendered undeniable by being a strict requirement of her agential self-understanding. While some commentators have claimed that Kant, at least in *GMM*,[11] tries to derive free will as a transcendental presupposition of pure theoretical reason, we contend that, while Kant does make claims linking free will as the *ratio essendi* of the moral law to 'a spontaneity' (a freedom) as the *ratio essendi* of pure theoretical reason (*GMM* AK 4:461; *CPrR* AK 5:46–47), he does so only on the premise that possession of pure practical reason *is* a presupposition of human agential self-understanding. In so doing, he does claim a unity between pure practical reason and pure theoretical reason. But, in this unity, it is pure practical reason that wears the crown, not pure theoretical reason. Furthermore, as Kant repeatedly insists, our knowledge of the primacy of pure practical reason over pure theoretical reason holds only in the realm of (i.e., for the purposes of) practical reason as a whole (see, e.g., *CPrR* AK 5:50, 56, 121, 133).

We anticipate that some will object to our attribution of *Pr7* to Kant in *SII*. While it is undeniable that 'Obey a categorical imperative' is a categorical imperative, it might be claimed that more is needed to give this practical significance than to show that understanding the concept of a categorical imperative requires a categorical imperative to be assigned a formula (the FUL) that is capable of differentiating what precepts comply with it from those that do not. Surely, it will be said, this does not show that Agnes must act in accord with the FUL, only that she must act in accord with the FUL *if a categorical imperative exists*. Thus, understanding what it means for an imperative to be categorical does not bring a categorical imperative into existence. However, we contend that Kant thinks otherwise, and clearly so, whether or not he is right to do so. And we maintain that the reason why he thinks this is that he holds that a categorical imperative is something that is constituted by and in human agential self-understanding and has no possible existence outside human agential self-understanding. Kant would be perfectly happy to concede 'Obey a categorical imperative' is elliptical for 'Obey any categorical imperative that exists' because he holds that a categorical imperative is brought into existence by having the idea of its existence (provided only that it is coherent for a human agent to have this thought). Its reality is posited in its ideation. That is just what makes it a fact of pure reason. We have already, to an extent, explained how we think he reasons this out in our discussion of the Pyrrhonian Dilemma in Chapter One, and the following three lines of reasoning, which are mutually supportive, are all at least not inconsistent with this, and we suggest that he would agree to all of them.

---

11 Most influentially, Dieter Henrich 1960.

Line One: 'If there is a categorical imperative then it is the FUL' is a proposition that Agnes categorically (unconditionally) must accept. But understanding the concept of a categorical imperative strictly requires Agnes to accept that there can be only one categorical imperative (the FUL). Therefore, because it is categorically imperative for Agnes to accept 'If there is a categorical imperative then it is the FUL', it is categorically imperative for Agnes to accept the FUL. To this it might be objected that 'If there is a categorical imperative then it is the FUL' is not an imperative for action, but an imperative for thought. However (see our discussion of the *sensus communis* of *CPoJ* in Chapter Four), by viewing the requirement to accept the categorical imperative as a requirement of human agential self-understanding, Kant views it as a matter of 'thinking in accord with oneself', which means that he thinks that an imperative for thought can lay down an imperative for action.

Line Two: If there is a categorical imperative, then if Agnes does not accept the FUL, she will make an error that, from a practical point of view, she categorically ought not to make. On the other hand, if there isn't a categorical imperative, yet Agnes thinks that there is, she will not make an error that, *from a practical point of view,* she categorically ought not to make. But, by the very idea of a categorical imperative, Agnes categorically ought to avoid making an error that she categorically ought not to make. So, provided that it is not possible to show that there isn't a categorical imperative (which is to say, provided that it is not possible to show that thinking that there is a categorical imperative – when there, *unknowably,* isn't – is an error from a theoretical point of view), merely understanding the concept of a categorical imperative strictly requires Agnes to accept that the FUL is the categorical imperative.

Line Three: Understanding the *concept of a categorical imperative* strictly requires Agnes to accept that its acceptance is a strict requirement of human agential self-understanding and understanding the *concept of human agential self-understanding* strictly requires Agnes to accept that it is categorically imperative to act in accord with human agential self-understanding. Since there can be only one categorical imperative and understanding the concept of a categorical imperative reveals its content to be the FUL, Agnes must accept that the FUL is the categorical imperative.

Finally, a few comments are needed about Kant's claim (*GMM* AK 4:420) that understanding what is contained in the concept of a categorical imperative immediately reveals any categorical imperative that might exist to be the FUL. Many commentators consider this claim to be astonishingly hasty. Part of their puzzlement derives from mooting the possibility that there might be an imperative that *Agnes* must think that she categorically ought to obey that another agent, say *Brian,* need not think that *he* categorically ought to obey. The thought is that what Agnes's agential self-understanding requires her to accept might not necessarily be what Brian's agential self-understanding requires him to accept, which is to say that Kant needs to show that/explain why Agnes's agential self-understanding strictly requires her to act in accord with Brian's agential self-understanding and vice versa.

The short answer to this concern is that Kant views a categorical imperative as one that binds human agents regardless of any of their contingent characteristics, including the things that make them the particular agents that they are. A categorical imperative, in his view, is one that binds human agents simply because they are human agents. As such, an imperative that unconditionally binds Agnes but not Brian is not a categorical imperative. In terminology that Kant uses in *GMM* (AK 4:429), it is only a 'subjective principle', not an 'objective' one.

However, while this is fine when depicting the FUL as contained in the idea of a categorical imperative as an impartial one, as we have depicted Kant's argument, *justifying* the categorical imperative as an impartial one places the onus on Kant to show that for Agnes to understand the concept of a hypothetical imperative she must have and understand the concept of a categorical imperative as the concept of an objective principle or practical law, not merely as the concept of an unconditional subjective (in the normative sense) principle (which he can only do by showing that Agnes must consider any unconditional subjective principles for her to be objective ones, which is to say, necessarily binding on all agents). Just how Kant deals with this is one of the trickiest matters to negotiate in Kant interpretation. But central to our construction is our view that Kant holds that for Agnes to understand what it is for her to act in accord with her *human* agential self-understanding strictly requires her to recognize that she unconditionally ought to act in accord with the strict requirements of *pure* agential self-understanding. We will comment specifically on this in Chapter Six when discussing Kant's claim at *GMM* AK 4:428–429 that 'rational nature is an end in itself' is the ground of the categorical imperative.

Chapter Three
A Priori Synthetic Practical Propositions as Strict Requirements of Human Agential Self-Understanding

In this chapter, we first explain why, *on the basis of what Kant says and does in GMM*, we think that his idea of an a priori synthetic practical proposition is that of a proposition that a human agent must accept because its acceptance is a strict requirement of human agential self-understanding. We then provide textual reasons for thinking that his claim in *CPrR* that the moral law is given to human agents as the sole fact of pure reason is the claim that the categorical imperative is established as an a priori synthetic practical proposition on the same grounds. Our emphasis in this chapter is on how Kant depicts his methodology in *GMM* and *CPrR,* rather than on the logical structure of his argument. However, it will by now be appreciated that, if we are right about the nature of his argument, it is not possible to keep elucidation of these two activities entirely separate from each other.

Human Agential Self-Understanding in *GMM*

Synthetic propositions are standardly contrasted with analytic ones, which are a priori. Thus, the idea of an a priori synthetic practical proposition contrasted with an analytic one requires an account of how a proposition can be a priori without being analytic. Modern philosophers who work within the empiricist tradition of David Hume, however, insist that only analytic propositions, the truth of which depend entirely on the meanings of their words, can be known a priori and hold necessarily. All non-analytic propositions are empirical and a posteriori and hold only contingently, and, *on such a basis*, the very idea of an a priori synthetic proposition is a contradiction in terms.

This thinking is, at least partly, responsible for the unwillingness of many commentators to take seriously the idea that Kant really means what he so clearly says; that he believes that he has shown that the categorical imperative holds with necessity as a synthetic proposition. But, as we have said, we are not concerned with whether Kant's claims are tenable, but with what they are, and no one should let their views of what is tenable drive their reading of what Kant's views actually are, *unless* this is the only way to make sense of him *on his own terms*. And, as we have already noted in the previous chapters, we consider that Kant's 'analysis' takes the form of exposition, which does not merely involve understanding what is contained in a concept *in vacuo*, but also understanding what is contained in a concept in and as being a representation of an 'I', which is to say, what is contained in the concept of an 'I' (e.g., Agnes) understanding what it is to have a concept (having a concept being to understand something). In other words, for Kant, an a priori synthetic practical proposition is the product of an analytic practical *understanding*.

So, what does Kant think are *analytic* practical *propositions?* He tells us that imperatives of skill (where what an agent ought to do is 'hypothetical' in being constituted by what the agent *understands* are the means necessary to achieve the agent's contingent impulses or inclinations) are analytic. Furthermore,

> If only it were as easy to give a determinate concept of happiness, imperatives of prudence would be just as analytic.[1] (*GMM* AK 4:417)

Indeed, the moral law, viewed as the law of a pure practical reason (a practical reason unfettered by interference by natural impulses and inclinations), is also analytic (*GMM* AK 4:412–413). This is supported by Kant's claim that the idea of action under the moral law is strictly analytically connected to the idea of free will, that if 'freedom of the will is presupposed, morality together with its principle follows from it by mere analysis of its concept' (*GMM* AK 4:447), and that a perfectly good will (one fully determined by pure practical reason) would necessarily act in accord with the moral law (*GMM* AK 4:414; 4:445). However, because Kant maintains that the categorical imperative is the only form that the moral law can take in application to an agent whose adherence to the moral law can be fettered by the agent's impulses or inclinations (*GMM* AK 4:412–413), the possible existence of a categorical imperative seems to presuppose that it is possible for an agent to have a will that can be subject to the laws governing heteronomy (hypothetical imperatives) and the law of autonomy (the moral law). But he also thinks that a will subject to the laws of heteronomy is subject to the universal law of mechanism, and that a

---

[1] According to Kant, happiness is a 'purpose that can be presupposed surely and a priori in the case of every human being, because it belongs to his essence' (*GMM* AK 4:415–416). (By this, we take him to mean that agents necessarily try to fulfil desires that correspond to their image of themselves as the particular agents that they are.) An imperative that 'refers to the choice of means to one's own happiness' is a 'precept of prudence' (*GMM* AK 4:416). The concept of happiness is indeterminate because human agents do not have the same self-images that determine what they need to be happy, and their self-images can change (*GMM* AK 4: 418–419).

will cannot be subject to the universal law of mechanism and be free 'in the very same actions' (*GMM* AK:455–456). Thus, the very idea of a categorical imperative is threatened with incoherence (with internal contradiction), as it seems to presuppose (though Kant does not phrase it this way) an addressee/addressor whose practical reason has two incompatible *rationes essendi* – free will and governance by the universal law of mechanism. So, for a categorical imperative to be shown to really exist,

> this seeming contradiction must be removed in a convincing way . . . to show that both [*rationes essendi*] not only can very well coexist but also must be thought as *necessarily united* in the same subject. (*GMM* AK 4:456)

If it is not the case that they *also must* be thought as *necessarily united* in the same subject, showing that they *can* coexist will not have shown that human agents *must* think that they have free will (and so are necessarily bound by the moral law) (*GMM* AK 4:456).

We can now see why Kant says that a categorical imperative must be an a priori synthetic practical proposition. If it is a strictly analytic one (here a construct of the idea *of being* a human agent), then the seeming contradiction cannot be removed. To be *categorical*, a requirement must be completely unconditional and, as such,

> must already be connected (completely a priori) with the concept of the will of a rational being as such [a being in whom pure reason necessarily determines the being's will]. (*GMM* AK 4:426)

But to be an *imperative*, an unconditional requirement cannot be contained in the concept of the will of a purely rational being (AK 4:420 fn). For there to be a categorical *imperative* it must be possible for the will *to be able* to conform to, but not *necessarily* conform to, the strict requirements of pure reason; but it is not possible for a purely rational will not to act for and in accord with the moral law.

This means that the key question is: 'On what basis can Agnes be required to accept that an a priori connection exists between the categorical imperative and the concept of governance by the law of pure practical reason that is not strictly analytic (i.e., not contained in the idea of being an agent)?' And to answer this question, we must discern what kind of a priori connection (if any) can coherently link the concept of being subject to the universal law of mechanism with the concept of being governed by the law of pure practical reason, given that Agnes cannot be constituted as an agent who is subject to a categorical imperative by her *existence* as an agent being constituted by subjection to the universal law of mechanism *and* the law of free will.

To assist us in answering this question, Kant tells us that an a priori connection between the concept of the categorical imperative and the concept of the will of a rational being as such is synthetic if the two concepts

> are bound together by their connection to a third in which they are both to be found
> (*GMM* AK 4:447)

and that it is the 'positive concept of freedom' (derived from the concept of pure practical reason) that points to 'this third concept' (which turns out to be the concept of membership of what he variously refers to as the 'world of understanding', the 'noumenal world', the 'intellectual world', or the 'intelligible world') (*GMM* AK 4:451–457). Now, it is possible for the concept of X and the concept of Z both to be contained (found) in the concept of Y without the concept of X and Z being contained in each other. But this is only possible if X and Z are *in themselves* compatible concepts, and this is not the case here if Y is the concept of a will since X is the concept of a purely autonomous will and Z is the concept of a heteronomously affected will contained in the concept of an imperative. X and Z, as incompatible concepts, can only be contained in Y if Y is something understanding which strictly requires X and Z to be entertained together without being brought into conflict with each other.

It is clear that Kant thinks that Y is something that requires Agnes to think of a purely autonomous will and a heteronomous will as properties simultaneously possessed by her will only in different aspects. Y requires Agnes to think of her will as heteronomously affected as a matter of empirical fact. But Y also requires her to think of her will as autonomous as a matter of what it ought to be. In other words, Y is something that presents the relation between heteronomy and autonomy, not as the relation between two empirical or metaphysical facts, but as the relation between what is posed for her recognition as what is the case and what ought to be the case. And it is also clear that Kant thinks that this 'ought' relation is imposed on Agnes by Y because Y is her membership of the world of understanding, which is constituted by her *having* the capacity for human agential self-understanding. What is not so clear is just what is involved in his account of how human agential self-understanding imposes a strict requirement for Agnes to recognize the 'is' to 'ought' relation.

According to Kant, when Agnes thinks of her will as under laws of mechanism, she thinks of her will as belonging to the world of sense, but when she thinks of her will as subject to the moral law *as such* (and she must do both to think of her will as governed by a categorical imperative) she thinks of her will as belonging to the world of understanding (*GMM* AK 4:451–453). But the world of understanding contains the ground of the world of sense and so too of its laws, and is therefore immediately lawgiving with respect to my [Agnes's] will (which belongs wholly to the world of understanding) and must accordingly also be thought as such, . . . [from which] it follows that I shall cognize myself as intelligence, though on the other side as a being belonging to the world of sense, as nevertheless subject to the law of the world of understanding, that is, of reason, which contains in the idea of freedom the law of the world of understanding, and thus cognize myself as subject to the autonomy of the will; consequently the laws of the world of understanding must be regarded as imperatives for me. (*GMM* AK 4:453–454)

This and other connected passages between *GMM* AK 4:451 and AK 4:457 are not easy to disentangle. However, it is clear that it is as concepts of reason/understanding (i.e., as products of use of the powers of human reason/understanding) that the idea of heteronomy (presupposed by the idea of a categorical imperative as an imperative) and the ideas of the moral law and free will (contained in the idea of a categorical imperative as categorical) are to be connected to make possible the idea of a categorical imperative. It is also clear that Kant is saying that Agnes's cognition that there are mechanistic causal laws (laws of the sensible world) and of the law of pure practical reason are laws given to Agnes by her understanding, the latter being given to her by understanding her agential self-understanding entirely on its own terms (i.e., without any reliance upon sense-experience or the idea of it). From this it follows that the a priori connection that Kant claims renders it possible for Agnes to hold that she is bound by a categorical imperative is not a construct of *being a human agent,* nor of the *concept of being a human agent,* nor even of *understanding the concept of being a human agent,* but of *Agnes understanding what it is for her to understand the concept of her being a human agent.*[2] On this basis, we suggest

---

[2] Some critiques of so-called 'Kantian constructivism' – we are thinking particularly of David Enoch 2006 – portray it as the view that normativity is a construction of agency, or of understanding the concept of agency (Enoch 2006, 170), with the implication that there are specific aims, desires or motives that are constitutive of agency (Enoch 2006, 173, 175). On this basis, Enoch says that even if there are specific aims that are constitutive of agency, this merely raises the question as to why anyone ought to be an agent. In effect, he claims that Kantian constructivism is impaled on the horns of the Pyrrhonian Dilemma. The position he attributes to Kantian constructivism is clearly ridiculous, as it implies that it is impossible for agents not to do what they ought to do, when the very idea that Agnes ought to do X entails that Agnes is both able to do X and able not to do X. No one with any idea of what 'ought' means could possibly entertain Enoch's 'Kantian constructivism' and Kant certainly holds no such position. According to Kant, if Agnes adopts any position incompatible with the FUL, she misunderstands what it is for her to be an agent and implies that she is not an agent. But this does not mean that he holds that if she misunderstands what it is for her to be an agent then she is not an agent. To misunderstand what it is to be an agent is not simply to fail to understand what it

that what is going on here is something like this: If Agnes, in thinking of herself *as an agent*, thinks of her practical reason as purely heteronomous, then she thinks of herself as a creature of nature as mechanism (as belonging to the world of sense) bound solely by hypothetical imperatives. As such, her agential self-understanding informs her that she *can* be bound only by hypothetical imperatives. On the other hand, if (in thinking of herself as an agent) she thinks of herself (strictly, thinks of *her will*) as constituted solely by her possession of pure practical reason, then her agential self-understanding informs her that she can only act in terms of the moral law *as such*. However, and this is key, Kant claims that Agnes is only able to think of herself as bound by hypothetical imperatives on the basis of possessing the powers of human agential self-understanding. In other words, he claims that Agnes's ability to see herself as belonging to the world of sense (governed by the universal law of mechanism) hence as subject to *hypothetical imperatives*, requires her to see herself also as subject to the world of understanding. As he puts it, 'the world of understanding contains the ground of the world of sense and so too of its laws' (*GMM* AK 4:453). This is because the fact that M is a necessary means to P can only require Agnes to think that she *ought* to pursue/have M if she understands (thinks) that M is a necessary means to P and that P is something that Agnes wants to have or pursue but does not feel that she necessarily will have/pursue or necessarily not have/not pursue. Hypothetical imperatives, which presuppose the possibility of Agnes's will being subject to the universal law of mechanism, do not apply to Agnes as products of nature but as constructs of Agnes's agential self-understanding.[3] However,

---

is to be an agent, which Agnes can do simply by failing to think. To misunderstand what it is to be an agent is to adopt a view incompatible with the idea that one is an agent, thereby implicitly denying that one is an agent. But one cannot deny that one is an agent without being an agent, because one requires the powers of agential self-understanding to do so. So, if Enoch's critique is directed at Kant himself (about which Enoch is somewhat coy), it is a complete straw man. It is equally misdirected in being applied (as Enoch 2006, 189 fn 42 does) to Alan Gewirth's claim (e.g., 1978) that the supreme principle of morality is established by its dialectical necessity', because Gewirth's claim that it is so established is no more and no less than the claim that it is established by its acceptance being a strict requirement of human agential self-understanding (see Chapter One, note 11). We consider that a cause of Enoch's error is that, while he correctly attributes an internalist view of reasons for action to Kant and Gewirth, he does not appreciate that neither Kant nor Gewirth subscribe to Humean internalism. Whether or not Enoch's critique is a straw man when directed at his main targets (Christine Korsgaard 2002, David Velleman 2004a and 2004b, and Connie Rosati 2003) we need not go into (though we think it is) (and Enoch [2011, fn 4] has accepted Rosati's protests that it is in her case). (For a more detailed critique of Enoch's reasoning, see Beyleveld 2017.)

3 It cannot be overstressed that for Kant a hypothetical imperative is not constituted by the empirical connection between 'means' and 'ends' that exists when M is necessary to achieve

understanding the nature of agential self-understanding as such reveals a capacity that Agnes 'really finds in herself'

> by which she distinguishes herself even from herself insofar as she is affected by objects, and that is reason. This, as pure self-activity [understanding the nature of self-understanding], is raised even above the *understanding* . . . [by the fact that the understanding] . . . can produce from its activity no other concepts than those *which serve merely to bring sensible representations under rules* and thereby unite them in one consciousness . . . [while reason, understanding the nature of self-understanding] proves its highest occupation in distinguishing the world of sense and the world of understanding from each other.
> (*GMM* AK 4:452)

Hence, Agnes's agential self-understanding requires her to think of herself as belonging to the 'intellectual world' (e.g., *GMM* AK 4:451) or the 'intelligible world' (e.g., *GMM* AK 4:454), a world governed by the laws of free will, the noumenal world, the world of 'things in themselves' (*GMM* AK 4:451).[4] In short, it requires her to govern her actions by reference to what is a law of pure agential self-understanding, the law that governs a purely rational will as a law of its nature.

However, as a being with heteronomous impulses, Agnes cannot coherently think of herself as constituted entirely as a purely rational agent either. Agnes's sound agential self-understanding also strictly requires her to think that *she* cannot be an agent without being the particular agent that she is. Because she must think that she is a member of the intelligible world, she must think that she is bound by the moral law *as such* and has free will (because, by being a member of the intelligible world, the 'causality' of Agnes's actions lies

---

P. A hypothetical imperative is one that is constituted by Agnes wanting to achieve P and perceiving (understanding) M to be necessary for P. It is, therefore, a *subjective* imperative in being from Agnes's perspective relative to her desire for P, and a subjective *imperative* on the basis of Agnes's perception that she cannot achieve P without M. So, for Kant, a hypothetical imperative is fully 'necessary'. However, unlike the categorical imperative, this necessity depends on Agnes's contingent choice of P. It is in this way that to view Agnes as being bound by a hypothetical imperative requires her to be viewed as belonging to the world of sense and the world of understanding. (Cf. the extensive discussion of the significance of the hypothetical imperative in *GMM* in Steigleder 2002, 23–58).

4 Kant does not assume the existence of a noumenal world but treats the need to recognize it as a requirement of human agential self-understanding. In this, his view is to be distinguished from intuitionist views that, in effect, see the possibility of a synthetic a priori connection as involving a direct a priori intuition providing access to a noumenal world independent of human agential self-understanding in which moral truths reside that normatively govern human agential self-understanding. For discussions of how genuinely Kantian views differ from such moral realism, see Beyleveld 2017 and Düwell 2017.

in 'reason alone', which 'gives the [moral] law [to Agnes]') (*GMM* AK 4:457). But, because she must also think that she is a member of the sensible world, she must think of the moral law *so given* as an 'unconditional *ought*', as a categorical imperative (*GMM* AK 4:454, 457). To human Agnes, the noumenal world, to which a purely rational Agnes would belong entirely, and in which the moral law would be a law of her nature, must be regarded as representing the state of nature towards which her actions unconditionally ought to be directed.[5]

This reasoning shows that, in *GMM*, Kant thinks that the problem of the *genuine* (*non-illusory*) existence of a categorical imperative is that of showing that such an imperative can be thought to exist without implying an antinomy in the idea of a will of a human agent. For, by this reasoning, Kant claims to explain how a categorical imperative *can be thought* possible (why it is coherent for Agnes to attribute free will to herself as a human agent), and, *thereby*, show that, by being found a priori in common human reason, the moral law is no phantom in the minds of human agents. There is no contradiction in Agnes thinking of herself as being bound by the universal law of mechanism and by the moral law (under which she must have free will), even though she must think that she is bound by both. This is because both thoughts are strictly required by Agnes's agential understanding as a human agent, but only as strict requirements of her understanding such understanding – in which the strict requirement to think of herself as bound by the universal law of mechanism is a strict requirement of seeing herself as merely the appearance of herself (for 'as a human being' Agnes 'is only the appearance of' herself, the representation of herself insofar as this is possible through her senses), while the strict requirement to think of herself as bound by the moral law is a strict requirement of understanding herself as given in understanding her*self* (which represents her 'proper self') (*GMM* AK 4:457).[6]

In this way, Kant holds that a (the) categorical imperative is established as an a priori (hence apodictic) synthetic practical proposition *in being* a strict requirement

---

[5] This is brought out clearly by Kant's provision of 'typics' for his various formulae for the categorical imperative. For example, the typic of the FUL is '*[A]ct as if the maxim of your action were to become by your will a* **universal law of nature**' (*GMM* AK 4:421). We consider that this is best read as 'You unconditionally ought to will as a purely rational agent necessarily would will'.

[6] Agential self-awareness is to be distinguished from agential self-understanding, even though they are connected. Agential self-understanding and agential self-awareness are both products of the possession and use of the powers of agential self-understanding; but, while anyone with the powers of agential self-understanding will have agential self-awareness, not everyone with the powers of agential self-understanding will achieve agential self-understanding.

of human agential self-understanding (*GMM* AK 4:456). In other words, Kant thinks that to show that the categorical imperative is an a priori synthetic practical proposition is to show that what must be viewed as a law of nature for a purely rational will can and must be thought to apply to beings who inhabit the world of sense as a categorical imperative.

This shows that, and why, Kant thinks that it is comprehensible for free will to be a deduction from pure practical reason to be a deduction from pure practical reason (as *GMM* III AK 4:447 claims he will do) in a human agent by purporting to show that Agnes, *as a heteronomously affected agent* can adopt the moral law *as such as such* (which he holds to be reciprocal to Agnes having free will) as a categorical imperative. What it does not do is show just how (as against that) in *GMM* Kant purports to show that Agnes must consider that pure reason is practical in her without any vicious circularity or *petitio* being involved.

We will attend to this in Chapter Six.

We will now provide reasons for thinking that Kant has essentially the same view of what makes the categorical imperative an a priori synthetic practical proposition in *CPrR*.

Human Agential Self-Understanding in *CPrR*

Kant continues to hold that the categorical imperative is an a priori synthetic practical proposition in *CPrR* (AK 5:31). However, he has much less to say explicitly about the nature of such a proposition here than in *GMM*. What he does say is that, *as such,* the categorical imperative 'is not based on any intuition, either pure or empirical' (AK 5:31), and 'that it is not an empirical fact but the sole fact of pure reason, which, by it [the categorical imperative], announces itself as originally lawgiving' (AK 5:31) Furthermore, as we have already noted, he says that, as a fact of pure reason (i.e., as an a priori synthetic practical principle), the categorical imperative is the supreme principle of practical reason and is shown to stand 'of itself altogether a priori and independently of empirical principles (which is to say that it is 'firmly established of itself', and is apodictically certain) by its *'exposition'* (given that speculative reason must permit of the possibility of free will) (AK 5:46–47).[7]

To this must be added three further facts.

---

[7] Others have interpreted AK 5:46–47 rather differently, and we will discuss this in Chapter Five.

First, Kant tells us that having moral consciousness (being aware of the categorical imperative) is the result of a process that involves activities of reason and understanding (*CPrR* AK 5:30; 50–57).

Secondly, recent attention to the etymology of the word 'Faktum' by various scholars has thrown new light on what Kant means by 'a fact [Faktum] of pure reason'. Most influentially in this direction, Marcus Willaschek (1990) points out that, in the German of the 18th Century, the word 'Faktum' is ambiguous: it can be used to mean 'fact' (as this is understood in English), but it can also be used to mean 'Tatsache', which is itself ambiguous. 'Tatsache' can bear the meaning of the English word 'fact', but it can also mean 'Tat' (which, in English, means 'deed'). Bettina Stagneth (2001) and Klaus Steigleder (2002), similarly, claim that Kant sometimes uses 'Faktum' in the sense of something that *has been* done ('Getanes'). Furthermore, according to Pauline Kleingeld (2010, 60–65), there is evidence that the term was used in this way in the 18th Century; and it is of particular relevance here that the term was used in this way in juridical contexts. So, the 'fact of reason' is to be seen, not as an empirical given (as Kant himself insists), but as a deed of reason, an activity of reason, or, as Willaschek proposes, as a deed of reason and a product of reason at the same time (1992, 181).[8] However, because reason can do nothing to require anything of an 'I' (as a categorical imperative must do) except through a representation of an 'I' by an 'I', these considerations themselves provide reason to think that Kant sees the categorical imperative as a product of our self-understanding 'in a way that permits of no doubt, making it a fact *for us* that reason determines it for us' (Steigleder 2002, 103). And, in direct support of this, in a passage where Kant actually tells us why he considers the moral law to be a fact (of pure reason), he says that we may regard the 'objective reality... of a pure practical reason' as 'a fact' because it is given by an a priori 'determination of the will that is unavoidable even though it does not rest on empirical principles' (*GMM* AK 5:55).

Thirdly, this etymological analysis has an independent textual basis in that Kant frequently refers to pure reason as doing something, as being practical. For example: pure practical reason proves its reality and that of its concepts (which include the moral law) by what it does (*CPrR* AK 5:3); pure reason 'announces itself as originally lawgiving' (*CPrR* AK 5:30); pure reason 'is practical of itself alone and gives [to the human being] a universal law which we call the *moral law*' (*CPrR* AK 5:30). And, perhaps most importantly, Kant makes very similar claims in *GMM*. For example: the existence of a categorical imperative

---

[8] To the list of those taking such a view, we can definitely add Klaus Steigleder (2002), David Sussman (2008), Michael Wolff (2009), and Jochen Bojanowski (2017).

depends on the existence of a will that 'determines itself immediately, just by the representation of an action' (*GMM* AK 4:444); 'reason alone, and indeed pure reason independent of sensibility gives the law' (AK 4:457). Such congruence was remarked on as early as 1960 by Lewis White Beck, who suggests that the fact of reason should be taken as a fact *for* reason derived from a fact *of* reason: '[t]he fact for reason . . . is a creation of the fact of reason as legislative' (1960b, 212),[9] and by Onora O'Neill (1989, 65) who suggests that the fact of reason might be seen as something 'made or constructed'.[10]

If we are correct that Kant derives the categorical imperative as a strict requirement of agential self-understanding in *GMM*, then these considerations imply (even if there are other possible not unreasonable interpretations, which we sincerely doubt) that what Kant means when he says that the categorical imperative is *given* as the sole fact of pure reason is that it is given as a strict requirement of human agential self-understanding. This follows from our default presumption that Kant presents the same argument for the categorical imperative in *GMM* and *CPrR*. For our default presumption requires no more than that it be possible to interpret *CPrR* as being in line with *GMM*, unless Kant makes unequivocal statements that negate the reasons we have given for treating congruence between *CPrR* and *GMM* as a default position or otherwise contradict congruence on the issue of Kant's justifying criterion.

Pauline Kleingeld, who contends (like the *WAV*) that, in *GMM*, Kant 'reasons from freedom of the will to the moral law' and reverses this in *CPrR* (2010, 70),

---

[9] This is an important insight, which needs more elaboration than Beck gives it. We will take this up again in Chapter Five.

[10] According to Ian Proops (2003), who applies Dieter Henrich's (1989) claim that Kant views his deductions in terms of a legal metaphor, to say that the moral law is the fact of pure reason is to say that it has its origin in pure reason, which is to say that it is justified on the basis of pure reason being practical, i.e., it is the law of pure practical reason in just the same way that to identify a legal right or obligation is to say that it is validated by a recognized legal authority. However, Proops claims (2003, 228) that this means that the idea of the moral law as a deed of pure practical reason fades from view. We do not see why. This is only the case if the validity of the moral law is viewed as entirely relative to validation by pure practical reason, regardless of whether pure practical reason actually exists and must be taken to be the supreme standard for all reason. In other words, Proops's claim holds up only if Kant sees pure practical reason as merely a rationally optional kind of reason rather than as presupposed by all practical reason. But Kant claims that the moral law is rationally undeniable, which can only be the case if the supreme authority of pure practical reason is rationally undeniable. Thus, we hold that Kant holds that the moral law is a fact (rationally undeniable) because it is the deed of pure practical reason, which is to say that it is the deed of pure practical reason to make the moral law a fact for agents.

nevertheless argues (unlike the *WAV*) that there is *methodological* continuity between *GMM III* and *CPrR* in that the transcendental deduction of *GMM III* and the argument in terms of the fact of reason are both arguments from human agential self-understanding. Regarding *CPrR,* she argues that Kant considers that the fact of reason is given to us with practical reasoning as such. Principles and reasons for action are revealed in one's reflection upon the very idea of one's pursuing means to ends (a finite embodied agent being someone who pursues means to his/her/its own ends). The very *question* as to *how one can understand* means to ends as *imperatival* reasons for one to act

> indicates that . . . deliberation about maxims presupposes a normative principle, and that this normative principle is conceived as independent from the inclinations. (2010, 68)

> Only when one realizes that one could act against all of one's inclinations . . . does one become aware of one's freedom in the sense required by Kant. In such cases it is not inclination which is conceived as determining the will, but pure practical reason. . . . Kants argument establishes that one must think that one can (i.e. that one must judge that one is free), not that one 'really' can. The latter claim would entail metaphysical knowledge of freedom from an objective and theoretical point of view. . . . Kant's account of the fact of reason is therefore, radically agent-based. (2010, 71–72)

This account, which interprets the fact of reason as both a deed and a product of reason is, in essence, our own view. However, she does not go into much of the detail of the process (the specific interplays) by which the powers of Agnes's agential self-understanding strictly require Agnes to be convinced of the validity of the categorical imperative, so it is not altogether clear whether she shares our view on these details. This said, we do differ from her in that, although we think she is right that Kant's justification can be put in terms of a theory of *justified* action that views Agnes's actions as products of her self-understanding (couched in terms of the strict requirements of human agential self-understanding), she is wrong to suggest (2010, 70) (for reasons we explained in Chapter One and Chapter Two) that it offers a morally-neutral justification of the categorical imperative.

We have already described the process that we think is involved in the last chapter. What we have not done is link our account of this process directly to the text of *CPrR*. We will do this in Chapter Five, where we will also consider whether there are any claims that Kant makes in *CPrR* that defeat our default assumption or otherwise make it unreasonable to interpret him as holding that the categorical imperative exists as a strict requirement of human agential self-understanding. In addition, we will there put our view to the test of what Kant is saying when he says that the moral law, justified in the way that it is, is the sole fact of pure reason.

Before we do so, however, we will show that our account of what Kant means by an a priori synthetic practical proposition is supported by the general aims and principles of his critical philosophy, and that this also supports our claims about the link between Kant's references to the common human understanding and the idea of human agential self-understanding.

Chapter Four
Kant's Justification in the Context of His Critical Philosophy as a Whole

As we have repeatedly said, Kant sees the central problem (indeed, the only real problem) of justifying the existence of a categorical imperative as being to show that the presuppositions of pure theoretical reason and pure practical reason can be united coherently in the idea of a human agent, and (in general) in the idea of a finite rational being who is subject to influence by heteronomous incentives, as a matter of the agential self-understanding of a finite embodied incompletely rational being. Because Kant views his philosophy as a system of transcendental presuppositions and frequently makes programmatic statements about its nature as such, placing his justification of the categorical imperative in relation to these statements is necessary to understand his justification.[1] In this chapter, we argue that attention to such statements provides systemic support for our position on how Kant views the task of establishing that the categorical imperative is an apodictic a priori synthetic practical proposition.

The chapter has two parts. In the first part, we place Kant's practical philosophy within the context of claims he makes about the fundamental questions for philosophy that he presents in *Jäsche Logic* and *CPuR,* and relate this to what he states to be the aim of *CPrR* in its Preface, particularly in order to establish that, when Kant claims that the categorical imperative is an apodictic a priori synthetic practical proposition, he means that its acceptance cannot rationally be questioned by any human agent.

In the second part, we argue that Kant's characterization of the *sensus communis* in *CPoJ* (as supported by related comments in *Jäsche Logic* and *Anthropology*) as the powers of thought that he claims are necessarily possessed by all humans (understood as beings capable of representing themselves as an 'I') provides direct and strong support for our claim that a priori synthetic practical propositions are strict requirements of human agential self-understanding.

---

[1] Some commentators take very lightly Kant's architectonic and schematic statements (which frequently classify things in threes), treating them as mannerisms that nod ritualistically to scholastic practice, which Kant does not really take seriously, and which frequently distract from the matter at hand. We consider this to be a colossal mistake. This is not just because Kant is aware of this attitude, to which he retorts that his three-part structuring is because 'that is in the nature of the matter' (*CPoJ* AK 5:197). Kant is right about this because it follows from the very idea that his critical philosophy deals in a priori synthetic propositions in which two ideas are connected to a third in which they are both to be found in agential self-understanding.

Kant's Justification in Context

In 'The Canon of Pure Reason' in *CPuR* (A804–805/B832–833), Kant declares that there are three fundamental questions for philosophy: 'What can I know?', 'What ought I to do?', 'What may I hope?' To this, in his lectures on logic, he adds a fourth question 'What is man?' commenting that '[a]t bottom all this could be reckoned to be anthropology, because the first three questions are related to the last' (*Jäsche Logic* AK 9:25).[2]

Kant's answers his first question in *CPuR*, according to which it is only possible for Agnes to have empirical knowledge on the assumption that every observable event has a mechanistic cause. He answers his second question foundationally in *GMM* and *CPrR* (though he has already given indications of it in *CPuR*), according to which Agnes categorically ought to act according to the moral law *as such* (the idea of the moral law *as such* being contained within the idea of an agent moved solely by pure practical reason), the application of which is later unpacked in *MoM*. His answer to his third question is along the following lines. Agnes cannot know on empirical or purely theoretical grounds that she is immortal or that God exists. However, the fact that she is bound by the moral law strictly requires her to hope that she herself and all other human agents will ultimately receive their just deserts as judged by the moral law, a state he calls the '*summum bonum*'. The *summum bonum*, however, cannot be realized unless Agnes and all other human agents are immortal and God (a perfectly good, i.e., perfectly rational, and omnipotent Being [*CPrR* AK 5:82]) exists. Therefore, Agnes categorically ought to have faith (be morally certain) (*CPrR* AK 5:125) that God exists and that human agents are immortal. As Kant also puts it, the existence of God and human immortality are practical postulates.[3] But, because theoretical reason cannot show that free will is impossible, the practical rational necessity of God and human immortality is rendered the apodictic rational necessity of God and human immortality for purely practical purposes. An outline of this is given in *CPuR* (A804–831: B832–859); it is the central pre-occupation of Book Two of *CPrR*; it

---

2 With regard to the previous note, it turns out that possibly the grandest of all Kant's statements actually involves four questions, though only three are active. In effect, the fourth question is *the* question, and it requires answers to three questions for its answer.

3 It must be remembered that, in *CPrR*, Kant defines a practical postulate as 'a *theoretical* proposition, though one not demonstrable as such, insofar as it is attached inseparably to an a priori unconditionally valid *practical* law' (*CPrR* AK 5:122). So defined, free will is also a practical postulate. But, see Chapter Five, note 12, Kant claims that free will has a different status from human immortality and God because only free will is reciprocal to the moral law.

is revisited in the last sections of *CPoJ*;[4] and it grounds *Religion*. Given that Kant's answer to his third question is derived from his answers to his first two questions, and that he says that his answer to his fourth question (which provides his view of the nature of humanity, i.e., human agency) synthesizes his answers to his first three questions, his answer to the question of how a categorical imperative is possible is the key to his entire critical philosophy. This is because only on the basis that a categorical imperative is possible can (according to Kant) the first two questions both arise coherently for Agnes. Thus, it is not surprising that the question of, and an explanation of, the unity between theoretical and practical reason occupies a prominent role in *CPuR* (in the form of addressing the Third Antinomy) (A444–451, 491–515, 532–558: B472–479, 519–543, 560–586),[5] as well as in Kant's justification of the application of the moral law *as such* to Agnes to render it the categorical imperative (in *GMM* and *CPrR*), and is the central concern of *CPoJ* (AK 5:176–179).

Indeed, how can *GMM/CPrR* be viewed as contributing to his critical philosophy at all unless this is so?

This is the context within which we must read Kant's claim, made when outlining the aim of *CPrR*, that

> the concept of freedom, insofar as its reality is proved by an apodictic law of practical reason, constitutes the *keystone* of the whole structure of a system of pure reason, even of speculative reason; and all other concepts (those of God and immortality), which as mere ideas remain without support in the latter, now attach themselves to this concept and with it and by means of it get stability and objective reality, that is, their *possibility* is *proved* by this: that freedom is real, for this idea reveals itself through the moral law... because it is the condition of ['the *ratio essendi* of' (*CPrR* AK 5:4 fn)] the moral law, which we do know.   (*CPrR* AK 5:3–4)

Once we do so (and taking his statements of his aims seriously is just as important as attending to his grand architectonic statements), it is evident that Kant treats the moral law as something that Agnes *unconditionally must* accept (as a categorical imperative), not merely as something that she *unconditionally may* accept. Even if there are problems with Kant's argument for God and human immortality (and we think that there are, as we will indicate in Chapter Nine), to think otherwise is revisionism not exegesis. For, only on the basis that Agnes must think that the categorical imperative exists can Kant even begin to surmise that Agnes *must* have faith in God's existence and her immortality. This is

---

4 On which see Deryck Beyleveld and Paul Ziche 2015, and Deryck Beyleveld 2016.
5 The third antinomy is constituted by pure reason leading to the thesis that causality in accordance with mechanistic causality is not the only causality because there is also the causality of freedom, and an antithesis that there is no freedom.

not gainsaid by the fact that Kant says that 'among all the ideas of speculative reason freedom is also the only one the possibility of which we *know* a priori' (*CPrR* AK 5:4). It is only relative to pure *theoretical* reason *by itself* that free will is to be conceived as *merely* possible (not impossible) rather than real. Relative to pure *practical* reason, free will must be held to exist, and so too must God and human immortality, for practical purposes with the *'force of law'* (*CPrR* AK 5:5). It is of the utmost importance here to distinguish Kant's concepts of knowledge, rational faith and rational hope. This is a very complex textual issue, and Kant's comments on it are sometimes very puzzling (see Beyleveld and Ziche 2015). But we can make sense of what Kant at least intends at *CPrR* AK 5:4–5, and throughout his discussion of the postulates of pure practical reason in *CPrR* and *CPoJ*, on the basis that he claims that we can have *knowledge* only of things that we can validate by experience, on the basis of pure theoretical reason, or on the basis of pure reason *as a whole*. It is as a postulate of pure reason *as a whole* that Agnes *knows* the moral law and that she has free will. Agnes must adopt the moral law and believe that she has free will because this is strictly required by *pure reason as a whole* for practical purposes. On the other hand, she must have *faith* (rationally necessitated belief that does not constitute knowledge) that God exists and that she is immortal, because this is only strictly required by pure *practical* reason, not by pure theoretical reason, so not by pure reason *as a whole*. She *may* merely hope that something S is the case if pure practical reason and pure theoretical reason both permit but do not strictly require belief or disbelief in S. So, from the perspective of pure theoretical reason alone, she *may* merely hope that God exists and that she is immortal. It would seem to follow from this that, given that Agnes must have faith that God exists and that she is immortal on the basis of pure practical reason, she *must* merely hope that God exists and that she is immortal on the basis of pure reason as a whole. However, Kant holds that pure practical reason has primacy over pure theoretical reason (see, e.g., *CPrR* AK 5:121), which means that Agnes must believe that God exists and that she is immortal on a rationally necessitated basis that is acceptable to pure reason as a whole for practical purposes. Pure reason as a whole does not permit knowledge of God and human immortality, but nevertheless requires faith (belief) in God and human immortality for practical purposes, not merely hope in God and human immortality. But why, then, does the fact that theoretical reason cannot show that God and human immortality cannot exist not render God and human immortality, alongside the moral law and free will, facts of pure reason as a whole? Kant's answer to this, we will argue in Chapter Five, confirms that the quasi-ontological reasoning that we claim is involved in an exposition of the concept of a categorical imperative is at the heart of his justification of the categorical imperative. Furthermore, it goes to the heart of what he is saying by calling the moral law the sole fact of pure reason.

Kant's Justification and the Three Maxims of the *Sensus Communis*

In *CPoJ*, Kant says that there are three principles of the common human understanding (*sensus communis*). These are:

1. To think for oneself; 2. To think in the position of everyone else; 3. Always to think in accord with oneself.[6] (*CPoJ* AK 5:294)

The first principle is the 'maxim of the understanding, the second that of the power of judgment, the third that of reason' (*CPoJ* AK 5:295). The maxim of reason is achieved 'by the combination of the first two' (*CPoJ* AK 5:295). The first maxim is 'the maxim of a reason that is never *passive*' (*CPoJ* AK 5:294); the second reflects on one's own judgments produced by thinking in accord with the first maxim 'from a *universal standpoint*' (*CPoJ* AK 5:295).

Crucially, Kant says that the *sensus communis* does not refer to 'common sense', if by this is meant what most persons just happen to consider to be reasonable or correct, which Kant calls '*sensus vulgaris*' in *Anthropology* (AK 7:139). The *sensus communis* is an *a priori faculty of judging* that represents the capacity of understanding 'which is the least that can be expected from anyone who lays claim to the name of human being', which *as a communal* sense, as a '*sensus communis*',

> in its reflection takes account (a priori) of everyone else's way of representing in thought, in order *as it were* to hold its judgment up to human reason as a whole and thereby avoid the illusion which, from subjective private conditions that could easily be held to be objective, would have a detrimental influence on the judgment.[7] (*CPoJ* AK 5:293)

---

[6] These three principles are also articulated by Kant in *Jäsche Logic*. There he describes them as '[g]eneral rules and conditions for avoiding error'. These are '(1) to think (by) oneself, (2) to think oneself in the place of another, and (3) to think consistently with oneself', which he labels, respectively, 'the *enlightened* maxim', 'the *broadened* maxim', and 'the maxim... of the *consistent* or *conclusive manner of thought*' (*Jäsche Logic* AK 9:57). They are referred to yet again in his lectures published in 1798, *Anthropology from a Pragmatic Point of View* as 'precepts for reaching 'Wisdom'' (AK 7:200).

[7] It must be everyone else's *a priori* way of representing in thought, as taking account of others' contingent ways of thought cannot contribute to an objective thought.

As we have said, many commentators take Kant's reference to 'common human understanding'understanding' or 'common human reason' to be reference to the *sensus vulgaris*. So, when Kant says that the moral law is to be found in common human reason, indeed, 'in the most common human reason' (*GMM* AK 4:411), they take him to be saying that it is the most commonly held view (or based in the most commonly held views). On the other hand, while it is true that Kant does think that belief in the moral law is the most commonly held view, *in all justificatory contexts* his reference to 'common human understanding' or 'common human reason' is to the *sensus communis* of *CPoJ*. In justificatory contexts, when Kant says that the moral law is found in common human reason/understanding, he means (as he sometimes says) that it is found in *sound* common (or 'natural') reason/understanding (e.g., *GMM* AK 4:397), and by this he means (*in the final analysis*) that it will be found by anyone who uses the powers of the *sensus communis* correctly, which is to say, by anyone who reasons as required by the maxims of the *sensus communis*. How else, when Kant holds that 'moral philosophy is based entirely on its pure part' and gives to the moral philosopher 'as a rational being, laws a priori' (*GMM* AK 4:389), are we to understand his statement that 'a philosopher... cannot have any other principle than that of common understanding' (*GMM* AK 4:404), which we can (and should) link to his claim in *CPrR* that

> the justification of moral principles as principles of *pure* reason could be carried out very well and with sufficient *certainty* by a mere appeal to the judgment of common human understanding.[8] [Our emphases added] (AK 5:91)

It should also be borne in mind that, if Kant's claim that the moral law is found in common human understanding means that it is the commonly held view that the moral law governs human action and practical thinking as a categorical imperative, then we should expect him to identify the moral law with the Golden Rule, 'Do unto others as you would have them do unto you'. After all, the Golden Rule can be found in scripture in Judaism, Christianity and Islam, and would have been held very generally by Europeans in Kant's time. But the moral law that Kant identifies in *GMM* I AK 4:402, *'I ought never to act except in such a way that I could also will that my maxim should become a universal law'* is not the Golden Rule. The Golden Rule prescribes 'a willing to will' condition on legitimate action. It demands that Agnes treat Brian in the way that she wishes to be treated herself. Kant's moral law demands that Agnes treat Brian

---

[8] It is worth noting, too, that Kant refers to the judgment of the common human understanding, not to the judgment of the common human person.

in the same way that she *rationally can* wish to be treated herself, which can only be identified within the frame of a categorical imperative by identifying what Agnes cannot rationally will for herself/rationally ought to will for herself. No such construction can be justified on the basis of what Agnes and Brian just happen to will. Thus, there must be something about what Kant refers to as 'the common human understanding' that strictly requires Agnes to will something in consequence of which she may adopt a maxim only if she can will it to be a maxim that all other agents also rationally can adopt. And, this something, we maintain, can be nothing other than conformity with common human understanding construed as an end in itself, which can only refer to human agential self-understanding construed in terms of the *sensus communis* of *CPoJ*.

This said, it should be noted that, in *Anthropology* (AK 7:139), Kant distinguishes what he there calls *'sensus communis'* – which he identifies with 'sound human understanding' *(bon sens)*, which he links to 'the application of rules to cases *(in concreto)*' – from 'scientific understanding', which is understanding belonging to 'a clear mind' (for which 'scientific principles *a priori* are required'). This suggests that Kant might not always be consistent in his terminology, for this suggests that the *sensus communis*/sound common human understanding of *CPoJ* is closer to the scientific understanding of *Anthropology* than to the *sensus communis* of *Anthropology*. In any event, what he seems to hold is that all human agents possess the powers of the *sensus communis* (per *CPoJ*), that many human agents have sufficient understanding of these powers to display *bon sens*, but that scientific understanding (use of clear and distinct understanding of the principles, i.e., the maxims, of the powers of the *sensus communis)* is necessary to determine what is *bon sens*. Discrepancies of use are also alleviated by the fact that Kant's focus on the 'precepts for reaching Wisdom' in *Anthropology* is very much in the context of applying the categorical imperative (rather than its construction), where the second principle is 'Think into the place of the other [person] (in communication with other human beings)'.

In any event, as Onora O'Neill insists (1989, esp. Chapter 2), by thinking from the viewpoint of everyone else (which Kant depicts as the aspect of the *sensus communis* that makes it a *communal* sense), Kant does not mean thinking from the viewpoint that everyone else actually accepts (after all, such a viewpoint does not actually, let alone necessarily, exist). He means thinking from the viewpoint that everyone else could possibly (i.e., could coherently) accept. And Kant is explicit about this. To take the universal viewpoint of others

> happens by one holding his judgment up not so much to the actual as to the merely possible judgments of others, and putting himself into the position of everyone else, merely by abstracting from the limitations that contingently attach to our own judging, which is in

turn accomplished by leaving out as far as possible everything in one's representational state that is matter, i.e., sensation, and attending solely to the formal peculiarities of his representation or his representational state. Now, perhaps this operation of reflection seems much too artificial to be attributed to the faculty that we call *common* sense; but it only appears thus if we express it in abstract formulas; in itself, nothing is more natural than to abstract from charm and emotion if one is seeking a judgment that is to serve as a universal rule. (*CPoJ* AK 5:294)

By representing the rules governing the essential powers of human understanding, the maxims of the *sensus communis*, as *general* rules and conditions for avoiding error,[9] Kant holds that they apply *a priori* to theoretical, practical, and aesthetic reasoning. Furthermore, applied practically, the generation of the maxim of reason clearly depicts nothing other than the essence of Kant's argument for the categorical imperative in the form of the FUL. As such, Kant's reasoning is something like this. For *Agnes* to be given a reason to act she must be given a reason to act *from the standpoint of the particular unique finite embodied agent that she is*. However, exercise of the power of reflecting judgment strictly requires Agnes to recognize that she cannot be the particular agent she is unless she is *an* agent (i.e., unless she possesses the powers of reason, judgment and understanding necessarily shared by all human agents, because they are the powers needed in order to be *an* agent). Consequently, to think that *she* has *a* personal understanding that she can oppose to, *or share with*, the personal understandings of others, she must reason in terms of any maxims she is strictly required to accept simply by virtue of understanding what it is for her to be *an* agent. Because requirements that Agnes, as a human agent *as such*, must accept are generated by the idea of being a human agent *as such*, and being a human agent *as such* is the same for all human agents, any maxim that Agnes must accept as a human agent *as such* will be a maxim that any other human agent must accept as a human agent *as such*. Hence, maxims that are requirements that Agnes must accept in order to understand what it is for her to be a human agent *as such* are collectively universal (i.e., normatively objective), not merely distributively universal (i.e., normatively subjective). *Understanding this*,[10] consistency strictly requires Agnes, *as the particular*

---

9 See Chapter Four, note 6.
10 This understanding is understanding of a unity of understanding effected by Agnes understanding what it is for her to be a human agent, which means that the maxim of reason is a construction of Agnes understanding what it is to understand what it is for her to be a human agent. This accords with the reading we gave to Kant's characterization in *GMM*. It is also worth noting that rendering the maxim of understanding consistent with the maxim of the power of judgment may, when thinking of the connection as involved in the justification of the maxim of reason, be viewed as requiring a solution to the problem of rendering application of the law of universal mechanism (linked to the maxim of understanding) with the presupposition of free

agent that she is, to accept the third maxim by also thinking in consistency with maxims that *any* human agent must accept (those that she must accept by understanding *what it is for her to be a human agent as such*). This yields the FUL read as

> Act only on practical precepts that you can act on consistently with universal laws (i.e., consistently with maxims that the agential self-understanding of any human agent strictly requires to be accepted).

This generation of the maxim of reason also reveals the sense/manner in which human agential self-understanding is inherently public or social. Its inherent public character lies in the maxim of reason being the product of a dialogue between first person Agnes (the particular agent that she is) and second person Agnes (Agnes representing all agents) and the bi-conditional relation that exists between Agnes as the particular agent that she is and Agnes as an agent *as such*. And it is in this way that the maxim of reason as a followability principle is grounded in public reason as against being the principle for public reason in its application.

We grant that there are terminological complexities in linking this to Kant's reasoning about the generation, possibility of, and requirements of moral consciousness in *GMM* and *CPrR*. This is because, in *GMM*, the operative powers are described as those of 'sensibility', 'understanding' and 'reason', whereas in *CPrR* only 'understanding' and 'reason' figure, as against 'understanding', 'power of judgment' and 'reason' in *CPoJ*. However, in *CPoJ*, Kant provides a table that we can use as a guide. He says that there are three a priori 'faculties of the mind' (we might, on the basis of what he says the *sensus communis* is, call them 'the three basic faculties required for human agential self-understanding'): 'the faculty of cognition', 'the feeling of pleasure and displeasure', and 'the faculty of desire'. He also tells us that the faculty of cognition is associated with itself as well as with the other two faculties. In its association with itself it constitutes 'understanding' ('Verstand' in the narrow sense we indicated in Chapter Two). In its association with the faculty of feeling of pleasure and displeasure it constitutes 'the power of judgment'. And in its association with the faculty of desire it constitutes 'reason' (*CPoJ* AK 5:196–198). However, when Kant talks of a '*critique of pure reason*', he is not talking about reason in this sense. He is talking about a critique of human agential self-understanding ('Verstand' in the broad sense we

---

will (linked to the power of judgment). Kant says that rendering the maxim of understanding consistent with the maxim of the power of judgment is the most difficult thing to do *CPoJ* AK 5:295). There are a number of things that he might think constitute this difficulty, but we consider that, at the most fundamental level, the problem is to resolve the third antinomy.

indicated in Chapter Two), where human agential self-understanding is viewed as being constituted and governed by the maxims of '*u*nderstanding', 'power of judgment', and 'reason' (which, because Kant often uses the words 'understanding' and 'reason' interchangeably, we may think of as the maxims of a priori 'Reason' or 'Understanding' as a whole). To this must be added that Kant tells us (at *CPoJ* AK 5:196–198) that the faculty of cognition through understanding cognizes (gains awareness of) nature as mechanism, the feeling of pleasure and displeasure through the power of judgment cognizes 'art' (objects as products of creative imagination), and the faculty of desire through reason (a product of understanding and the power of judgment) cognizes free will. Since Kant holds that cognition of nature as mechanism presupposes sensibility and posits mechanistic causal laws, and cognition of free will presupposes the moral law and postulates the *summum bonum* (which he repeatedly tells us requires God and human immortality for it to be possible for it to be brought about), while cognition of art presupposes imaginative creativity and posits purposivity and meaningfulness and 'mediates' between the domain of nature and the domain of free will (thereby uniting the concepts of nature as mechanism and free will in the same subject while 'at the same' time promoting 'the receptivity of the mind for the moral feeling'),[11] connections can be made to the processes Kant describes in the language of *GMM* and *CPrR*.

Just how these connections are to be made is not altogether clear; but, given the importance that Kant assigns in *CPoJ* to the power of judgment, we consider that it is crucial to focus on the role played by the power of imagination (the capacity for free creativity, the power of reflecting judgment – as against determining judgment) that he holds enables the concept of the moral law *as such* to be generated from the concept of a hypothetical imperative.

We suggest, albeit rather tentatively, that Kant thinks of the power of imagination as the power of thought that enables agents not only to *live/feel* the actual (the now) but to *think* the possible, thereby to *think* the past and future, and hence to *think* the actual. Without this power (which is implicated in the use of all three

---

[11] By 'the moral feeling', Kant means the feeling of reverence, awe, or respect for the moral law that characterizes the mind of Agnes when she not merely acts *in accordance with* the moral law, but purely *for the sake of* the moral law (*CPrR* AK 5:81). It is a capacity for this feeling that Kant thinks is necessary to be able to be moved to act by pure agential self-understanding *alone*, a capacity necessary for free will to be active in human agents (*GMM* AK 4:460; *CPrR* AK 5:76). If it can be said to explain the capacity of human agents to be motivated by pure agential self-understanding, Kant certainly does not think that a capacity for moral feeling can be explained by anything, though we must presume that we have it, while recognising the ease with which it can be confused with heteronomous incentives to act in accord with the moral law, and that we can never be certain when we act from it (see, e.g., *GMM* AK 4:419).

powers of the *sensus communis*), but which is connected in its purest form to the reflecting power of judgment, there could be no thought at all. The power of imagination enables Agnes to think herself in the position of someone else, just as it enables her to imagine herself to possess characteristics, and to occupy a position other than the one she thinks of herself as contingently occupying. Furthermore, it enables her to imagine what it would be like for her to be a purely rational being, one whose existence is constituted entirely by the powers of the *sensus communis*. And the other powers of the *sensus communis* inform her that if she were such a being then the moral law *as such* would be a law of her nature. The fact that she possesses sensibility, however, tells her (through the determining power of judgment) that she is not such a being, and does not (indeed, cannot) necessarily act according to the moral law *as such*. However, the reflecting power of judgment tells her that she not only can imagine what it would be like for her to be a purely rational being. It tells her that to understand what she is as a heteronomously affected being, she must imagine what it would be like for her to be a purely rational being because she cannot be Agnes without possessing the a priori powers of the *sensus communis*, which all other agents necessarily possess. Thus, she must think of herself as both governed by the maxim of understanding (the maxim of heteronomous practical reason) and the maxim of the power of judgment (the maxim of pure practical reason), and this means that she must view herself as governed by the maxim of reason (the maxim of a heteronomously affected being who has the powers of a purely rational being), which means that she must consider that she is bound by the moral law as the categorical imperative.

In this way, according to Kant, Agnes must view herself as occupying two worlds, the world of sense and the intelligible world, both of which are aspects of the world of understanding (to which she belongs by virtue of possessing the powers of agential self-understanding).

The problem for Kant in this picture is then solely to show that it is coherent for Agnes to view herself as governed by the maxim of reason.

Furthermore, although this claim is beyond the scope of this book to justify, we consider that viewing the role of the power of imagination in this way helps us to see what Kant means when he says that the beautiful is a symbol of/for morality (*CPoJ* AK 5:346–354), while the sublime is a symbol of/for the categorical imperative (the moral law *as such* conceived of in relation to resistance to its command) (*CPoJ* AK 5:274–276). This is because Kant holds that what is judged beautiful is an expression in feeling occasioned by having the concept of negative freedom derived from exercising the reflecting power of judgment; whereas that which is judged sublime is an expression occasioned in feeling by that which mentally opposes the idea of being wholly free with the idea of belonging to a world governed by the universal law of mechanism derived from exercising the determining power of judgment (thus, when rationally felt, generates a sense of awe that is a symbol of/for respect for the moral law). It is in this way, we suggest, that Kant holds that, in the power of judgment mediating between the power of understanding and the power of reason, having the capacity for aesthetic judgment is necessary to have the capacity for moral judgment.

As we signalled early on in this book, this (and much else that we say about the precise details of the interplay of the powers of thought of the *sensus communis*) is to a degree speculative. However, we consider that whatever the details of how Kant reasons in *CPoJ*, and howsoever the terminological connections with *GMM* and *CPrR* are to be made, how he reasons in *CPoJ* relates sufficiently to how he reasons in *GMM* and *CPrR* to support the claim that he regards an a priori synthetic practical proposition as one that is a strict requirement of thinking in accord with oneself, which is a matter of synthesising the strict requirements of thinking for oneself (as a heteronomously affected agent) with thinking from the viewpoint of an agent *as such* (as a non-heteronomously affected agent), and that this is what must be done to achieve human agential self-understanding, thereby justifying the existence of the moral law as the categorical imperative.

It is also important to appreciate that, by stating that the principles of the *sensus communis* are maxims (practical precepts), Kant implies that the maxim of reason is the supreme principle of all human reason,[12] and that he thinks of all *a priori* synthetic rules of *human* thought as rules of human agential self-understanding. This is witnessed, not only by his claim that the concept of free will as derived from the moral law is the keystone of the entire system of pure reason (*CPrR* AK 5:3–4), but also by his saying, in *GMM*, that

> I require that the critique of pure practical reason, if it is to be carried through completely, be able at the same time to present the unity of practical and speculative reason in a common principle, since there can, in the end, be only one and the same reason, which must be distinguished merely in its application. (*GMM* AK 4:392)

This is also stated in the following passage from *CPrR*:

> [I]f pure reason of itself can be and really is practical, as consciousness of the moral law proves it to be,[13] it is still only one and the same reason... Thus, in the union of pure

---

12 Onora O'Neill (1989, 20) draws the same inference.
13 It is this kind of statement that leads Dieter Schönecker (2013) and others to identify the fact of reason with moral feeling. This requires 'consciousness of the moral law' to be read as 'moral feeling', whereas we consider that 'consciousness of the moral law' refers to agentially required awareness on the part of humans of the concept of a moral law *as such*, a law of pure agential self-understanding. While Kant says that having the power of judgment requires a capacity to feel pleasure and displeasure, and that for an embodied being exercise of the power

speculative with pure practical reason in one cognition, the latter has primacy, assuming that this union is... based a priori on reason itself and therefore *necessary*. For, without this subordination [i.e., 'if they were merely juxtaposed'] a conflict of reason with itself would arise.... But one cannot require pure practical reason to be subordinate to speculative reason and so reverse the order, since all interest is ultimately practical and even that of speculative reason is only conditional and is complete in practical use alone.

(*CPrR* AK 5:121)

The effect of linking Kant's programme in *CPoJ*, and what he says about the *sensus communis*, to his reasoning about the generation and possibility of moral consciousness in *GMM* and *CPrR* and its place in his transcendental project as a whole, also confirms that Kant holds that he has established that the categorical imperative is an apodictic a priori synthetic practical proposition *for* all human *agents*, not merely for those who happen to be morally committed. In our opinion, an overarching problem that Kant is addressing in *CPoJ* is the possibility that causal laws of mechanism (knowledge of which is only possible within the frame of human agential self-understanding) do not constitute a consistently ordered system (AK 5:385–415) But, according to Kant, Agnes must believe that all laws grounded in (i.e., regulated by) human agential self-understanding are purposively ordered because it is 'morally necessary to assume the existence of God' (*CPrR* AK 5:125) and human immortality (*CPrR* AK 5:122) (see *CPoJ* AK 5:416–484). In relation to this, Kant is adamant that his moral argument for God, which

is meant to prove that if his [anyone's] moral thinking is to be consistent, he must include the assumption of God's existence [as postulated by his free will] among the maxims of his practical reason.[14]   (*CPoJ* AK 5:451)

does not relate God to morality in such a way

that whoever cannot convince himself of... [the existence of God] can judge himself to be free from the obligations of the [moral law]... [For] [e]very rational being would still have to recognize himself as forever strictly bound to the precept of morals.[15]   (*CPoJ* AK 5:451)

---

of judgment will necessarily involve a capacity for feeling in general, such feeling is not to be confused with the distinctively moral feeling generated by acceptance of the moral law. (See further Chapter Five, note 8.)

14 Kant's claim that belief that God exists is a maxim, a practical precept, implies that to be required to believe that God exists is to be required to act in accord with 'God ought to exist', which is to be required to act as though God exists. As we interpret this, Kant is saying that, from the perspective of theoretical reason, 'God exists' is an 'ought', but from a practical perspective it is an 'is', a fact of pure *practical* reason (i.e., a *practical* postulate).

15 This shows that Kant does not consider God and the moral law-free will coupling to be reciprocal concepts, and we are sure he would say the same about the relationship between human immortality and the moral law-free will coupling.

Everything we have said in this chapter is implicit in the famous peroration with which Kant concludes *CPrR*.

> Two things fill the mind with ever new and increasing admiration and reverence, the more often and steadily one reflects on them: *the starry heavens above me and the moral law within me*. I see them before me and connect them immediately with the consciousness of my existence. The first begins from the place I occupy in the external world of sense... The second begins from my... personality... but... can be discovered only by the understanding... [by which] I cognize that my connection with... [the intelligible] world (and thereby with... [sensible worlds]) is not merely contingent... but universal and necessary. The first view of a countless multitude of worlds annihilates, as it were, my importance as an *animal creature*, which after it has been for a short time provided with vital force (one knows not how) must give back to the planet (a mere speck in the universe) the matter from which it came. The second, on the contrary, infinitely raises my worth as an *intelligence* by my personality, in which the moral law reveals to me a life independent of animality and even of the whole sensible world, at least so far as this may be inferred from the purposive determination of my existence by this law, a determination not restricted to the conditions and boundaries of this life, but reaching into the infinite. (AK 5:161–162)

Given the aims of *CPrR* stated in its Preface, we consider that this is (as it should be) a succinct and integrated statement of what Kant thinks human agential self-understanding strictly requires Agnes to think constitutes her existential condition. In other words, it is the answer to his question, 'What is the nature of man?' that *Jäsche Logic* implies is contained in Kant's answers to his other basic questions for philosophy. For us, at least, it also has enormous poetic force in opposing the image of a being who is an almost infinitesimally small part of a cosmos that is devoid of meaning to the image of that same being nonetheless being able to contemplate being in that position and thereby standing outside of it and beyond it, which encapsulates the essence of what Kant considers to be the sublime.

Chapter Five
The Moral Law as the Sole Fact of Pure Reason in *CPrR*

It is uncontroversial to say that, in *CPrR*, Kant continues to accept *GMM*'s analysis of the tenor of a categorical imperative *if one exists*. We have, thus far, argued that he also holds (in both works) that understanding the concept of a categorical imperative reveals that establishing the categorical imperative as an apodictic a priori synthetic practical proposition is a matter of showing that acceptance of it is strictly required by human agential self-understanding. Thus, we have argued that what it *means* to say that the moral law is given to human agents as the sole fact of pure reason in *CPrR* is that the moral law is justified as a categorical imperative in the form of the FUL[1] by the fact that Agnes's agential self-understanding strictly requires her to accept the FUL. What we have not yet done is show that the way in which Kant argues this in *CPrR* conforms to what we claim is the logical structure of his argument for the existence of the categorical imperative, and this is what we will now do.

It will be recalled that we claim that Kant's argument (which we presented in ten moves in Chapter Two) has three Stages. In short, these are:

SI Agnes's agential self-understanding strictly requires her to have and understand the concept of a categorical imperative.

SII Thus, because *understanding the concept of having the concept of a categorical imperative strictly requires Agnes to think that she is bound by a categorical imperative* (and that it has the content given by the FUL),[2] Agnes's agential self-understanding strictly requires her to think that she is categorically bound by the FUL.

SIII Therefore, because it is coherent for Agnes's agential self-understanding to strictly require her to think that she is categorically bound by the FUL, she cannot coherently deny or doubt that she is categorically bound by the FUL *on any grounds*.

We must show that his reasoning in *CPrR* conjoins *SI*, *SII* and *SIII*.

While spelling out the aims of *CPrR*, Kant says that, as 'a *Critique of Practical Reason* generally', *CPrR*

---

[1] Or the equivalent statement of it in *CPrR*: viz.,'So act that the maxim of your will could always hold at the same time as a principle in the giving of universal law' (AK 5:30).

[2] Kant does not mention the other formulations of the categorical imperative of *GMM* in *CPrR*, but he does allude to the FoH at *CPrR* AK 5:87.

> has merely to show *that there is pure practical reason*, and for this purpose it criticizes reason's entire *practical faculty*. . . . [I]f as pure reason it is really practical, it proves its reality and that of its concepts by what it does [by giving us the moral law], and all subtle reasoning against the possibility of its being practical is futile. (AK 5:3)

By establishing the reality of pure practical reason, he will have shown that 'transcendental *freedom* is also established' in the 'absolute sense' of something '*unconditioned* in the series of causal connection' (cf., something that is of itself the causality of a will *[GMM* AK 4:461]) that speculative reason needs but can 'put forward only problematically, as not impossible to think, without assuring its objective reality' (*CPrR* AK 5:3).³

Jochen Bojanowski (2017, 83) cites the passage from *CPrR* AK 5:3 indented above as evidence that Kant holds, because the moral law is given by pure practical reason by pure practical reason's deed, that this makes it futile to question the possibility of pure reason being practical. We are not sure just how Bojanowski thinks pure practical reason performs its deed, but he seems to share our view that Kant thinks that understanding the concept of pure practical reason posits the existence of the moral law.

> I take [it] . . . that Kant only needs to show that there is a fundamental practical principle constitutive of pure practical cognition. The question whether and how this relates to an object need not be addressed, for this cognition first brings the object of cognition into existence. As an a priori cognition of what ought to be, it is by its very nature transcendent. (2017, 84)

If by 'pure practical cognition' Bojanowski means that even human reason strictly requires Agnes to have the concept of pure practical reason, then it looks like he holds *SI* and *SII* of our construction. However, this does not show that Agnes must accept that she is really bound to accept the moral law as the criterion for all her permissible maxims, *unless* it is coherent for her to do so. So, it must be noted that Kant does not say *sans caveat* that pure practical reason proves its reality by what it does. He says that *if pure reason is really practical*, then it proves its reality by what it does. And what needs to be shown to establish that pure reason is really practical is to show that pure reason *as a whole* permits Agnes to think that pure reason is practical in her as a human agent. In other words, what must be shown is that pure reason *as a whole* permits pure *practical* reason to govern Agnes's human will by showing that pure theoretical reason can raise no valid objection to the commands of pure practical reason. It is because of this that Kant says that it is necessary to critique reason's entire practical faculty (rather than its pure practical faculty).

---

3 Here Kant alludes to his resolution of the Third Antinomy.

Chapter Five The Moral Law as the Sole Fact of Pure Reason in *CPrR*

This might be thought to be gainsaid by what Kant says at *CPrR* AK 5:121: viz.

> [I]f pure reason of itself can be and really is practical, *as consciousness of the moral law proves it to be* [our emphasis added], it is still only one and the same reason.

But this is not so, because he goes on to emphasize that this is because the union of pure theoretical reason with pure practical reason has been shown to be necessary in a priori reason as a whole.

In any event, we take what Kant says at AK 5:3 to sum up what he will claim to have done by the end of Book One of *CPrR*. The aim of Book Two is to give 'stability and objective reality' to the concepts of God and human immortality on the basis that

> freedom is real, for this idea reveals itself through the moral law . . . because it is the condition of the moral law, which we do know. (*CPrR* AK 5:4)[4]

Kant begins Book One by elucidating the concept of a categorical imperative as the law of pure practical reason that governs the will of a finite, embodied, imperfectly rational being. Significantly, he tells us that if there is a categorical imperative then

> it is requisite to reason's lawgiving that it should need to presuppose only *itself,* because a rule is objectively and universally valid only when it holds without the contingent, subjective conditions that distinguish one rational being from another. (*CPrR* AK 5:21)

He then tells us that such a rule (principle) can only be thought if it contains the determining ground of the will (the reason for the will to comply with the rule), not by its matter, but only by its form (*CPrR* AK 5:27); that such a principle can only exist if the will is free (*CPrR* AK 5:28–29); and that 'freedom and unconditional law reciprocally imply each other' (*CPrR* AK 5:29).

Given Kant's justificatory methodology, that he thinks that showing that the categorical imperative exists requires *SI*, *SII*, and *SIII* to be conjoined is implicit in these statements. This is reasonably clear if, as we have interposed, reference to the determining ground of the will is reference to what reason requires the will to do rather than to what impels the will to act.

He then begins a discussion in which he presents his justification of the moral law as the categorical imperative, which renders this explicit.

SI of our construction involves the following claim.

---

4 This means that the correctness of our construction is signalled strongly right at the beginning of *CPrR* by Kant's own statement of intention as soon as one takes Kant's 'rational theology' seriously.

If Agnes is a human agent (defined in part by her possession of the *a priori* powers of the common human understanding), which she must be in order to be an intelligible addressee/addressor of hypothetical imperatives, the question of the possible existence of a categorical imperative necessarily arises for her (whether or not she is aware of this). Consequently, in order to understand adequately what it is for her to be an agent, Agnes must engage with and understand the concept of a categorical imperative.

Directly relevant to this, Kant tells us that

> we become immediately conscious . . . [of the *moral law*] . . . as soon as we draw up maxims of the will for ourselves . . . inasmuch as reason presents it [the moral law] as a determining ground not to be outweighed by any sensible conditions and indeed quite independent of them. (*CPrR* AK 5:29)

In other words, Agnes becomes immediately aware of the moral law as soon as she guides herself by hypothetical imperatives (which she necessarily does as an agent) through reason giving her the idea of the moral law as a categorical imperative. Note that, despite the fact that Kant says that we become immediately conscious of the moral law as soon as we draw up maxims for ourselves, this consciousness is not a pre-existent fact for reason to take on board but the result of the exercise of reason. Consciousness of the moral law is not something human Agnes necessarily possesses. It is not strictly analytic that she possesses moral consciousness. Being conscious of the moral law is not a necessary truth about what it is for her to have a will and be an agent. It is not a brute fact. It is possible for her to be an agent and not be conscious of the moral law. But one necessary truth about her being an agent is that she possesses the powers of reason (the a priori powers of the *sensus communis*) necessary for her to have a will; and it is also a necessary truth that the sound use of these powers strictly requires her to be conscious (think the idea) of the moral law (this latter truth being a fact of, i.e., elicited by, these powers of reason). That this is what Kant thinks is revealed by his claim that agents become morally conscious only *inasmuch* as reason presents the moral law to them, upon which he elaborates by proceeding immediately to ask, 'But how is consciousness of that moral law possible?' (*CPrR* AK 5:30), to which he answers:

> We can become aware of pure practical laws just as we are aware of pure theoretical principles, by attending to the necessity with which reason prescribes them to us and to the setting aside of all empirical conditions to which reason directs us. The *concept* of a pure will arises from the first, as *consciousness* of a pure understanding arises from the latter. [Our emphases added.] (*CPrR* AK 5:30)

This connects the process of the prescription of pure practical laws to those passages in *GMM* III (esp. AK 4:451–454, 457) where Kant discusses the relation between having the idea of a hypothetical imperative and having the idea of the moral law that Agnes must accept by understanding the relations between viewing herself as belonging to the sensible world, the world of understanding, and the intelligible world.[5] Although this process is something he appeals to in relation to *SIII* of our construction of his argument, this does not preclude part of his 'three worlds' analysis[6] being employed in *SI*. This is because the 'three worlds' analysis performs two functions. The first shows that understanding the idea of a hypothetical imperative requires understanding the idea of a categorical imperative. The second shows that this linkage does not reveal an antinomy. We suggest that Kant only appeals to the first function at *CPrR* AK 5:30. That it can be viewed in this way is also supported by a statement he makes at *CPrR* AK 5:63 that indicates that he thinks that the first function can be separated from the second. Here, given that there are hypothetical imperatives, he says that the basic issue he is addressing is

> [w]hether there is not also an a priori determining ground of the will [free will] (which could never be found elsewhere than in a pure practical law, and indeed insofar as it prescribes to maxims only their lawful form without regard to an object). (*CPrR* AK 5:63)

However, in relation to this, he has a few sentences back said:

---

[5] Note, too, that Kant makes direct reference to his *GMM* III discussion of this, when he later says that 'it has been sufficiently proved elsewhere that freedom, if it is attributed to us, transfers us into an intelligible order of things' (*CPrR* AK 5:42).

[6] The three worlds we are referring to are the 'worlds' of sensibility, understanding and reason. It is customary to portray Kant as employing a 'two worlds' analysis, the two worlds being the noumenal world and the phenomenal world. But, from the point of view of construction through cognitive self-recognition, there are three relevant players: the sensible world (linked to the phenomenal world), the world of understanding, and the intelligible world (the noumenal world linking to the intelligible world, which is a construction of understanding reflecting upon itself by abstraction). With reference to the maxims of the *sensus communis* of *CPoJ*, the phenomenal world relates to the maxim of understanding, while the maxims of the power of judgment and of reason relate to the noumenal world/its connection to the phenomenal world in ways that we do not find absolutely clear. It is tempting to say that the maxim of the power of judgment governs the world of understanding and that the maxim of reason governs the intelligible world. But what better seems to fit how Kant reasons is to say that the power of judgment by abstraction generates the intelligible world (the maxim of the power of judgment governing the noumenal world) while the maxim of reason governs existence in both the phenomenal world and the noumenal world. But this does not quite fit statements Kant makes in *CPoJ* to the effect that the power of judgment mediates between free will as the object of reason and nature as the object of sensible cognition (see the Second Introduction to *CPoJ* especially). We will have more to say about this later, but everything we say about this aspect of Kant's reasoning is tentative, though we do not think that our uncertainty about this affects the validity of our construction.

> Even if we did not know that the principle of morality is a pure law determining the will a priori, we would at least have to leave it *undecided* in the beginning whether the will has only empirical or also pure determining grounds a priori. (*CPrR* AK 5:63)

This latter quote implies that the idea of a pure practical law and that of a hypothetical imperative must be had by anyone able to understand the question being addressed, and it is obvious that no-one can understand the idea of a hypothetical imperative who does not (at least negatively) grasp the idea of a categorical imperative. And it is this abstractive process of reasoning that is integral to our claim that Kant thinks that Agnes's agential self-understanding requires her to be aware of and understand the concept of a categorical imperative. It also distinguishes (when read with the first passage we quoted) the process of having the concept of a categorical imperative from that of proving the tenability of holding that there is free will.

It is also significant that Kant is explicitly concerned in *CPrR* AK 5:30 with the generation of, and the relationship between, the *concepts* of free will and the moral law, or *consciousness* of free will and *consciousness* of the moral law, not with the relationship between *the proposition* that Agnes has free will and *the proposition* that Agnes is bound by the moral law. Also, that there is a difference between these two concerns might explain why his only reference to the moral law as a 'fact of *reason*' is through reference to 'consciousness of' the fundamental law of pure practical reason (*CPrR* AK 5:31) and 'consciousness of freedom of the will' (*CPrR* AK 5:42), whereas he always refers to the moral law itself (or free will as an unavoidable determination given in the moral law) as the fact, or the sole fact, 'of *pure reason*' (*CPrR* AK 5:31, 47, 55, 91). So, if he intends us to be sensitive to these nuances, then it is at least plausible (on the basis of the process by which consciousness of the moral law is made possible) to interpret him as saying that Agnes can only (adequately) understand what it is for her to be guided by a hypothetical imperative if she is aware of the *idea* of a categorical imperative. As such it is very plausible to think that what he means by 'consciousness of the moral law is a fact of reason' is 'having the concept of pure practical reason (having the concept of the moral law) is a strict requirement of agential self-understanding', which implies that he holds that Agnes's agential self-understanding strictly requires her to understand the concept of pure practical reason (the concept of the moral law).

Anyway, Kant now says that the concept (read 'consciousness') of a pure will (a free will) arises from the necessity with which reason makes us aware of a pure practical law, and that this is the *only* way in which we can become aware of (become conscious of) free will. This is because empirical science cannot possibly generate the concept of free will since 'nothing in appearances can be explained by the concept of freedom', and the idea of 'a mechanism of nature' is antithetical to the idea of the causality of free will (*CPrR* AK 5:30). Thought of in this way, he is claiming that the *concept* of the moral law is the *ratio cognoscendi* of the *concept* of free will and the *concept* of free will is the *ratio essendi* of the *concept* of the moral law that reason (human agential self-understanding) necessarily makes us aware of.

Matters might, however, be thought to be complicated by the fact that Kant then says that 'experience *also* [our emphasis added] confirms this order of concepts in us', which he illustrates with the following much discussed example.

> Suppose someone asserts of his lustful inclination that, when the desired object and the opportunity are present, it is quite irresistible to him; ask him whether, if a gallows were erected in front of the house where he finds this opportunity and he would be hanged on it immediately after gratifying his lust, he would not then control his inclination. One need not conjecture very long what he would reply. But ask him whether, if his prince demanded, on pain of the same immediate execution, that he give false testimony against an honourable man whom the prince would like to destroy under a plausible pretext, he would consider it possible to overcome his love of life, however great it may be. He would perhaps not venture to assert whether he would do it or not, but he must admit without hesitation that it would be possible for him. He judges, therefore, that he can do something because he is aware that he ought to do it and cognizes freedom within him, which, without the moral law, would have remained unknown to him. (*CPrR* AK 5:30)

Some commentators who hold the *WAV* think that Kant uses this example to tell us what he means when he says that moral consciousness is a fact of reason at *CPrR* AK 5:31. He is telling us that the responses to his questions that he envisages the lustful man to make are ones that ordinary people will make, and that they can only make them if they are aware of the moral law. In doing so, he is assuming that such awareness *is* part of the consciousness of anyone who possesses 'common human reason'. So, when he says that moral consciousness is forced on us by reason, he means either that

(a) only agents who believe that they are bound by the moral law can and must hold that they have free will, and that he is merely addressing those who have this belief, which he is happy to do because reasonable people generally have moral consciousness (which implies that 'common human reason' refers to 'common sense' – i.e., to generally or customarily thought to be reasonable reasoning); or;

(b) all agents know in their hearts what they ought to do, even if they won't admit it to themselves, because they necessarily possess conscience (a faculty of moral intuition), which is a fact that needs and admits of no justification (which implies that 'common human reason' refers to 'the a priori conscience of humankind').

But option (a) does not match the apodictic aspirations that Kant's Book Two claims require justification of the moral law to secure; and, while it might be thought that option (b) can ground these aspirations, it flatly contradicts Kant's claim that the moral law is not grounded in any a priori intuition (*CPrR* AK 5:31).[7] So, we need to find another explanation of the role that the example performs.

We submit that Kant is not using the gallows example to reveal the cognitive status of the moral consciousness that is the *ratio cognoscendi* of consciousness of free will. He is showing that his claim about the cognitive relation between the concept of the moral law and the concept of free will *can* be confirmed by all human agents by using the powers of the common human understanding (the powers of the *sensus communis* of *CPoJ*), the powers that make them intelligible addressors/addressees of any practical precepts, and claiming that this will be confirmed by anyone who uses these powers properly. He is well aware that philosophical reflections on morality are pointless unless they can speak to real agents, and that he believes that they can do so is illustrated by his belief that the exercise of the powers of human agential self-understanding, which all human agents necessarily have, is sufficient for them to grasp the concept of morality and its significance for them. In effect, Kant is claiming that this is confirmed by the fact that his readers (and the lustful man) are able to understand the practical predicament of the lustful man and the questions that he is asking.

Furthermore, unless *GMM* also does not purport to establish the rational necessity of the categorical imperative, such a reading is supported by the fact that, in *GMM*, Kant provides 'an example' of 'the most hardened scoundrel' to very much the same effect as his gallows example, as a case of the 'practical use of common human reason' confirming 'the correctness of' the 'deduction' of the categorical imperative (*GMM* AK 4:454) that he gives in *GMM* through his 'three worlds' analysis. When he talks of 'confirmation' here, he is not to be read as referring to 'justification' or 'validation' but to the ability of the result of his deduction to be understood and used by ordinary human agents in their practical reasoning, once they think the concept of the moral law distinctly (*CPuR* A807: B835).

That this reference and other references to the use of common human reason can be read as reference to the possible effective use of the capabilities of recognition of those with the capacity of human agential self-understanding,

---

[7] Kant is so emphatic that pure reason cannot be grounded in anything outside of itself that it is beyond credulity to think that there is some way of interpreting what he says so as to allow of a grounding in a priori intuition, unless we are to take nothing he says seriously.

and not as reference to a universal or general actual recognition of the categorical imperative, is (as we argued in Chapter Four) also supported by what Kant has to say about the *sensus communis* in *CPoJ*. In this regard, it is possible that, when he says that the order of concepts is confirmed by common experience, he is presuming that human agential self-understanding has an autonomous capacity to generate moral feeling, an autonomous respect or reverence for the moral law, that is necessarily involved in acting out of respect for the moral law, but that might not be involved in merely acting in accord with it (as it could be driven by heteronomous incentives to care about what is strictly required by human agential self-understanding) (see *GMM* AK 4:397; *CPrR* AK 5:81), and that the recognition of this feeling is needed for human agents to feel that they have free will. But, if so, it must (as we have emphasized) be noted that Kant says that the ordering of concepts is *also* confirmed by experience. Because this implies that the ordering is justified without this 'experiential confirmation', this alone implies that the example as an experiential confirmation does not tell us how moral consciousness is cognized in any justificatory sense and tells us that it must be consistent with his justificatory account. Thus, what Kant means is that the necessitated a priori ordering is *conformable* to experience, without this *conformability* being necessary or able to establish the ordering.[8]

---

8 We can, therefore, agree with Onora O'Neill (2002) or Pawel Łuków (1993) that the gallows example is an explication of how pure practical reason can register in the lives of ordinary people. But we cannot agree with Łuków that, by his doctrine of the fact of reason, Kant has abandoned the idea that the categorical imperative can be justified as such altogether. And we also cannot agree with O'Neill that Kant's discussion of the fact of reason is tangential to his justification of the categorical imperative, which (like us) she maintains presupposes the justification given in *GMM*. As the linkage Kant makes to his argument for God that we will shortly consider, makes clear, Kant's claims about the fact of reason/pure reason are integral to the cognitive status he assigns to the categorical imperative.

We definitely do not agree with Dieter Schöneker (2013), Jeanine Grenberg (2013), or Heiko Puls (2011, 2014, 2016), who maintain that Kant's 'fact of reason' signals that our awareness of the moral law is possible only through the feeling of respect that Kant associates with the moral law. We agree with Heiko Puls (2011, 2014, 2016), against Dieter Schonecker (2014), that Kant holds that the categorical imperative is is a product of common human understanding in both *GMM* and *CPrR*. But Puls's characterization of this process (because of his characterization of common human understanding) does not accord with our view that awareness of, and understanding the concept of, pure practical reason is a strict requirement of human agential self-understanding unmediated by the respect that human agents ought to have (so can have, but might not have) for the strict requirements of human agential self-understanding. As we understand Kant, free will is constituted by the capacity to act out of respect for the moral law. Since free will is not the *ratio cognoscendi* of pure practical reason (thus, of the moral law), any feeling of respect for the requirements of pure practical reason cannot be the *ratio cognoscendi* for moral consciousness. The existence of the moral law/categorical imperative does

Kant, then, returns to the line of justification rather than one of illustration or autonomous explanation. Having, in effect, told us that common human reason requires agents to have the concept of the moral law/categorical imperative, thus the concept of free will, he follows this immediately with a statement of the moral law (the 'Fundamental Law of Pure Practical Reason'), which brings us to *SII* of our construction.

He now says what we take to be a declaration that it follows from this that understanding the concept of the moral law strictly requires Agnes to consider that she is bound by it (or, what amounts to the same thing, that understanding the concept of having free will *on the basis of understanding the concept* of the moral law, strictly requires Agnes to hold that she has free will, and, thus must think that she is bound by the moral law).

> [The moral law] says: one ought absolutely to proceed in a certain way. The practical rule is therefore unconditional and so is represented a priori as a categorical proposition by which the will is objectively determined absolutely and immediately (by the practical rule itself, which accordingly is here a law). For, pure reason, *practical by itself*, is here immediately lawgiving. The will is *thought* [our emphasis] as independent of empirical conditions and hence, as a pure will, as determined *by the mere form of law*, and this determining ground is regarded as the supreme condition of all maxims. The thing is strange enough, and has nothing like it in all the rest of our practical cognition. For the a priori thought of a possible giving of universal law, which is thus merely problematic, is unconditionally commanded as a law without borrowing anything from experience or from some external will. (*CPrR* AK 5:31)[9]

We take Kant to be saying that merely by understanding the concepts of the moral law, pure practical reason, the categorical imperative *as categorical*, and free will, all of which are reciprocal to each other in being given to Agnes a priori,

---

not rest on feeling motivated to act in accordance with it, even if the absence of feeling motivated to act in accordance with it *might* lead to failure to recognize its existence. Failing to accept the categorical imperative cannot mean that the categorical does not exist, simply because the existence (the 'is') of the categorical imperative is constituted by rationally required recognition that it ought to exist, and such existence presupposes the capacity of agents to fail to recognize its existence as well as the capacity to recognize its existence. For Kant, respect for the moral law is a requirement of its recognition not the basis of the requirement to recognize it (see, e.g. *CPrR* AK 5:23, and 71–89, esp. 78–82); and while having a feeling of respect cannot be commanded, it can be commanded to strive to have this feeling (*CPrR* AK 5:83).

9 Kant leads us into this by relating it by contrast with the postulation in pure geometry of propositions the content of which is that one can do something if one needs to do it. The difference is that in pure geometry the postulation is in order to do something not itself absolutely commanded. Onora O'Neill (1989) and particularly Michael Wolff (2009) also take this contrast to be central to Kant's reasoning. We consider Wolff's analysis in Chapter Seven.

Agnes must think that the moral law as the FUL *is* categorically binding on her and that she *has* free will. This is because, in the last sentence of the passage we have just quoted, Kant is saying that, merely by being rationally compelled to recognize the possibility of a categorical imperative (which rationally compels Agnes to accept 'If there is a categorical imperative, then it is the FUL'), Agnes is rationally compelled to accept 'The FUL is the categorical imperative'.

As we have said, it is on account of this that we call Kant's argument a 'quasi-ontological' one by linking this reasoning (dis)analogically to Anselm's ontological argument for the existence of God (according to which the idea of God, being the idea of a being containing all perfections, is the idea of a being that necessarily exists, so that anyone who can form the idea of God must accept that God exists).

It is, therefore, of considerable moment that Kant explicitly draws attention to such a (dis)analogy when he claims that, in his argument for the moral law,

> unconditioned causality [pure reason that is practical] and the capacity for it, freedom, . . . is not merely *thought* indeterminately[10] and problematically[11] (speculative reason could already find this feasible) but is even *determined with respect to the law* of its causality and *cognized* assertorically; and thus the reality of the intelligible world is given to us. . . . We could not, however, take a similar step with respect to the . . . idea of a *necessary being* [God] [because] the necessary being is to be cognized as given *outside us*.

whereas free will is cognized (given) within our reason (*CPrR* AK 5:105). In other words, whereas having free will and being bound by the moral law (thus the existence of the categorical imperative) are facts that can be and are produced by human reason, the existence of God is not the kind of fact that can be produced by human reason. Put bluntly, whereas human reason brings the categorical imperative into existence by its own activity, it cannot make God exist. If God exists, then God exists whatever human reason might or might not strictly require.

However, it is not the classical ontological argument of Anselm that Kant himself is commenting on here. The specific purpose of his remarks is to explain why, given his own argument for the existence of God and human immortality,

> among all the ideas of pure speculative reason, [free will] alone provides . . . a great extension in the field of the supersensible, though only with respect to practical cognition.
>
> (*CPrR* AK 5:103)

---

10 That is, is not merely thought without any determinate content.
11 That is, as something merely not impossible.

This means that his comments should be linked to the distinction between knowledge and faith that we drew attention to in Chapter Four in connection with free will being something Agnes knows, whereas God and human immortality are only things that she must have faith in. There we said that Kant regards free will as a postulate of pure reason as a whole, whereas he considers God and human immortality to be only postulates of pure practical reason as necessary conditions for the possible attainment of the *summum bonum*.[12] However, since pure reason as a whole is comprised of pure practical reason and pure theoretical reason, and Agnes's requirement to believe in her free will and assume the existence of God and human immortality requires no more than that pure theoretical reason not be able to demonstrate the impossibility of free will, God and human immortality, we queried how Kant can differentiate between Agnes's required commitment to the moral law and free will and her required commitment to God and human immortality in this way. We think that his answer is this. The existence of the moral law for Agnes, its undeniable factual (ontological) nature, its 'is-ness', is constituted by its categorical 'ought-ness'. This facticity is constituted by pure practical reason/understanding and it can (and must) be recognized by pure theoretical reason (because there can be only one pure reason and pure theoretical reason necessarily presupposes a freedom that it cannot characterize), on the basis of which the moral law-free will is given to Agnes as the sole fact of pure reason (as a whole). On the other hand, the facticities of God and human immortality (their ontological natures) are ideated inherently as 'is-es', as non-idealities, as things that in themselves cannot be brought into existence by reason/the understanding. So, while the existence of God is a postulate (fact) of pure practical reason, by being necessary for the *summum bonum*, that pure theoretical reason cannot disprove, it is not a fact of pure reason as a whole on that account. And it is this that Kant is

---

12 We have already noted that Kant claims (at *CPrR* AK 5:122) that free will as well as God and human immortality are practical postulates. Insofar as the moral law is the *ratio cognoscendi* of free will, it is apposite to say that free will is a practical postulate. But, insofar as having free will and the moral law are reciprocal concepts, free will also ought to be regarded as a postulate of pure reason as a whole, in contrast with human immortality and God which are postulated by the moral law/free will but not reciprocal to them, and so not postulates of reason (as a whole). Indeed, when Kant says that the moral law is a postulate of reason he means that it is a fact of pure reason, and though he calls it the sole fact of pure reason, he also says that free will is a fact of pure reason. This means that his view is really that the moral law-free will coupling is the sole fact of pure reason (postulate of reason). So free will has an aspect in which it is a postulate of reason and an aspect in which it is only a practical postulate, and it is, perhaps, this ambivalent character that leads Kant to regard free will as the keynote concept in his critical philosophy.

explaining when he says that one can (indeed, must) reason from the non-impossibility of free will to its reality for pure reason as a whole (albeit only for practical purposes), but from the theoretical non-impossibility of God only to God's reality for pure practical reason (again, only for practical purposes).

In any event, that the quasi-ontological argument (dis)analogy is about the moral law being given as the sole fact of pure reason is also supported by the explanation that Kant himself gives as to why he says that the moral law is given to human agents as the 'fact' of pure reason. We quoted parts of this passage before in Chapter Four, but we will now quote it in full. The

> [r]elation in which the *understanding* [Kant's emphasis] stands [to objects in theoretical cognition] . . . has also a relation to the faculty of desire, which is therefore called the will, and is called the pure will insofar as the pure understanding (which in this case is called reason) is practical *through the mere representation of a law* [our emphasis added]. The *objective reality of a pure will or, what is the same thing, of a pure practical reason* [our emphasis added] is given a priori in the moral law, as it were by a fact – for so we may call a determination of the will that is unavoidable even though it does not rest on empirical principles. In the concept of a will, however, the concept of causality is already contained, and thus in the concept of a pure will there is contained the concept of a causality with freedom, that is, a causality that is not determinable in accordance with laws of nature and hence not capable of any empirical intuition as proof of its reality, but that nevertheless *perfectly justifies its objective reality* [our emphasis added] a priori in the pure practical law. (*CPrR* AK 5:55)

What Kant's quasi-ontological move tells us is that what he thinks is special about pure practical reason is that the mere *possibility* of pure practical reason (which can only exist in agential self-understanding) is that it *entails*, not only the possibility of free will, but the *existence* of free-will. In other words, the *existence* of free will is not only the *ratio essendi* of the existence of *pure practical reason*, but the *ratio essendi* of the mere *possibility of pure practical reason!* Since Kant holds that Agnes's agential self-understanding strictly requires her to at least consider the possibility of pure practical reason, it requires her to accept that she has free will. Because she can only have free will if pure reason is practical, she must hold that pure reason is practical. Consequently, *within her agential self-understanding*, Agnes must hold that the possibility of pure practical reason, equivalent to the possibility of the moral law, entails the existence of pure practical reason and thus of the moral law.

As we have already noted, Kant is very clear that once someone is presented with the idea of pure practical reason, this person must consider the possibility of pure practical reason and may not dismiss it out of hand.

> [E]ven if we did not know that the principle of morality is a pure law determining the will a priori, we would at least have to leave it *undecided* in the beginning whether the will

has only empirical or also pure determining grounds, in order not to assume principles quite gratuitously (*gratis*); for, it is contrary to all basic rules of philosophic procedure[13] to assume as already decided the foremost question to be decided.[14]   (*CPrR* AK 5:64)

In other words, in order to deny, or even to doubt, that there is a categorical imperative, a sceptic has to engage with the idea of a categorical imperative and understand it. So any possible justification of scepticism concerning a categorical imperative rests on claiming *either* that Agnes's agential self-understanding does not necessarily present her with the idea of a categorical imperative *or* that the idea of a categorical imperative, whether necessarily presented to Agnes by her own agential self-understanding or contingently to her by the claims of others, is an incoherent idea (*or both*). Since Kant thinks that Agnes is necessarily presented with the idea of a hypothetical imperative, and that she cannot understand this idea without having the idea of a non-hypothetical imperative, it is clear that he thinks that the agential self-understanding of any sceptic (who might be Agnes herself),[15] requires the sceptic to be presented with the idea of a categorical imperative and to understand it. This leaves the sceptic with only one card to play, which is to claim that (having) the concept of a categorical imperative, though a strict requirement of human agential self-understanding, is incoherent. And it is this move that is addressed and rejected by *SIII* of Kant's argument.

This reasoning does not merely explain what Kant means when he says that

> in regarding this [the moral] law as *given*, it must be noted carefully that it is not an empirical fact but the sole fact of pure reason which, by it, announces itself as originally law giving.   (*CPrR* AK 5:31)

It also elucidates the process by which pure reason gives the moral law to Agnes. Pure reason gives the moral law to Agnes *by* Agnes understanding that understanding the concept of pure practical reason strictly requires her to think that she is bound by the law of pure practical reason, which is thereby practical of itself alone. And this coheres with the fact that, in Kant's numerous references to the moral law being given to Agnes as a deed or product of reason, he always says things like 'pure reason is practical *of itself* in being lawgiving' (*CPrR* AK 5:31; 5:42); the moral law provides a fact (free will) that gives a law

---

13 Kant might just as well have said 'contrary to all the basic tenets of critical thinking', which for him are the three maxims of the *sensus communis*.

14 Here Kant shows that he is aware of the Pyrrhonian Dilemma of the Criterion and sets up his response to it in the way we explained it in Chapter Two.

15 Indeed, strictly speaking, it is Agnes herself who is envisaged as the putative sceptic. We will comment further on this in Chapter Eight.

(the FUL) to itself (*CPrR* 5:43);[16] that the moral law establishes itself (*CPrR* AK 5:47); that 'the idea of the law of a causality (of the will) itself has causality or is its determining ground' (*CPrR* AK 5:50). How else can this be so unless by understanding the concept of pure practical reason Agnes is strictly required to assent to pure reason being practical?[17] And it is this latter thought that leads us to hold that, when Kant says that the moral law is given to human agents as the sole fact of pure reason, he means that rational nature is an end in itself and, in being so, is the ground of the moral law (*GMM* AK 4:428–429), where a rational nature is something that a human agent can exhibit, and to do so is to reason according to the strict requirements of human agential self-understanding (the requirements set by understanding the capacities of the *sensus communis* that Agnes needs to be an intelligible addressee/addressor of any practical precepts). This contention is at the heart of our preferred version of our claim in Chapter Six that Kant's argument in *GMM* is concordant with his argument in *CPrR*.

Although Kant never expresses things this way, we also consider that Lewis White Beck's (1960b) distinction between a fact *of* reason and a fact *for* reason suggests a helpful way to understand how Kant views the process by which

---

16 If this is not to be vacuous, Kant can only mean that Agnes understanding the concept of the moral law gives the moral law to Agnes.
17 It might be claimed that such an interpretation renders the argument viciously circular (tautologous). We disagree. It is viciously circular if Kant is claiming that Agnes must, by virtue of presuming that pure reason is practical, hold that pure reason is practical. But he is claiming that it is on the basis of having to understand the concept of pure practical reason (given that the concept of pure practical reason is the concept that pure reason *is* practical) in order to achieve human agential self-understanding that Agnes must hold that pure reason is practical. This is not viciously circular, because (as we explained in Chapters One and Two), Kant holds that to act in accord with the strict requirements of agential self-understanding must be recognized to be an end in itself because all claims about agential self-understanding presuppose the powers of agential self-understanding.

Pauline Kleingeld (2010, 58–59) responds to a charge of circularity in Kant arguing from 'the Fundamental Law of Pure Practical Reason to freedom and from freedom to the fundamental law', by saying that the argument is not circular because the grounding relationship between the moral law and freedom is different in each direction (as *ratio cognoscendi* in one direction and as *ratio essendi* in the other). But this does not suffice, because it does not answer the question as to why the fundamental law must be taken to be categorically binding. We are left with 'If Agnes must hold that she is bound by the moral law then she knows that she has free will; and if she has free will then she is bound by the moral law'. This is fine if the question is 'Why is Agnes bound by the moral law because her agential self-understanding strictly requires her to hold that she is?' But it is not. The question is 'Does Agnes's agential self-understanding strictly require her to hold that she is bound by the moral law???' Kant answers this question affirmatively, but not simply by asserting that free will is the *ratio essendi* of the moral law.

commitment to the moral law is generated in human agential self-understanding. However, in order to apply Beck's distinction adequately, it must be recognized that there are *three* facts that are at work, that the same fact can be a fact of reason and a fact for reason, and that the relationship between a fact as a fact of reason and the same fact as a fact for reason is dynamic. The first fact (which is undeniable) is that human agents possess practical reason, which is to say that they possess the powers of human agential self-understanding of the *sensus communis* (the powers of the common human understanding/reason). These powers are, however, self-reflective powers. *As such,* utilising them requires Agnes to treat the fact that she has practical reason, which (because it is undeniable) may be called a fact *of* practical reason, as at the same time a fact *for* practical reason, a fact that her practical reason must reflect on. The second fact is that doing so presents Agnes with the concept of pure practical reason, as a fact *of* the first fact *for* practical reason, which she must now also treat as a fact *of* pure practical reason. The third fact is that self-reflection on this, in turn, makes it necessary for Agnes to treat the existence of pure practical reason as a fact *for pure* practical reason, understanding which (with input from *SIII*) requires her to accept that it is a fact (the sole fact) of pure reason that she is bound by the moral law as the FUL. This, we contend, is built into Kant's idea that acceptance of the categorical imperative as a strict requirement of human agential self-understanding is something that is both legislated by her (so artificial or invented) yet legislated to her (so not arbitrary, but obligatory) (because, by understanding the concept of her having agential self-understanding, Agnes must consider acceptance of its strict requirements to be an end in itself).[18]

---

18 The idea that Kant holds that the moral law is legislated to agents is questioned by Pauline Kleingeld and Marcus Willaschek in a recent article (2019). They reject not only the widely held view that Kant holds that the moral law is legislated by free will, but that it is legislated by anything at all, including by pure practical reason to itself. Instead, they maintain that Kant holds that the moral law is simply the fundamental a priori law of pure practical reason (2019, 2). While there are numerous places where Kant might appear to assert that *the* moral law is legislated by the will/freedom/pure practical reason, careful inspection shows that it is only moral *laws* that are legislated (by *the* moral law) (2019, 2, 6). It might, therefore, be thought that their analysis challenges our position. And such a contention might be thought to be reinforced by the fact that Kant holds that the moral law has and needs no grounds (e.g., at *CPrR* AK 5:47) (see 2019, 3) because it is central to our view that Kant holds the moral law to be grounded in the fact that rational nature is an end in itself (see *GMM* AK 4:429). Nevertheless, we do not think that their analysis is incompatible with our own. This is because they distinguish between the moral law being imposed on agents by pure practical reason and it being legislated to agents by pure practical reason, and claim that, for Kant, 'legislation' always implies a contingent act of will (2019, 9). We consider this claim to be questionable. But, even if it is correct, when we say that that the moral law is legislated to Agnes by her agential self-understanding, no contingency is

So, what about *SIII*? Having reached the point where he is able to declare that

> [p]ure reason is practical of itself alone and gives (to the human being) a universal law
> which we call the *moral law* (*CPrR* AK 5:31)

Kant draws attention to the fact that the moral law as the categorical imperative has two *rationes essendi* (free will, and heteronomy – which requires subjection to the universal law of mechanism) (*CPrR* AK 5:32). Thereafter, he moves on to what distinguishes the categorical imperative from all other principles, returning to the establishment of the categorical imperative at *CPrR* AK 5:42–50. Here, he declares that

> [t]he *exposition* of the supreme principle of practical reason is now finished, that is, it has
> been shown, first, what it contains, that it stands of itself altogether independently of empirical principles, and then what distinguishes it from all other practical principles.
> (*CPrR* AK 5:46)[19]

But then he says

> With the *deduction*, that is, the justification of its [the supreme principle of practical reason's] objective and universal validity and the discernment of the possibility of such a
> synthetic proposition a priori, one cannot hope to get on so well as was the case with the
> principles of the pure theoretical understanding. (*CPrR* AK 5:46)

Many commentators take this to disqualify any suggestion that Kant thinks that he has established that the FUL (as the categorical imperative) is an apodictic a priori synthetic practical proposition *by a transcendental deduction*.[20] Another interpretation must be given for what Kant means when he continues to refer to the categorical imperative as an apodictic a priori synthetic practical proposition.

---

involved. In our view, the moral law *as such* is the fundamental a priori law of pure agential self-understanding (pure practical reason), the categorical imperative the fundamental a priori imperative of human agential self-understanding. In our view, to say that the moral law (*as such*) is legislated by pure practical reason is to say only that it is presupposed in and by (pure) agential self-understanding. Furthermore, on such a basis, there is no inconsistency between holding that the moral law has and needs no grounds and that the ground of the moral law is that rational nature (i.e., agential self-understanding) is an end in itself, for this implies that it has and needs no grounds beyond itself, which Kant, in any event, makes clear is his view at *CPrR* AK 5:47.

19 The fact that Jochen Bojanowski (2017, 77–80) sees the moral law as justifying itself by exposition is the main reason why we attribute *SII* of our construction to his account of the process by which practical reason gives the moral law to agents by a deed.

20 Many taking their cue from Dieter Henrich 1960.

There are no grounds for this. The reason why one cannot hope to get on so well with 'the *deduction*' (which Kant clearly regards as necessary to establish the truth of a categorical imperative as an a priori synthetic proposition) is that the principles of pure theoretical understanding refer to 'objects of possible experience, namely appearances' and these can only be '*cognized* as objects of experience' on the presupposition that they conform to the principles of pure theoretical understanding. But

> the moral law is not concerned with cognition of the constitution of objects that may be given to reason from elsewhere. (*CPrR* AK 5:46)

It is concerned only with the constitution of objects given by reason to itself. Indeed, 'pure but practical reason, by its very concept, cannot possibly be held to be dependent' on a deduction from the principles of experience and does not need *such* a deduction. The fact that such a deduction is impossible does not and cannot affect the fact that

> the moral law is given, as it were, as a fact of pure reason of which we are a priori conscious and which is apodictically certain. (*CPrR* AK 4:47)

So, when Kant says that the moral law 'itself has no need of justifying grounds' (*CPrR* AK 5:47), he is not saying that the moral law needs no justification, let alone that it has no justification, but merely that it needs no justification on any grounds other than *those it undeniably gives to itself by its very idea*. What the idea of the moral law gives to itself is the existence of the moral law (cognition of the binding character of the moral law) and the idea of free will, and free will is rendered not merely possible (merely an idea) but real 'in beings who cognize this law [the moral law] as binding on them' (*CPrR* AK 4:47). To cognize the law as binding on oneself is not merely to be committed to it. Kant never maintains that to 'know' (even when this is 'moral knowledge', based on pure practical reason, as against knowledge supported empirically or by pure theoretical reason) is merely to believe. To cognize the moral law as binding on oneself is to be required unconditionally by reason to be committed to it, and Agnes is shown to be unconditionally required to be committed to the moral law because the moral law is given to her as 'a fact of pure reason'[21] in Kant's '*exposition* of the supreme principle of practical reason'.

---

[21] In our interpretation, strictly speaking, this should be 'the fact of pure practical reason purporting to be the sole fact of pure human reason as a whole'. That Kant refers to 'a fact of pure reason' not 'the fact of pure reason' at this point is consistent with this. For, at this point, he is yet to say that being the fact of pure practical reason is enough to render the moral law the sole fact of pure reason (which he does in the next paragraph and at *CPrR* AK 5:48).

Chapter Five The Moral Law as the Sole Fact of Pure Reason in CPrR — 103

Given that the reasoning underlying Kant's quasi-ontological move is that the concept of a categorical imperative is so related to human agential self-understanding that being strictly required to accept its possibility means being strictly required to think that it exists, the fact that pure theoretical reason cannot show that it is impossible for Agnes to have free will shows that the categorical imperative is possible, and (*as constituted in Agnes's agential self-understanding*) it cannot be possible without being actual. This is all that Kant needs to show to establish that the categorical imperative is an apodictic a priori synthetic practical proposition by a practical transcendental deduction. However, he adds to this, we think mistakenly, and unnecessarily for his argument for the categorical imperative (though not for his dialectical purposes concerning the existence of God and human immortality), on the assumption that there can be only one pure reason, that the

> moral law proves its reality, so as to satisfy the *Critique* of speculative reason, by adding a positive determination to a causality [noumenal free will] thought only negatively, the possibility of which was incomprehensible to speculative reason, which was nevertheless forced to assume it. (*CPrR* AK 5:48)²²

However, this addition holds only for practical purposes (*CPrR* AK 5:50).

It is astonishing that any plausibility should be attached to the claim that Kant is here rejecting the transcendental deduction he offers in *GMM*. Kant says that, although

> the moral law cannot be proved by any deduction, *by any efforts of theoretical reason, speculative or empirically supported* [our emphasis added], . . . it is nevertheless firmly established of itself.

> But something different and quite paradoxical takes the place of this vainly sought deduction of the moral principle, namely that the moral principle, conversely itself serves as the principle of an inscrutable faculty which no experience could prove *but which speculative reason had to assume as at least possible* [our emphasis added] . . . namely the faculty of freedom of which the moral law, which itself has no need of justifying grounds, proves not only the possibility but the reality in beings who cognize this law as binding upon them. (*CPrR* AK 5:47)

For Kant to be rejecting the deduction he offered in *GMM*, 'this vainly sought deduction' must be the deduction he offers in *GMM*.²³ But it is not, and this is because he says exactly what he is saying here in *GMM*.

---

22 We will indicate why we think this reasoning, in so far as it makes free will a property of noumenalnoumenalnoumenal reality, is invalid on Kant's own premises in Chapter Nine.
23 Which, e.g., Jens Timmermann (2010, 74) takes him to be doing.

104 — Chapter Five The Moral Law as the Sole Fact of Pure Reason in *CPrR*

> [W]e can explain nothing but what we can reduce to laws the subject of which can be given in some possible experience.[24] Freedom, however, is a mere idea . . . [that] holds only as a necessary presupposition of reason in a being that believes itself to be conscious of a will.[25] . . . Now, where determination by laws of nature ceases, there *explanation* ceases as well, and nothing is left but *defense,* that is to repel the objections of those who pretend to have seen deeper into the nature of things and therefore boldly declare that freedom is impossible. We can only point out to them that the supposed contradiction they have discovered in it [vanishes as soon as they] . . . acknowledge, as is equitable, that things in themselves (though hidden) must lie behind appearances as their ground and that one cannot insist that the laws of their operation should be the same as those under which their appearances stand. (*GMM* AK 4:459)

Thus, the vainly sought deduction of *CPrR* AK 5:47 is clearly that attempted by those, *who certainly do not include Kant,* who try to do so via a theoretical deduction, and this is his view in both *GMM* and *CPrR*.[26]

Jochen Bojanowski's account of what Kant is saying at *CPrR* AK 5:46–47 puzzles us. He explicitly takes Kant to be saying that no transcendental deduction is necessary to establish the application of the moral law to human agents. Yet he says that Kant *uses and needs*

> an argument that will fend off determinist sceptics. . . . Against this kind of scepticism, Kant attempts not to prove the theoretical actuality of the concept of freedom but rather its logical possibility. (2017, 84–85)

Apart from the fact that it is the coherence of the idea that free will can be applied to human agents, not the coherence of the concept of free will as such, that is at stake, this is correct. But this, and nothing else, is the transcendental

---

[24] By saying this, Kant does invite misunderstanding, because this conflicts terminologically with his claim that we can explain free will as the necessary presupposition of the moral law (the reality of which is not given in a possible experience) (see *GMM* AK 4:461). But the general context and the fact that the claim about autonomous explanation comes after what he says here, makes it sufficiently clear that the explanation that Kant holds to be confined to subject matters given in experience is explanation in terms of mechanistic causes.

[25] By 'a being that believes itself to be conscious of a will', Kant means 'any agent'. There is no conditionality asserted here that differentiates some agents from others. The only conditionality asserted is what differentiates agents from non-agents, because he claims to have already shown that Agnes must cognize the moral law and it is in relation to this cognition, not to any contingent belief of Agnes, that he is referring.

[26] Onora O'Neill (2002), Michael Wolff (2009), and Owen Ware (2017) also reject the claim that Kant is here abandoning the transcendental deduction he offers in *GMM*. Unlike O'Neill, Wolff, and ourselves however, Ware thinks that Kant does not consider that this deduction renders the existence of the categorical imperative absolutely certain (to which we respond in Chapter Eight).

argument that Kant uses in *GMM* that constitutes *SIII* of the argument. As we will show in Chapter Six, Kant employs no transcendental argument in *GMM* that attempts to establish a necessary presupposition of free-will on any grounds different from those appealed to in *CPrR*. If Bojanowski is saying that Kant thinks that the moral law *as such* needs no deduction, we agree. The moral law *as such* exists analytically in the concept of pure practical reason. But the issue for the deduction (*SIII* of our construction) is whether the moral law (the law of pure practical reason) can apply to human agents, which it can do only as a categorical imperative. That moral consciousness necessarily exists in common human understanding is also not at issue between us, on which basis we attribute Bojanowski's agreement to *SI* of our account (though our accounts of the reason why this is so might differ, for it is not clear to us that he sees Kant's reasoning in terms of human agential self-understanding in quite the way that we do). But Bojanowski cannot legitimately finesse this to say that this means that the question of the existence of a categorical imperative does not arise. It still arises and the defence against determinist scepticism that Bojanowski treats as not being necessary to establish the existence of the moral law as the categorical imperative is precisely what Kant thinks is needed to establish the existence of the categorical imperative. Bojanowski's claim, that Kant thinks that it is not necessary to establish the possibility of free will in *CPrR* to establish the apodictic rational necessity of the categorical imperative, rests on claiming that Kant does not think that free will or even its possibility is the *ratio essendi* for the moral law and thus a *ratio essendi* of the categorical imperative. For reasons we will give in Chapter Nine, as against Kant, we think that the *possibility* of free will (not the existence of free will) is a *ratio essendi* for the categorical imperative (the existence of free will being the *ratio essendi* of the moral law *as such)*, which means that the moral law is only the *ratio essendi* of the possibility of free will *for human agents*. Even so, establishing that acceptance of the moral law is a strict requirement of human agential self-understanding still requires the possibility of free will to be established to show that the idea of a categorical imperative is coherent to justify the reality of the categorical imperative (i.e., render the existence of the categorical imperative unassailable), which requires defence against the claims of determinism. For this reason, we doubt that our disagreement with Bojanowski concerning Kant's view in *CPrR* is merely terminological (though it might be). We have no doubt, however, that our disagreement with him about Kant's view in *GMM* is not terminological.

Although Henry E. Allison (1990) subscribes to the *WAV*, his incorrect view about *CPrR* enables us to highlight the importance of appreciating that Kant's argument is conducted from and within human agential self-understanding and not a freestanding analysis of the concept of rational agency. As a *WAV* proponent, Allison claims that *GMM* attempts to establish the existence of the categorical imperative by combining

(a) an analysis of the concept of rational agency to establish that Agnes necessarily presupposes, in a morally neutral way, that she has free will, with
(b) the reciprocity thesis to establish that Agnes must accept that she is bound by the moral law as the categorical imperative, with
(c) a defence of the coherence of this result in the face of a threat posed by the claim that Agnes must believe that every observable event has a mechanistic cause (1990, 214–229).

However, *CPrR* abandons *GMM's* claim that the categorical imperative is shown to exist by a morally neutral transcendental deduction. This is because Kant *now* realizes that the existence of the categorical imperative

> cannot be derived from any higher principles or from reflection on the nature of rational agency ([because the concept of a categorical imperative itself implies that] 'one cannot ferret it out from antecedent data of reason'). (1990, 233)

Thus, because Kant holds that consciousness of free will is not, and cannot be, given in experience, he *now* maintains that consciousness of free will can only derive from prior consciousness of the moral law.

This is standard *WAV* fare. However, an interesting feature of Allison's construction is his view that, because Kant holds that consciousness of the moral law provides consciousness of free will, Kant now holds that Agnes is required to think that the categorical imperative exists simply by understanding the concept of a categorical imperative. Indeed, he claims that Kant ought to have concluded this at the end of *GMM* II:

> [T]he desired goal [deduction of the moral law] has been already attained, implicitly at least, in and through the analysis of the nature of morality and its principle contained in the first two parts of the *Groundwork*[27] and the first chapter of the Analytic of Pure Practical Reason in the second *Critique*. (1990, 236)

This means that Allison also thinks that the quasi-ontological reasoning of our *SII* is part of Kant's argument in *CPrR!*[28] Furthermore, like us, he does not consider

---

27 In the next chapter, we will argue that the best interpretation of the way in which Kant presents his argument in *GMM* represents him as explicitly reaching this conclusion by the end of *GMM* II.

28 It is worth remarking that it is for this reason that Allison shares our view that Kant does not deny that the categorical imperative is derived by a deduction at *CPrR* AK 47. In his opinion, Kant claims that it is derived by a metaphysical deduction (i.e., a metaphysical exposition)

Chapter Five The Moral Law as the Sole Fact of Pure Reason in *CPrR* —— 107

that Kant thinks this is enough (even given the coherence of the concept of a categorical imperative, argued for by *SIII* of our construction) to establish that the categorical imperative exists. *SII* presupposes that Agnes has moral consciousness (engages with the concept of the moral law), but for *SII* to show that Agnes has reason to think that the moral law exists it must be shown that Agnes has reason to be morally conscious. Therefore, when Kant tells us that moral consciousness is a fact of reason, he is telling us that Agnes has reason to be morally conscious and that what provides this reason (what makes moral consciousness a fact of reason) conditions the operation of *SII* and *SIII*. Regarding this, Allison tells us that

> [b]y referring to this [moral] consciousness as a fact, Kant is emphasizing both its presumed universality (at least with regard to those capable of moral deliberation) and its status as a brute given, which cannot be derived from any higher principles or from reflection on the nature of rational agency. (1990, 233)

However, to say that moral conscuousnees has the status of a brute given (brute fact) in that it cannot be derived from higher principles or from reflection on the nature of agency does not tell us what positively makes moral consciousness a brute fact. According to Allison,

> Although the texts are far from unambiguous on this score, the bulk of the evidence suggests that the fact is best construed as the consciousness of standing under the moral law and the recognition of this law 'by every natural human reason as the supreme law of its will' (KprV 5:91). This cannot mean, however, that everyone is supposed to have a distinct and explicit awareness of the moral law as Kant defines it . . . It is rather that the consciousness attributed to 'every natural human reason' is of particular moral constraints as they arise in the process of practical deliberation . . . Kant claims explicitly that 'everyone does, in fact decide . . . [on the basis of the constraints set by the moral law] whether actions are morally good or bad' (KprV 5:69 [in Allison's translation]). (1990, 233)

From the perspective of our construction, this suggests that Allison thinks that this fact performs the function in *CPrR's* argument that our construction attributes to its *SI*, which is to explain why the result achieved by combining the quasi-ontological reasoning of our *SII* with our *SIII* is *practically relevant for Agnes* by explaining how the question of the existence of a categorical imperative arises for Agnes.

Does this mean that Allison's view is that our construction correctly depicts the structure of Kant's argument in *CPrR*, and that Allison only disagrees with us about the structure of the argument in *GMM*?

(not by a morally neutral transcendental deduction) which is defended by a transcendental exposition. (See 1990, 235.)

By no means! For one thing, Allison's account, having initially distinguished moral consciousness (having the concept of morality) from acceptance of the moral law, conflates them, and then locates moral consciousness (having the concept of morality) in 'natural human reason' in a way that does not assign it the same status as our *SI*. Furthermore, we think that what drives Allison's account of this phase of the argument in *CPrR* is a major reason why he fails to see that Kant presents the same argument in *GMM*.

The first problem we have with Allison's depiction of moral consciousness/the moral law as the fact of reason is that it does not square with Kant's clearly and persistently stated claim that he has shown the categorical imperative to be an *apodictic* a priori synthetic proposition *(CPrR 47)*. This is because it is obvious that Kant cannot reasonably make this claim *unless* he holds that *no agent can intelligibly evade* engagement with the concept of pure practical reason. Yet, as Allison rightly points out, grounding moral consciousness/the moral law in natural human reason *as Allison interprets 'natural human reason'* will not require anyone to accept that the categorical imperative exists who does not think that their practical reason *unconditionally must* engage with the concept of a categorical imperative. The thrust of Allison's construction is that Kant's strategy in *CPrR* is no more than 'reasonably successful' in

> authenticating the moral law and establishing the reality of transcendental freedom . . . [because] it can hardly be expected to convince someone who rejects . . . the account of morality as based on a categorical imperative. (1990, 230)

A second problem is that the claim that everyone who deliberates practically actually recognizes the existence of moral contraints is manifestly false. Even if it is not false, it is either an empirical claim or a claim about what all agents necessarily do by virtue of being agents. In either case, this possibility contradicts Kant's claim that to say that the moral law is given to Agnes as the sole fact of pure reason is not to say that it is given on the basis of any intuition, a priori or empirical *(CPrR 5:31)*. Furthermore, Kant will not accept that there is anything *human* agents *necessarily* do *as agents* because the fact that they are heteronomously influenced agents precludes this. To avoid this problem, Kant must be understood to mean (at *CPrR* AK 5:69) only that *everyone who reasons as natural human reason requires them to reason* will necessarily reason in line with the constraints set by the moral law. Even then, reference to 'natural' human reason cannot be understoood to refer to what is merely a widespread practice of reasoning (no matter how widespread); and, of course, we claim that Kant's reference to natural human reason is reference to reasoning as required by sound exercise of the a priori powers of the *sensus communis*.

Chapter Five The Moral Law as the Sole Fact of Pure Reason in *CPrR* — **109**

A third problem is that Kant does not think (as we have explained in relation to our discussion of the Pyrrhonian Dilemma, upon which we will elaborate still further in Chapter Eight) that there can be any brute (i.e. presuppositionless) facts. Kant simply does not believe that there can be any presuppositionless knowledge or, as Allison describes a brute fact, 'something directly accessible' (1990, 238).

Consequently, we consider that Allison's depiction of what it is for moral consciousness/the moral law to be a fact of reason is inconsistent with too many of Kant's clearly and persistently stated positions for it to be plausible to portray it as the best fit to the bulk of the available textual evidence.

In our opinion, the root cause of the inconsistencies between Allison's account of the fact of reason and many of Kant's clearly stated claims lies in the way in which he interprets Kant's contention that moral consciousness/the moral law cannot rest on any antecedent data of reason. While it is true that Kant holds that neither moral consciousness nor the moral law is contained in understanding the concept of practical reason, it does not follow from this that Kant thinks that either moral consciousness or the moral law can only be given by something that does not require recourse to any data of reason to establish it. The reason for this *non sequitur* is, of course, that Kant actually claims that moral consciousness (having the concept of morality) is strictly required by Agnes for her to understand the concept of understanding having the concept of practical reason (*SI*) with the moral law (the fact of pure reason) being a strict requirement of understanding the concept of pure practical reason (the concept of moral consciousness) *so generated* (*SII*). In other words, the moral law itself is given to Agnes as a strict requirement of understanding the concept of agential self-understanding. On this basis, we can see why Kant holds that moral consciousness (engagement with the concept of a categorical imperative) does not rest on any *antecedent* data of reason yet considers that it is an intelligibly unquestionable fact of reason (strict requirement of agential self-understanding). Moral consciousness does not rest on antecedent data of reason (antecedent data of agential self-understanding) because it necessarily rests on understanding the idea of agential self-understanding. Though this should no longer need repeating, this is because he holds that possession of the a priori powers of agential self-understanding, the a priori powers of the *sensus communis*, is presupposed by any being able to assert deny or even question any claims about practical reasoning.

Furthermore, on this basis, it cannot be correct to claim that

> it seems quite possible both to accept the outlines of Kant's analysis of morality and to evade much of the force of the conclusion regarding the unconditioned nature of moral requirements. Thus one might very well admit that these requirements stem from reason

> and even that their rational origin entails that we have a reason to obey them . . . and yet deny that these requirements need to be recognized as overriding. (1990, 238)

This is because, on Kant's analysis of morality, in making such a denial, an agent implies that the agent is unable to recognize anything as applying to the agent, so cannot intelligibly deny that the requirements are overriding. Consequently, whether or not Kant's analysis of morality is correct, to deny that the requirements are overriding is not to accept the outlines of Kant's analysis of morality, which is nothing other than an analysis of having the concept of human agential self-understanding.

The upshot of all this is that, unlike Allison, we do not consider that the textual evidence is ambiguous about the fact of reason/the fact of pure reason. It is also not the case that our construction merely better fits the bulk of the textual evidence in *CPrR* than Allison's. To think that our construction merely better fits the bulk of the textual evidence is to imply that there is some textual evidence that it does not fit, which implies that the textual evidence is not consistent, when what we claim is that it is reasonable to hold that our construction fits *all* the pertinent *clear* textual evidence in *CPrR*. Of course, it is open to Allison to claim that Kant's reasoning in the way our *SI* portrays it is invalid and that the strongest grounding Kant can provide for the categorical imperative is via Allison's construction of moral consciousness/the moral law as a brute fact. But, whether or not Allison is right about this, this is a revisionary reconstruction of Kant. We will stick to exegesis; and, if we do, there is still more to be said. For, as we will now argue, the account we have given of what it is to be a fact of reason and the fact of pure reason in *CPrR* also fits Kant's argument in *GMM*. In other words, we will argue that Allison's claim that *CPrR*, 'in sharp contrast to the *Groundwork*, [maintains] that morality is "firmly established of itself"' (1990, 238) is also false on the clear textual evidence. This is because, once it is understood what Kant actually means when he says that morality is firmly established of itself, it becomes clear that he also holds this to be the case in *GMM*. In this regard, the only thing that Kant does not do in *GMM* is *label* what he designates in *CPrR* as a fact of reason and the fact of pure reason a 'fact of reason' and the 'fact of pure reason'.

Chapter Six
The Moral Law as the Sole Fact of Pure Reason in *GMM*

We will now argue that the *logical* structure of Kant's justification of the categorical imperative in *GMM* is identical to that in *CPrR*. However, how Kant presents his justification is less transparent in *GMM* than it is in *CPrR*.[1] Indeed, we think that there are four different tales that can be told about how Kant presents his justification in *GMM* that are consistent with our construction. Because all four tales are consistent with our construction, choice between them is not imperative. It should also be noted that each of the four tales is not necessarily entirely exclusive of the others, as some things we say in support of one tale might also be used to support some aspects of another, even if we do not say so. We will, however, give reasons to prefer one of them.

Four Tales

In line with what Kant claims is achieved by exposition of a categorical imperative at *CPrR* 5:46, all four of our narratives agree that Kant holds that *exposition* of a categorical imperative does more than reveal what Agnes must believe about a categorical imperative only on the assumption that one exists. *Exposition* of a categorical imperative, the analytic part of Kant's discussion of the idea of a categorical imperative *also* reveals that Agnes is strictly rationally required to engage with the concept of a categorical imperative (*SI* of our construction), by virtue of understanding which she is strictly required to consider that a categorical imperative exists (*SII* of our construction). All four narratives also agree that the deduction that establishes that the categorical imperative, so postulated, really is an apodictic a priori synthetic practical proposition consists of showing that there are no grounds on which the idea of a categorical imperative can be shown to be incoherent (*SIII* of our construction).

Where the four tales differ is in where they think Kant puts *SI* and *SII* in place, all four tales agreeing that *SIII* is put in place by showing that it cannot be shown to be incoherent for Agnes to hold that she has free will while thinking

---

[1] This is well observed by Michael Wolff (2009), who views Section 1 of Book I of *CPrR* ('On the Principles of Pure Practical Reason') as a concise and better structured summary of *GMM*. See Chapter Seven.

that her will is capable of being subject to the universal law of mechanism, which Kant does beginning only at the end of AK 4:450.

Put briefly, Tale 1 maintains that all that Kant claims to establish by exposition by the end of *GMM* II (i.e., by AK 4:445) (though, to be more accurate, by AK 4:447, just before the heading 'Freedom Must be Presupposed as a Property of the Will of All Rational Beings')[2] is that *if Agnes holds that there is a categorical imperative* then she must hold the following: that there is only one categorical imperative; that it is an apodictic a priori synthetic practical proposition; that it is formulated by Kant's formulae for it (which include the FUL and FoH); that rational nature exists as an end in itself; that pure reason is practical in Agnes; and that she has free will. The quasi-ontological inference of *SII* is made in AK 4:448; the problem of an antinomy (still part of the exposition) is pointedly explained in AK 4:449 450, and the rest of the exposition (*SI*) is carried out alongside the deduction (*SIII*), beginning at the end of AK 4:450.

On the other hand, Tale 2 has it that everything that Kant claims to cover by exposition of the concept of a categorical imperative (*which is all of SI and SII*) is complete by the end of *GMM* II (AK 4:445) (or, at the latest, AK 4:447). AK 4:448 until the end of AK 4:450 elaborates on how the exposition raises the suspicion of an antinomy *(so is really an analytic comment on the exposition)*, and the rest of *GMM* III is concerned with showing that the concept of a categorical imperative is not incoherent (*SIII*).

Tale 3 claims, like Tale 2, that Kant has already put *SII* in place by the end of *GMM* II, but claims, like Tale 1, that *SI* is only put in place when *SIII* is put in place (i.e., after AK 4:450).

According to Tale 4, in addition to what Tale 1 says is accomplished by the end of *GMM* II, *SI* is put in place (per Tale 2); and *SII* and *SIII* are put in place in *GMM* III per Tale 1.

Tale 1

When Kant says (*GMM* AK 4:444–445) that showing that the concept of a categorical imperative is possible (and necessary) is the task for *GMM* III, he addresses those who have the concept of a categorical imperative and have at least partly understood it. After all, by the time he gets to *GMM* 4:447, he has presented any of his readers who are not already so primed with the concept of a categorical imperative and told them something of what he thinks understanding

---

[2] This is because free will is not explicitly linked to the moral law until AK 4:446.

it provides. However, he has not claimed that Agnes's agential self-understanding strictly requires her to think and understand the concept of a categorical imperative, nor that understanding it requires her to think that the categorical imperative exists. Thus, he has not claimed that Agnes must think that pure reason is practical in her. So, when he says (*GMM* AK 4:447) that the purpose of the passages that follow is to make comprehensible the deduction of free will from pure practical reason from pure practical reason in order to make comprehensible the concept of a categorical imperative, he asks his readers to imagine (for the sake of argument) how Agnes would think if she were a purely rational agent, an agent whose agential self-understanding would strictly require her to think and understand the concept of pure practical reason.

Kant thinks that, because the *concepts* of pure practical reason and free will and free will are reciprocal (*GMM* AK 4:447), Agnes's imagined pure agential self-understanding would strictly require her *to think* that she has free will.

> I say now: every being that cannot act otherwise than *under the idea of freedom* [which is any being *with a purely rational will*][3] is just because of that really free in a practical respect, that is, all laws that are inseparably bound up with freedom hold for him [her] just as if his [her] will had been validly pronounced free also in itself and in theoretical philosophy [i.e., as a law of her nature, rather than as an imperative]. (*GMM* AK 4:448)

So, because having free will and having her actions governed by the moral law are reciprocal, Agnes would necessarily hold that she is bound by the moral law as a law of her nature. Right here, Kant makes the quasi-ontological move, the move from understanding the concept of pure practical reason to having to think that the moral law (*as such*) exists. The form of this reasoning may be put in different ways because Kant holds that the concepts of pure practical reason, the moral law *as such*, and free will are all reciprocal. But the best way of putting it here (because Agnes is imagining that her will is necessarily pure) is that Kant claims that having the concept of pure practical reason is the *ratio cognoscendi* for having the concept of free will and that, for a being with a purely rational will, the thought that she might possibly have free will is for her not only the *ratio essendi* for the possibility that pure practical reason is practical in her (that the moral law possibly governs her will) but the *ratio essendi* for actually having a pure practical reason.

---

[3] As Tale 1 reads Kant, he is saying *here* only that every purely rational agent must and can only act under the idea of its free will. He is not saying that every agent (purely rational or not) can only act under the idea that the agent has free will, though he will assert this immediately afterwards.

On the assumption that Agnes is a purely rational agent, this is fine. As such an agent, it is rationally undeniable that Agnes's agential self-understanding necessitates her to reason like this, and this is enough to show that purely rational Agnes is really bound by the moral law as a law of her nature. As a purely rational agent, she necessarily thinks and understands the concept of pure practical reason, and there can be nothing other than understanding the concept of pure practical reason that can possibly be thought to cause her behaviour. Agnes cannot do anything other than think that her will is bound by the moral law as a law of her will's nature, simply because her will is nothing but a will that operates in accord with the moral law as a law of its nature.

However, now Kant says

> I assert that to every rational being with a will [which includes our human Agnes] we must necessarily lend the idea of freedom also, under which alone [s]he acts.[4]
>
> (*GMM* AK 4:448)

Consequently, human Agnes must think that she is bound by the moral law as the categorical imperative.

But why must human Agnes think that the quasi-ontological reasoning (which is applicable to her in imagining herself to be a purely rational agent) can apply to her as a human agent? For it to be legitimate to claim that human Agnes necessarily presupposes that she has free will, it must be shown that her *human* agential self-understanding strictly requires *her* to think and understand the concept of pure practical reason. Even then, the quasi-ontological reasoning that is applicable to a purely rational Agnes can only be applied to human Agnes *if* the law describing the will of a purely rational agent can coherently be thought by human Agnes to regulate her will. So, as things stand, Kant has put *SII* in place, but its applicability to human Agnes has not been established. Kant needs *SI* and *SIII* as well. Only then will he have shown that Agnes's human agential self-understanding strictly and unassailably requires her to consider that she has free will, and so is really bound by the moral law as the categorical imperative.

This is what Kant acknowledges when he says that, if deriving the moral law from the concept of pure practical reason via the concept of free will, as he has done, is held to show that human Agnes is really bound by the categorical imperative, then his reasoning will be a *petitio principii*.

> It must be freely admitted that a kind of circle comes to light here from which, as it seems, there is no way of escape. We take ourselves as free in the order of efficient causes in order

---

4 In our view, to be precise, Kant should really say 'is strictly required to act'.

to think ourselves under moral laws in the order of ends; and we afterwards think ourselves as subject to these laws because we have ascribed to ourselves freedom of the will.

(*GMM* AK 4:450)

However, this is not because he has derived the existence of the moral law (the existence of pure practical reason) from the concept of pure practical reason (the concept of the moral law). To infer that Agnes's human agential self-understanding strictly requires her to think that the moral law exists because it strictly requires her to think and understand the concept of a moral law (and understanding the concept of the moral law strictly requires her to think that it exists) is not circular.[5] The problem is that Kant is not entitled to apply this quasi-ontological reasoning to human Agnes unless Agnes's agential self-understanding strictly requires her to think and understand the concept of pure practical reason *(SI)* and, even then, Kant's quasi-ontological reasoning (in *SII*) will not establish that Agnes is really bound by the moral law unless it is shown that it is coherent for her to think that the moral law can govern her heteronomously affected will (which needs *SIII*).[6]

It is at this point that Kant launches into his 'three worlds' analysis, which is designed to put *SI* and *SIII* in place (*GMM* AK 450–457). By arguing that Agnes cannot intelligibly have the concept of a hypothetical imperative (which as a human agent she necessarily ought to have, and which she must have in order to be strictly required to hold that the idea of the universal law of mechanism has application to her actions) *unless* she has and understands the idea of the moral law as a categorical imperative, he argues for *SI*. By arguing that reflection upon the possibility of *SI* being sound shows that the fact that her agential understanding strictly requires her to think that the universal law of mechanism applies to her is unable to show that she cannot coherently suppose that she has free will for practical purposes, he argues for *SIII*. With all three stages now in place, Kant concludes that Agnes (regardless of whether she in fact thinks that pure reason is practical in her) really is bound by the moral law as the categorical imperative.

This, according to Tale 1, completes Kant's argument in *GMM* for the contention that the categorical imperative is a strict requirement of human agential self-understanding. And if we want a clear statement that this argument is to the effect

---

[5] At any rate, if it is, so too is Kant's reasoning in *CPrR*.
[6] Jochen Bojanowski (2017, 86) says that Kant's reasoning is circular, not because he cannot reason from the concept of pure practical reason to the existence of the moral law, but because pure practical reason is a proxy for free will not for the moral law. This is not so. Pure practical reason is *for human agents* a construct of understanding the imperatival nature of a hypothetical imperative not of understanding the concept of free will. In any event, Kant does not think it circular in *GMM* (telling us at AK 4:453 that any suspicion of a hidden circle is now removed) and there is no evidence that Kant came to think that it is circular in *CPrR*.

that the moral law is given to human agents as a fact of pure reason (*ala CPrR*) then Kant now makes it. The causality of actions of a free will 'lies in' 'the human being'

> as intelligence and in the laws of effects and actions in accordance with principles of the intelligible world, of which he knows nothing more than in it *reason alone, and indeed pure reason independent of sensibility, gives the law, and,* in addition, that it is there, as intelligence only, that he is his proper self (as a human being he is only the appearance of himself), [and] *those laws apply to him immediately [i.e., without mediation by any other proposition] and categorically.* [Our emphases added]. (*GMM* AK 4:457)

But this does not complete what Kant has to say *about* his argument and what it accomplishes. At this point, Kant tells us that:

> [R]eason would overstep all its bounds if it took it upon itself to explain how pure reason can be practical, which would be exactly the same task as to explain how freedom is possible.
> (*GMM* AK 4:458–459)

> [T]he question, how a *categorical imperative* [our emphasis] is possible, can indeed be answered to the extent that one can furnish the sole presupposition on which alone it is possible, namely the idea of freedom . . . but how this presupposition [free will] itself is possible can never be seen by any human reason. (*GMM* AK 4:461)

> [I]t is impossible for us to explain . . . how pure reason can be practical, and all the pains and labor of seeking an explanation of it are lost. (*GMM* AK 4:461)

> [W]e do not indeed comprehend the practical unconditional necessity of the moral imperative, but we nevertheless comprehend its *incomprehensibility*. (*GMM* AK 4:463)

Do these remarks show that Kant realizes, as some like H. J. Paton (2000) and Dieter Henrich (1975) suggest, and Owen Ware (2017) thinks, that he has not established and cannot establish that 'the categorical imperative, and with it the autonomy of the will, is true and absolutely necessary as an a priori principle' (*GMM* AK 4:445)? Alternatively, does this show that Kant at times contradicts the claim he makes at others that he has established that the categorical imperative really exists as such? Not if we pay scrupulous attention to what Kant says, and see that he very clearly and carefully distinguishes showing that Agnes categorically must (as a strict requirement of her human agential self-understanding) consider that she has free will from explaining how Agnes can have free will. Explaining *how it is possible* for free will to exist, is not the same as showing *that it is possible* for free will to exist (or, to be precise, showing that it is impossible to show that free will cannot exist). That the former cannot be done does not mean that the latter cannot be done. The reason why it is impossible to explain the existence of free will (as against to show its existence for practical purposes) is that the

> impossibility of *explaining* the freedom of the will is the same as the impossibility of discovering and making comprehensible an *interest* which the human being can take in moral laws, and yet he does really take an interest in them, the foundation of which in us we call moral feeling . . . [which is] the *subjective* effect that the law exercises on the will, to which reason alone delivers the objective grounds. (*GMM* AK 4:460)
>
> For us human beings it is quite impossible to explain how and why the *universality of a maxim as law* and hence morality interests us. This much is certain: it is not *because the law interests us* that it has validity for us (for that is heteronomy and dependence of practical reason upon sensibility, namely upon a feeling lying at its basis, in which case it could never be morally lawgiving). (*GMM* AK 4:460–461)
>
> It is therefore no censure of our *deduction* of the supreme principle of morality . . . that it cannot make *comprehensible as regards its absolute necessity* an unconditional practical law (such as the categorical imperative must be) . . . *by means of some interest laid down as a basis* . . . since then it would not be the moral law, the supreme law of freedom. [Our emphases added.] (*GMM* AK 4:463)

What we take Kant to be saying is that to show that free will exists (must be taken by Agnes to exist) requires nothing more than showing that Agnes's agential self-understanding strictly requires her to think the moral law, for which free will is the *ratio essendi*, and that this thought is coherent. To show that free will is possible does not require, nor can it have, an explanation of how it is possible that goes beyond showing that it *can coherently* be thought to be a *ratio essendi* of the categorical imperative. Such *further* explanation, which can only be in terms of mechanistic causality (or some additional a priori intuition), is impossible and unnecessary. It totally misses the point by misunderstanding what is involved in having the concept of a categorical imperative.

In effect, Kant agrees with Hume that it is impossible to derive an unconditional 'ought' from any theoretical cognition. If one could do so, it would not be an unconditional 'ought'. But, against Hume, he claims that it is unnecessary, and (indeed) unintelligible (incomprehensible) to demand that this be possible as a condition of reason strictly requiring acceptance of a categorical imperative. To do so is to demand that a categorical imperative be conceived to be a hypothetical imperative or not an imperative at all. Apart from this demand involving a contradiction in terms, it is unintelligible on the grounds that Kant has shown that it is only possible for Agnes to think coherently of herself as bound by any hypothetical imperatives on the basis that she accepts that there is a categorical imperative. In other words, although Kant accepts that hypothetical imperatives can provide reasons for action (indeed he starts from this assumption), he denies that only hypothetical imperatives can do so (which is to say that he rejects Humean internalism) on the grounds that hypothetical imperatives can only be thought to provide reasons for action coherently on the presupposition that there is a categorical imperative.

Far from Kant now demanding that, to justify the categorical imperative, 'unconditional ought' must be derived from 'theoretical is', which he considers to be incomprehensible, his actual reasoning here is that an unconditional 'ought' is a necessary 'is' (fact) of pure practical reason, which is given to human Agnes by her agential self-understanding (common human reason) as a categorical 'ought' (imperative). In relation to the question of its existence, all heteronomous considerations and factors are simply irrelevant because the categorical imperative exists purely as the creation of the a priori cognitive faculties of the human mind. The moral law *as such* is, as much as free will, purely an idea of pure practical reason. But, *in the moral law being a necessitated idea of pure practical reason*, the *reality of the moral law as the categorical imperative* is established simply by the fact that pure theoretical reason cannot show the impossibility of the moral law governing a heteronomously affected will as an imperative; which makes the moral law the fact of pure reason *as a whole* an 'unconditional ought' (i.e., an undeniable fact for practical purposes).[7]

This is supported by attending to what Kant means by 'comprehensibility'. In *Jäsche Logic* (AK 9:64–65), he says that there are seven levels of increasing cognition, of which the fifth is understanding, the sixth is cognition through reason, and the seventh is comprehension.[8] To understand something is 'to cognize something *through the understanding by means of concepts*, or to *conceive*', which 'is very different from comprehension as '[o]ne can conceive much, although we cannot comprehend it, e.g., a *perpetuum mobile*'. To 'cognize something through reason' is '*to have insight* into it'; while to '*comprehend* something' is

---

[7] Jochen Bojanowski (2017, 76) calls the incomprehensible deduction that Kant rejects a 'strong deduction', and he calls the deduction that Kant accepts (which Kant calls 'a defence') a 'weak deduction'. By doing so, Bojanowski suggests that Kant thinks that if only the 'strong deduction' were possible it would provide a stronger justification for the categorical imperative than the 'weak deduction' can achieve if valid. This is clearly not what Kant thinks. He does not think that anything more than the 'weak deduction' is needed or can be given to establish the absolute *normative* necessity of the categorical imperative. And the reason why this is so is that Kant, unlike many of his commentators, does not think that a transcendental deduction can only be a theoretical one/a morally neutral one. Bojanowski is right to say that Kant draws a distinction between theoretical and practical a priori synthetic cognition in *CPrR* (AK 5:83); but he is wrong to suggest that Kant only recognizes this distinction in *CPrR*. The distinction that Kant recognizes is articulated in his claim (at *CPrR* AK 5:105) that his quasi-ontological reasoning works for free-will but not for God, and this goes back to at least *CPuR*.
[8] In *Blomberg Logic*, 106, Kant says that there are five levels, of which levels three to five are the same as levels five to seven of *Jäsche Logic*.

to cognize it through reason or *a priori* to the degree that is sufficient for our purpose. For all our comprehension is only *relative*, i.e., sufficient for a certain purpose; we do not comprehend anything *without qualification*.

In more modern terms, Kant is saying that there is no presuppositionless knowledge. In the present context, he is saying that all human understanding, reason and comprehension is relative to human agential self-understanding, which is relative to itself. As such, human comprehension cannot be absolute (i.e., presuppositionless). But what it is relative to, can and need presuppose nothing other than itself, which is fully sufficient to render the categorical imperative undeniably rationally necessary for all agents (provided only that its concept is coherent). That knowledge of the strict requirements of human agential self-understanding is not, and cannot be, presuppositionless does not mean that Agnes's commitment to the categorical imperative cannot be absolutely rationally necessary. It is, and can be, because the strict requirements of human agential self-understanding are presuppositions of all intelligible questions and claims about anything, including themselves. And it is an unintelligible idea that Agnes's commitment to the categorical imperative can only be absolutely rationally necessary if her acceptance of the strict requirements of her agential self-understanding is necessitated by an incentive to accept these requirements. This is because this idea can only be validated as a strict requirement of Agnes's agential self-understanding in a context in which the idea that the existence of a categorical imperative rests on Agnes having an incentive to obey it contradicts the idea of a categorical imperative (thereby, contradicting the idea of a strict requirement of human agential self-understanding).[9]

Tale 2

Contrary to Tale 1, Kant has already put *SI* and *all of SII* in place by *GMM* AK 4:447. When he claims that human Agnes necessarily presupposes that she has free will (*GMM* AK 4:448), he considers that he has already established that her

---

[9] It is also worth noting that, on this basis, Kant's claim that all of our comprehension is relative to a purpose helps us to understand why he claims that his moral argument for God renders the existence of God certain, even though this is only for practical purposes. Given that human agential self-understanding is the basis of all human comprehension and that the purpose of all human agential self-understanding is (by the very idea of agential self-understanding) directed at the achievement of human agential self-understanding (which is inherently practical), it follows directly that all postulates of pure practical reason hold only for practical purposes in a way that makes belief in God as rationally necessary for Agnes as her required commitment to human agential self-understanding, which is rationally unquestionable.

agential self-understanding strictly requires her to think and understand the concept of pure practical reason and that this strictly requires her to think that pure reason is practical in her. His task now is *solely* to explain how this is possible, by showing that the normative product of understanding what it is to have human agential self-understanding is not annulled by an antinomy within it. In other words, all he needs to put in place is *SIII*.

This means that when, in *GMM* III (AK 4:453), Kant claims that understanding the concept of a hypothetical imperative requires engagement with the idea of a categorical imperative, he is merely repeating what he has already claimed in *GMM* II (or even earlier) and the reason for reciting this claim is that he needs to have it in focus in order to show that there is no antinomy in human agential self-understanding for the purposes of practical reason. This is because the reason why there is no practical antinomy is that understanding the fact that human agential self-understanding strictly requires engagement with the concept of a categorical imperative presupposes that the presuppositions of Agnes being bound by a hypothetical imperative cannot conflict with the presuppositions of Agnes being bound by the moral law *within Agnes's agential self-understanding*. In other words, it is the possibility of *SI* of his argument being coherent that *SIII* addresses, because it is only through *SI* that *SII must* be applied to *human* Agnes.

There is a general reason for thinking that Kant puts *SI* and the quasi-ontological inference of *SII* in place before AK 4:447. This is that, given that he is ultimately going to argue that the principle of morality is the supreme principle of all practical reason, it makes no sense for him to say in *GMM* II (AK 4: 419–420), immediately after completing his description of the distinction between a categorical imperative and two kinds of hypothetical imperatives (imperatives of skill and prudential imperatives), that the *only* question *that arises* (in regard to imperatives in general) is 'how the necessitation of the will, which the imperative expresses in the problem, can be *thought*' (our emphasis added) (*GMM* AK 4:417), and that the *only* question *needing a solution* (i.e., the only question for which the answer is problematic) is that of how the necessitation expressed in a categorical imperative can be *thought* (*GMM* AK 4:419), which is the task for *GMM* III to address (*GMM* AK 4:420). This only makes sense if Kant thinks that Agnes's agential self-understanding strictly requires her to understand the concept of a categorical imperative (*SI*), and then thinks (quasi-ontological inference of *SII*) that there is an a priori reason why Agnes is strictly required to think that she is unconditionally bound by the moral law (the law of pure practical reason) as the categorical imperative prior to an explanation of why this is not impossible being provided. Otherwise, there is no reason why we should think that the only thing that *GMM* III needs to do is to explain how Agnes can think coherently that a categorical imperative is possible. Showing that it is possible for her to be bound by the moral law will not, without more, establish that she is *necessarily* bound by the moral law, only that it is *possible* for her to be bound by the moral law. And the fact of the matter is that Kant can only think that nothing more than this is required if he holds that, simply by understanding the idea of a categorical imperative that she must have, Agnes must think that the categorical imperative exists.

In any event, there is explicit evidence that Kant puts *SI* and the quasi-ontological inference of *SII* in place before AK 4:447.

Regarding *SI*, Kant implies (in *GMM* II) that Agnes's agential self-understanding strictly requires her to engage with the concept of pure practical reason/a moral law/a categorical imperative when he says:

> From what has been said it is clear that all moral concepts have their seat and origin completely a priori in reason, and indeed in the most common reason.   (*GMM* AK 4:411)

And this should not be surprising, as it is very much like his claim in *CPrR* that we become conscious of the moral law as soon as we draw up maxims for ourselves (AK 5:29).

Indeed, even earlier (in *GMM* I), he says:

> [W]e have then to explicate the concept of a will that is to be esteemed in itself and that is good apart from any further purpose, as it already dwells in natural sound reasoning and needs not so much to be taught as only to be clarified.   (*GMM* AK 4:397)

So what is this sound natural reasoning? One needs to be alert to detect it, but it is implicit in Kant's statement that, in order to explicate the concept of a will good in itself,

> we shall set before ourselves the concept of duty, which contains that of a good will though under certain subjective limitations and hindrances, which, however, far from concealing it and making it unrecognizable, rather bring it out by contrast and make it shine forth all the more brightly.   (*GMM* AK 4:397)

How so? By having the idea of a hypothetical imperative, which Agnes must have to understand what it is for her to be a human agent, she must have the concept of an *imperative* as such, and so of a categorical imperative 'by contrast' or 'abstraction' (as not a hypothetical one) (just as one cannot understand what 'minus' means if one does not understand what 'plus' means), which is to say that Agnes can only understand what it is for her to be an agent by understanding the idea of a categorical imperative.

The same contention is implicit in the following passage:

> Only a rational being has the capacity to act *in accordance with the representation of laws*, that is, in accordance with principles, or has a *will*. Since *reason* is required for the derivation of actions from laws, the will is nothing other than practical reason. If reason infallibly determines the will [i.e., if it is pure practical reason], the actions of such a being that are cognized as objectively necessary are also subjectively necessary . . . However, if reason solely by itself does not adequately determine the will . . . then actions that are cognized as objectively necessary are subjectively contingent. (*GMM* AK 412–413)

In other words, to think of any kind of imperative (i.e., of any practical principle), so of a hypothetical *imperative*, Agnes must have the idea of a determination of her desires by reason as well as the idea of a will serving something not given by reason alone. But she cannot understand the idea of reason that serves something not given by reason alone unless she has and can understand the idea of pure practical reason, of a will serving pure reason alone. Thus, Agnes's agential self-understanding strictly requires her to think and understand the concept of pure practical reason.

What, then, about the quasi-ontological reasoning of *SII*? Where does Kant say or imply directly that to understand the concept of pure practical reason/a moral law/a categorical imperative strictly requires human Agnes to think the existence of pure practical reason?

There are at least four contentions, or sets of contentions, that can be read in this way.

The first contention provides a reason similar to that invoked by Tale 1. Kant tells us at *GMM* AK 4:414 that if Agnes were a purely rational agent then it would be analytic that she would necessarily act for and in accord with the moral law. However, understanding this requires her to recognize that if the moral law has any possible application to her as a human agent it will do so in the form of a categorical imperative. And this entails that if Agnes understands the concept of a categorical imperative she must think that it exists. If being governed by the moral law *as such* means that Agnes necessarily acts in accord with it, then being governed by the moral law as the categorical imperative means that Agnes categorically ought to act in accord with the moral law *as such*.

The second set of contentions is what Kant says about why understanding the concept of the moral law strictly requires Agnes to hold that it is expressed by the FUL *if it exists*, and then about what is needed to establish that it does actually exist.

> [W]hen I [Agnes] think of a *categorical* imperative I know at once what it contains. For, since the imperative contains, beyond the law, only the necessity that the maxim be in conformity with the law, while the law contains no condition to which it could be limited,

nothing is left with which the maxim is to conform but the universality of a law as such; and this conformity alone is what the imperative properly represents as necessary.

(*GMM* AK 4:421)

As Kant explains in a footnote, in being categorical, a categorical imperative is a law, which is an objective principle, one that binds (is valid for) all agents (thus universal) that cannot be limited by any condition. The concept of a categorical imperative is the concept of an imperative that all maxims must be consistent with unconditionally. Although Kant does not say so, it follows directly that, if Agnes understands the concept of a categorical imperative *and must engage with this concept,* then she must think (must regard it as categorically imperative) that she may not adopt any maxim that is inconsistent with the categorical imperative (i.e., with the universality of a practical law as such).

However, despite this, Kant tells us that

[w]e have not yet advanced so far as to prove a priori that there really is such an imperative, that there is a practical law, which commands absolutely of itself and without any incentives, and that the observance of this law is duty [i.e., a categorical imperative].

(*GMM* AK 4:425)

Why not? The reason Kant gives is that for 'duty' to

be practical unconditional necessity for action . . . it must hold for all rational beings . . . and only because of this be also a law for all human wills. (*GMM* AK 4:425)

So, what do we need to do to prove it? According to Kant, we must show that a 'necessary law for all rational beings' to act in accord with the FUL is necessarily already

connected (completely a priori) with the concept of the will of a rational being as such

(*GMM* AK 4:426)

though, as a categorical imperative, it cannot be contained in it (*GMM* AK 4:420 fn).

As we hardly need to remind ourselves, the problem now is that, for this condition to be met, it must be shown that Agnes is coherently able to think that the law governing the will of a purely rational being as a law of its nature necessarily governs her heteronomously influenced will as an 'ought' (*SIII*).

However, if this is *all* that is needed for 'duty' to be a concept that contains 'significance and real lawgiving for our actions' (*GMM* AK 4:425), then Kant is presuming that simply by understanding the concept of a categorical imperative, Agnes must be required to think that she unconditionally ought to adopt the FUL, and he is plausibly read as making this quasi-ontological move in the very way in which he depicts the derivation of the content of the FUL from the concept of a categorical imperative.

Most commentators maintain that Kant's aim, in insisting that to establish that a categorical imperative exists is to establish that it is an apodictic a priori synthetic practical proposition, is to show that all human agents (not merely those who are already morally committed) must accept the FUL (which is to say that he is addressing moral scepticism in *GMM* III). This, despite what Owen Ware (2017) says – see Chapter Eight – is true about the conclusion to be reached. But it is not specific enough about the means to be used to reach it. The point is that Kant is not trying in *GMM* III to show that human agential self-understanding strictly requires all human agents to think that they are bound by the FUL. *He thinks that he has already shown this to be true.* After all, right from the outset, he maintains that the moral law is to be found in *sound* common human reason. He thinks that all he has to do now is refute the sceptic who wishes (by alleging that there is an antinomy in the idea of pure human practical reasoning) to challenge the claim that the fact that acceptance of the FUL is a strict requirement of human agential self-understanding means that Agnes's will is bound by the FUL with the force of law (categorical 'ought'). Given this, merely by showing that all human agents can coherently think that they are bound (as a categorical imperative) by the natural law of a purely rational agent, Kant will claim to establish that the commands of human agential self-understanding are not phantoms, and therefore authentically apodictic.

The third reason for thinking that Kant makes the quasi-ontological move before *GMM* AK 4:447, is that, *once we have it in mind that he holds that Agnes's agential self-understanding strictly requires her to understand the concept of a categorical imperative*, he makes numerous statements that suggest that he views the concept of the moral law as the concept of a law that imposes itself on Agnes's will by the fact that by understanding the concept of the moral law she is strictly required to think that she is bound by the FUL.

For example,

> [T[he ground of obligation . . . must not be sought in the nature of the human being or in the circumstances of the world in which it is placed, but a priori *simply in concepts of pure reason*. [Our emphasis added]. (*GMM* AK 4:389)

The concept of a categorical imperative is one that represents

> an action as objectively necessary of itself, without reference to another end.
> (*GMM* AK 4:414)

The question of an objective practical principle is one

> of the relation of a will to itself insofar as it determines itself only by reason.
> (*GMM* AK 4:427)

> [T]he ground of all practical lawgiving lies . . . objectively in the rule and the form of universality which makes it fit to be a law. (*GMM* AK 4:431)

The concept of a categorical imperative is of an imperative in which the will gives the law to itself (*GMM* AK 4:441).

In a categorical imperative, the 'will determines itself immediately, just by the representation of an action' (*GMM* AK 4:444).

These statements all imply that Kant thinks that, merely by understanding the concept of a categorical imperative, Agnes must think that it exists; for Agnes cannot understand what it means for an action to be objectively necessary of itself without reference to another end without thinking herself required to act in accord with an objectively necessary action. Nor can she understand what it means for a will to determine itself only by reason, without thinking that she unconditionally ought to act in accord with such a will, and so on. So, all of these involve quasi-ontological reasoning, which (given *SI*) must be regarded as strict requirements of Agnes's agential self-understanding.

The fourth reason that supports the claim that Kant puts the quasi-ontological inference of *SII* in place before *GMM* AK 4:447 is a contention that we might have included amongst the set of contentions just considered. This is Kant's claim that the fact that rational nature exists as an end in itself is the ground of the categorical imperative. But it is so important that it merits separate attention. Indeed, we consider that this contention reveals the very essence of Kant's critical philosophy. However, just what Kant is saying about this in *GMM* II is not as clear as it could be, and to make sense of it we need to come to grips with the following passages.

> The will is thought as a capacity to determine itself to acting in conformity with the *representation of certain laws*. And such a capacity can only be found in rational beings.
>
> . . . Now I say that the human being and in general every rational being *exists* as an end in itself, *not merely as a means* to be used by this or that will at its discretion; instead he must in all his actions, whether directed to himself or also to other rational beings, always be regarded *at the same time as an end*. (*GMM* AK 4:427–428)

> If then, there is to be a supreme moral principle and, with respect to the human will, a categorical imperative, it must be one such that, from the representation of what is necessarily an end for everyone because it is an *end in itself*, it constitutes an objective principle of the will and thus can serve as a universal practical law. The ground of this principle is: *rational nature exists as an end in itself*. The human being necessarily represents his own

existence in this way; so far it is thus a *subjective* principle of human actions. But every other rational being also represents his existence in this way consequent on just the same rational ground that also holds for me;[10] thus it is at the same time an *objective* principle from which, as a supreme practical ground, it must be possible to derive all laws of the will. The practical imperative will therefore be the following: *So act that you use humanity, whether in your own person or in the person of any other, always at the same time as an end, never merely as a means.*[11] (*GMM* AK 4:428–429)

Rational nature is distinguished from the rest of nature by this, that it sets itself an end. This end . . . must here be thought not as an end to be effected but as an *independently existing end* . . . that is, as that which must never be acted against and which must therefore in every volition be estimated never merely as a means but always at the same time as an end . . . Now, this end can be nothing other than the subject of all possible ends itself, because this subject is also the subject of a possible absolutely good will; for, such *a will* [our emphasis] cannot without contradiction be subordinated to any other object.[12]

. . . [F]rom this it follows incontestably that every rational being, as an end in itself, . . . must be able to act as if he were by his maxims at all times a lawgiving member of the universal kingdom of ends. The formal principle of this maxim is, act as if your maxims were to serve at the same time as a universal law (for all rational beings).[13]

(*GMM* AK 4:437–438)

These passages raise several questions. For present purposes, the most important are these:

(1) What does 'rational nature' refer to, and consequently what does it mean to say that rational nature exists as an end in itself?
(2) Kant asserts that all rational beings exist/necessarily represent their own existence as an end in itself, and also that rational nature exists as an end in itself. Which (if any) of these assertions are made unconditionally, and which (if any) of them are only made conditional upon presuming the existence of a categorical imperative?
(3) What exactly are the grounds for the proposition that Kant declares at AK 4:429 to be a postulate that will be grounded in *GMM* III?

---

10 To which Kant adds a footnote: 'Here I put forward this proposition as a postulate. The grounds for it will be found in the last Section'.
11 This being the Formula of Humanity (FoH).
12 There are reasons to doubt the validity of Kant's reasoning here, at least when this leads to the FoH) being interpreted in the way that does not permit agents to commit suicide or cause bodily harm to themselves (unless to save their own lives or the lives of others) as Kant does at *GMM* 4:429. We comment further on this in Chapter Nine).
13 This being the Formula of the Kingdom of Ends (FKE).

(4) Why does Kant think that the fact that every rational being rationally must represent its existence as an end in itself on the same ground entail that the categorical imperative is the FoH)?

Re Question (1). According to our construction, to act rationally is to act in accord with the strict requirements of agential self-understanding.

We understand Kant's claim that rational nature exists as an end in itself as the claim that to be rational, to act and think rationally, is an end in itself, meaning that it makes no sense for Agnes to ask 'Why ought I to act or think rationally?' because to ask 'Why ought I to do X?' is to ask 'Why do I have sufficient reason to do X?' when to act or think rationally is to act or think in a manner for which there is sufficient reason. So, to ask 'Why ought I to act or think rationally?' is to ask 'Why do I have sufficient reason to do what I have sufficient reason to do?' or 'Why ought I to do what I ought to do?'

Of course, it might be said that there are different criteria of rationality, that different agents might and do have different criteria of rationality. On *this* basis, rational nature exists as an end in itself for Agnes only in terms of the criteria for rationality that Agnes accepts. But, on *this* basis, 'rational nature exists as an end in itself' cannot (as Kant claims) be the basis for a categorical imperative, which is an objective principle, one that is necessarily valid for all agents.

This is true. However, when Kant refers to 'rational nature', he is not referring to criteria that Agnes just happens to adopt. He is referring to criteria that Agnes unconditionally ought to adopt. He is referring to criteria of rationality that Agnes must accept for it to be intelligible for her to accept any contingent Agnes-specific criteria of rationality. And we have argued that these necessary criteria of rationality are constituted by the strict requirements of agential self-understanding. So, when he says that rational nature exists as an end in itself, he is saying that to act in accord with the strict requirements of agential self-understanding is an end in itself.

Construing possessing rational nature as the strict requirement to *act and think* rationally in this sense is necessary because practical reason, even pure practical reason, does nothing by itself (it only does anything by virtue of being thought of by an agent as a capacity that the agent possesses, the exercise of which requires the agent to think and do something). Thus, in telling us that to say that rational nature exists as an end in itself is to say that to follow the strict requirements of agential self-understanding is an end in itself, Kant is telling us that pure reason is practical of itself alone through agential self-understanding.[14]

An objection to this interpretation might be made by alleging that this relies, in part, on a mistranslation by Mary Gregor in the 1998 translation we are using of 'die vernünftige Natur existiert als Zweck an sich selbst' as 'rational nature exists as an end in itself'. For example, Jens Timmermann (in his 2012 revision of this translation) translates this as 'a rational nature exists as an end in itself' and says in a footnote that 'a rational nature' means 'a rational being with a will'.

But why does Timmermann think that the German 'die' may, let alone should, be translated as 'a' ('ein')? Literally it should be 'the rational nature exists as an end in itself'. But, in English, use of 'the rational nature' is ungrammatical except in the context of, e.g., 'the rational nature of agents'. So, if one wants to refer to the nature of reason as such, one must say 'rational nature' not 'the rational nature'. However, in German, it is natural to say 'die vernünftige Natur' whether one means 'the rational nature' or 'rational nature' and it would be uncommon to skip the definite article when meaning the latter. On this basis, 'rational nature exists as an end in itself' is the correct translation. Then, as regards Timmermann's footnote, why should Kant suddenly refer to a rational being with a will as 'a rational nature' when he does this nowhere else? And if 'die vernünftige Natur existiert als Zweck an sich selbst' is taken to *mean*, as Timmermann wants us to believe, 'a rational being with a will exists as an end in itself', this renders it at least puzzling

---

14 The linkage of this to the idea that the moral law, the law of pure practical reason, is a fact of pure reason in *CPrR* is strongly suggested by the following passage from *CPrR*.

> Either a rational principle is already *thought* [our emphasis] as in itself the determining ground of the will without regard to the possible objects of the faculty of desire (hence through the mere lawful form of the maxim), *in which case* [our emphasis] that principle is a practical law a priori and pure reason is taken to be practical of itself. In that case, the law determines the will *immediately,* the action in conformity with it *is in itself good,* and a will whose maxim always conforms with this law is *good absolutely, good in every respect* and the *supreme condition of all good.* (*GMM* AK 5:62)

On the basis that Kant views human agential self-understanding as governed by the three maxims of the *sensus communis* of *CPoJ*, a clear link is also made between the idea that 'rational nature exists as an end in itself' and the idea that 'agential self-understanding is an end in itself' when he says that an absolutely good will is one 'whose maxim . . . can never conflict with itself' and that this principle is the supreme law of an absolutely good will (*GMM* AK 4:437). This is because, the maxim of human agential self-understanding, in which the first two maxims of human agential self-understanding are united, is the maxim of reason, 'Act in accord with yourself', which is the maxim that Agnes must be able to accept if she is to be able to conceive of her will as one that is not in conflict with itself, thus one that she can coherently think that she possesses.

why Kant should, as he does (*GMM* AK 4:437–438), find it necessary to argue that, on the basis that 'Die vernünftige Natur nimmt sich dadurch vor den übrigen aus, daß sie ihr selbst einen Zweck setzt' (which we think, if not quite a literal translation, states 'Rational nature is distinguished from all other things by the fact that it sets an end by itself'), Agnes ought to consider her existence as an agent to be an end in itself. For Timmermann wants us to read this as 'A rational being is distinguished from every other thing/being by setting itself an end which is its own existence', which has the consequence that if 'die vernünftige Natur existiert als Zweck an sich selbst' *means* 'a rational being exists as an end in itself', it is a mere tautology that a rational being regards its own existence as an end in itself, which serves no justificatory purpose. But, in fact, Kant argues that, because Agnes must regard her agential self-understanding as an end in itself, she must regard herself as the subject of all setting of ends, hence consider her existence as an agent to be an end in itself.

Re Question (2). Per Tale 2, Kant asserts unconditionally both that rational beings (those with the powers of pure agential self-understanding) necessarily represent their own existence as an end in itself and that rational nature exists unconditionally as an end in itself, not merely on the presumption that there is a categorical imperative. This is because he derives that all agents necessarily represent their own existence as an end in itself from the premise that rational nature exists as an end in itself and says that the proposition that all rational beings represent their own existence as an end in itself on the same grounds is a postulate from which the categorical imperative as the FoH follows. Since Kant defines a postulate as

> a practical, immediately certain proposition, or a principle that determines a possible action, in the case of which it is presupposed that the way of executing it is immediately certain (*Jäsche Logic* AK 9:112)

all of the propositions that Kant links here must have the status of a practical postulate with respect to certainty. Indeed, because the certainty of a postulate is unmediated by any other proposition, all these propositions must be derived from the postulate that rational nature exists as an end in itself as expressions of understanding this postulate.

Related to this, it must also be borne in mind, as we have explained in Chapter Four, that 'achieving human agential self-understanding', equivalent to 'thinking in accord with the three maxims of the *sensus communis*' is, according to Kant, the basis of his entire critical philosophy. It is something that Agnes must accept in order to be able to ask any questions at all within the sphere of practical or theoretical reason. So, Kant simply cannot consistently think that Agnes's mandatory acceptance of it *depends* at any point on her contingent supposition that there is a categorical imperative. She must, according to the rationale for holding that achieving human agential self-understanding is the criterion for all synthetic critical thought, be something that Agnes necessarily presupposes in order to be able even to question whether or not it is. And it is equally necessary for Agnes to think that she unconditionally must accept the strict requirements of her human agential self-understanding. This is because she presupposes this in the very moment of asserting that she needs to establish that the moral law can exist as an a priori synthetic practical proposition – which, in turn, is because for it to so exist is for it to be a strict requirement of her agential self-understanding. This leaves us with the axiomatic idea that agential self-understanding, as such, is something the requirements of which any agent must accept as governing the agent's will. Since 'rational nature exists as an end in itself' is (given the answer to Question (1)) to be understood as 'agential self-understanding exists as an end in itself', Kant cannot be asserting 'rational nature exists as an end in itself' as being merely conditional on acceptance of a categorical imperative.

Despite this, it might be objected that the statement with which Kant closes *GMM II* negates the claim that he asserts unconditionally that rational nature exists as an end in itself. This is because he claims that

> whoever holds morality to be something and not a chimerical idea without any truth must also admit the principle of morality brought forward. *This section then, like the first, was merely analytic.* [Our emphasis added.] That morality is no phantom – and this follows if the categorical imperative, and with it the autonomy of the will, is true and absolutely necessary as an a priori principle – requires a possible *synthetic use of pure practical reason* [establishing which is the task for *GMM* III]. (GMM AK 4:444–445)

On the contrary, that everything in *GMM* II is analytic does not conflict with the claim that Agnes unconditionally must think that rational nature is an end in itself. This is because the quasi-ontological inference of *SII* relies on the idea that Agnes must think that pure reason is practical merely by understanding the concept of pure practical reason. Furthermore, if Kant wants us to be sensitive to his reference to 'a chimerical idea', the problem is not the existence of the categorical imperative directly, but the threat to its postulated existence due to the possibility that the *idea* of morality is a phantom *in the mind of a human agent*, in consequence of which the *possible* synthetic use of pure practical reason is being asserted to be enough to establish the *absolute normative necessity* of the categorical imperative as an a priori principle.

However, supposing that this is accepted, it might still be objected to Tale 2 that, while this applies to the quasi-ontological inference of *SII*, it does not apply to *SI*, for *SI* is not supposed to be established by understanding the concept of a categorical imperative.

But this objection is misconceived. It would have considerable force if Kant confines 'analysis' to understanding what is contained within the concept of a categorical imperative. But it has no force because, as we explained in Chapter One, Kant also regards 'analysis' ('exposition') as covering understanding that and why it is necessary to have the concept of a categorical imperative.

Re Question (3). On the basis of the answer to Question (2), Kant is not saying that *GMM* III will establish that all agents necessarily represent their existence as an end in itself on the same ground, in consequence of which their agential self-understanding strictly requires all agents to accept the FoH). He already considers this to be the case. The task for *GMM* III is to show that the ground that agential self-understanding requires agents to cite as the *ratio essendi* for the moral law/categorical imperative (here possession of pure practical reason) (possession of free will in *GMM* III) is something that can validly (coherently) be attributed to human agents.

Re Question (4). The issue here is why Kant thinks that the fact that all agents must consider that they are ends in themselves because they are able to exercise the powers of pure practical reason (have free will) (have free will) strictly requires them to treat all other agents as ends in themselves. In our opinion, three lines of reasoning are available to him.

(a) The idea that Agnes's existence is an end in itself contains the idea that no agent may treat Agnes's existence as merely a means. Thus, if Agnes must hold her existence *to be* an end in itself, *she* must hold, 'All other agents categorically ought to treat my existence as an end in itself, never merely as a means'. However, it is clear that if Agnes's agential self-understanding strictly requires *her* to regard *her* existence as an end in itself then, then another human agent's (e.g., Brian's) agential self-understanding strictly requires *him* to consider *his* existence to be an end in itself, and Agnes must recognize that this is so. But, just as Agnes cannot coherently think that she ought to do anything that requires her to treat herself merely as a means, so she cannot coherently think that Brian can coherently accept anything that requires him to consider that his existence is not an end itself. It follows that Agnes must accept that it is not intelligible for her to think that Brian ought to do anything (including, treat Agnes's existence as an end in itself) if this requires Brian to think contrary to how being required to regard his own existence as an end in itself requires him to think. Consequently, Agnes must consider Brian's existence also to be an end in itself.

(b) Because Agnes's agential self-understanding strictly requires her to consider that having the powers of pure agential self-understanding is the *ratio essendi* for her existence being an end in itself, she must attribute being an end in itself to the existence of any being (all agents) who possess the powers of pure agential self-understanding.

(c) Agents are, and can only be, strictly required to consider that their own existence is an end in itself because acceptance of this is strictly required by their agential self-understanding, which, as an end in itself, sets categorically binding ends that presuppose that pure reason is practical in them (that they have free will). But the moral law is the law of pure practical reason, an *objective* law which takes (and must take) the form of the categorical imperative for human agents.

Which of these does Kant appeal to? Places can be found in his writings where he appeals to (a) (e.g., *CPoJ* 5:294), and this fits well with viewing human agential self-understanding in terms of the three maxims of the *sensus communis*. On the other hand, (b) is a logical construction of the idea that agential self-understanding requires human agents to consider their possession of free will to be the *ratio essendi* of the moral law.[15] But it is (c) that we think is most likely to reflect Kant's intentions here. This said, we are not sure; but what is important for Tale 2 is that it does not really matter, because, if any of these lines is valid, then the other two also are. What is really important for Tale 2 is that the

---

15 According to Alan Gewirth (1978, 110), if Agnes's agential self-understanding strictly requires her to think that she has rights to the necessary conditions of her agency then it follows logically that her agential self-understanding strictly requires her to consider that the sufficient reason (*ratio essendi*) why she has these rights is that she is an agent. Thus, her agential self-understanding strictly requires her to grant these rights to all agents. The reasoning for this is as follows. If Agnes denies that being an agent is the *ratio essendi* for having these rights, she must hold that she needs some property only contingently connected to being an agent in order to have these rights. But if she holds this, she must hold that she can be an agent and hold *permissibly* that she does not have these rights. But for her to hold this is for her to deny that her agential self-understanding strictly requires her to hold that she has them. Thus, her agential understanding strictly requires her to hold that the *ratio essendi* why she has these rights is that she is an agent. Therefore, her agential self-understanding requires her to grant these rights to all agents. On the premise that Kant holds that Agnes's agential self-understanding strictly requires her to consider her existence to be an end in itself and that the *ratio essendi* for this is that she has free will, we may infer that he holds that Agnes's agential self-understanding strictly requires her to consider the essence of her being an agent to reside in her possession of free will. On this basis, he can be construed as arguing from Agnes being strictly required to consider her existence as an end in itself to Agnes being strictly required to regard Brian's existence as an end in itself in a parallel way to Gewirthds reasoning.

task for *GMM* III be not to provide the reasoning of (a), (b) or (c); but to show that what is strictly required by pure agential self-understanding is coherent for human agents to adopt, that the fact that even human agential self-understanding requires human agents to think that they have free will does not reveal an antinomy in human agential self-understanding.

Cue *GMM* III. The task for *GMM* III posed by this account is now simply to explain how pure reason can be thought to be practical in human agents, how *heteronomously* affected agents can be required by their agential self-understanding to consider that pure reason is practical in them. In terms of the maxims of the *sensus communis*, the problem is to show that it is possible for the maxim of understanding and the maxim of the power of judgment to be rendered consistent with each other in the maxim of reason. Consistency (the unity of theoretical and practical reason), which human agential self-understanding demands, requires this, but the *rationes essendi* of the maxim of understanding and of the maxim of the power of judgment seem to be in conflict, and it must be shown that this conflict is not real.

We are hesitant to say just how Kant makes these connections, not because we think that there is some doubt that *SI* ties to the operation of the maxim of understanding, the quasi-ontological inference of *SII* to the operation of the maxim of the power of judgment, and *SIII* to generation of the maxim of reason by rendering the maxims of understanding and the power of judgment consistent with each other, but because we are not absolutely certain just where the operation of one maxim ends and that of another maxim takes over. And this is because there are difficulties with the way that Kant reasons this out and he does not explain it very clearly. The difficulty we have in mind is this. According to Kant,

> The understanding legislates *a priori* for nature, as object of the senses, for a theoretical cognition of it in a possible experience. Reason legislates *a priori* for freedom and its own causality, as the supersensible in the subject, for an unconditioned practical cognition
> (*CPoJ* AK 5:195)

and neither can legislate for the other by itself. That it is possible (indeed, necessary) to view the moral law *as such* as laying down what Agnes ought to do is due to the power of judgment, which

> provides the mediating concept [ought] between the concepts of nature and the concept of freedom, which makes possible the transition from the purely theoretical to the purely practical, from lawfulness in accordance with the former to lawfulness in accordance with the latter, in the concept of a *purposiveness* of nature.   (*CPoJ* AK 5:196)

However, it is the understanding that gives an 'indication of its supersensible substratum' though leaving it 'entirely *underdetermined'*, the power of judgment that 'provides for its supersensible substratum (in us as well as outside us) *determinability through the intellectual faculty'*, and reason that 'provides *determination* for the same substratum through its practical law *a priori*' (*CPoJ* AK 5:196).

As we understand this, Kant is saying that the understanding points to a noumenal reality behind the phenomenal reality that its application to sensibility requires must be thought to be governed by the law of universal mechanism; the power of judgment provides that this must allow for a determination that is not mechanistic (a spontaneity or freedom); and reason (through requiring strict adherence to the moral law) fills in the nature of the freedom that the power of judgment provides as free will for practical purposes. This, however, seems to suggest that reason operating on desire generates the moral law, hence the idea of free will *sui generis*, and this suggestion seems to conflict with the idea that the maxim of reason (for which Kant clearly thinks free will is the *ratio essendi*) is a synthesis of the maxims of understanding and the power of judgment. To render what Kant says consistent, it is necessary to distinguish the maxims of the *sensus communis* from the powers of the *sensus communis* in some way (which at least does not contradict anything Kant says). But how exactly do they relate? We are not at all sure. Perhaps the description that treats reason as *sui generis* is apt for the sub-faculties of cognition viewed as pure faculties *in se* (i.e., as pure powers: pure theoretical reason, pure judgment, pure practical reason), whereas the description in terms of maxims is apt for what is generated by the application of these powers to the agential self-understanding of human agents as such.[16] This enables the maxims to be seen as products of the interplay of the powers as such with the faculties of cognition, feeling, and desire. It is, however, beyond the scope of this book to attempt a definitive analysis, let alone evaluation, of exactly how this interplay is structured.

In any event, we do not consider that our vacillations or speculations about this affect the validity of our exegetical account of the logical structure of Kant's justification of the categorical imperative, even though (see Chapter Nine) we suspect that Kant's own unclarities about precise details negatively affect the validity of his argument for the categorical imperative and his philosophical anthropology.[17]

---

[16] Indeed, it should be noted that Kant says that only finite agents can have maxims (*CPrR* AK 5:79).

[17] Since Kant, in effect, regards both a hypothetical imperative and the moral law *as such* as analytic, and only a categorical imperative as a priori synthetic, some may also wonder how we can correctly claim that Kant holds both hypothetical imperatives and the moral law *as such* to be requirements of, respectively, human agential self-understanding and autonomous agential self-understanding, given that we say that requirements of agential self-understanding are a priori synthetic. We can, because what we are concerned with is how agents can coherently regard whatever laws are applicable to them as applicable to them (which is a matter of agential self-understanding) and how a human agent can regard the moral law *as such* as being applicable to a

However, whatever is to be made of this, according to Tale 2, what Kant does in *GMM* III does not differ from the account given by Tale 1, except that he does not begin with Agnes merely imagining that pure reason is practical in her, but starts from the premise that it has been established that Agnes's agential self-understanding strictly requires her to think that pure reason is practical in her. Tale 1's device of asking Agnes to imagine that she is a purely rational agent is now, however, not used to put *SII* fully in place. Its purpose is merely to clarify further what the problem is that *SIII* is needed to solve. To repeat: the important thing for Tale 2 is that the task for *GMM* III is not to show that human agential self-understanding strictly requires Agnes and Brian to think that pure reason is practical in them. It is merely to show that it is possible (coherent) for them to think this. All that *GMM* III is about is whether Kant's exposition *of the concept of a categorical imperative*, which declares that practical reason strictly requires human agents to accept the moral law, is a coherent (and so unassailable) self-justifying story to tell about the practical reason of human agents.

Tale 3

Tale 3 follows Tale 2 in holding that Kant puts the quasi-ontological inference of *SII* in place by AK 4:447 but follows Tale 1 in maintaining that *SI* (as well as *SIII*) is only put in place in *GMM* III after AK 4:450.

GMM I claims that the idea of a categorical imperative, indeed, that of the FUL, exists in sound common human reason. But, according to Kant, although there

> is something splendid about innocence . . . what is bad about it . . . is that it cannot protect itself very well and is easily seduced. . . . [Because] reason issues its precept unremittingly, without thereby promising anything to the inclinations, and so, as it were, with disregard and contempt for those claims . . . there arises a *natural dialectic*, that is, a propensity to rationalise against those strict laws of duty and to cast doubt upon their validity, or at least upon their purity and strictness, to make them better suited to our wishes

---

purely rational agent even if only so applicable. In effect, Kant implies that the reason Agnes must consider herself bound by the moral law *as such* as an imperative is that Agnes can only conceive of a purely rational agent being so bound if Agnes can conceive of herself as being bound by the moral law as an imperative. That the relation between the moral law and the categorical imperative can be turned around like this reflects the bi-conditional relationship between Agnes's idea of herself as the particular agent that she is and her idea of herself as an agent *per se*. It also follows from the fact that this bi-conditional relationship is a compound relationship, as it really incorporates two bi-conditional relationships: that between Agnes's idea of herself as the particular *human* agent that she is and her idea of herself as a *human* agent *per se*, and that between Agnes's idea of herself as a *human* agent *per se* and her idea of herself as *an* agent *per se*.

and inclinations. . . . In this way *common human reason* is impelled . . . to seek help in philosophy. (*GMM* AK 4:405)

GMM II starts the process of help by analysing the concept of a categorical imperative, which involves thinking the concept of a categorical imperative distinctly. This analysis not only shows what must be the case if the categorical imperative exists, it shows that the categorical imperative is given to agents as the fact of pure practical reason. In doing so, Tale 3 appeals to the quasi-ontological reasoning of *SII* (understanding having the concept of a categorical imperative requires assent to its existence) but does not ground this in the claim that human agential self-understanding requires engagement with the concept of a categorical imperative (*SI*). However, the idea that the quasi-ontological reasoning of *SII* can be grounded in *SI*, which is necessary to establish that the categorical imperative exists, raises the possibility that there is an irresolvable dialectic between pure practical and pure theoretical reason that renders the categorical imperative a phantom.

GMM III then, by means of Kant's 'three worlds' analysis, puts *SI* and *SIII* in place as described by Tale 1, thereby showing that Agnes's agential self-understanding strictly requires her to have the concept of a categorical imperative (*SI*) and at the same time resolving the dialectic between pure practical and pure theoretical reason, thereby establishing the moral law in the form of the categorical imperative as the fact of pure reason as a whole for human agents.

Tale 4

According to Tale 4, in addition to what Tale 1 says is accomplished by the end of *GMM* II, *SI* is put in place (per Tale 2); and *SII* and *SIII* are put in place in *GMM* III per Tale 1.

Which Tale?

We prefer Tale 2 to Tales 1, 3 and 4 for four main reasons.

The first reason is that Tale 2 fits Kant's statement (*CPrR* AK 5:46) that his '*exposition*' of the categorical imperative (in, effect, his analysis) does everything needed to show that the FUL is the categorical imperative *except* show that it is coherent for Agnes to think that she can be bound by the law of pure practical reason as the categorical imperative.

The second reason is that it enables us to understand why Kant says in *GMM* II that the only thing that needs to be done to establish the categorical imperative as an apodictic *synthetic* proposition is to show that what *SIII* asserts is true.

The third reason is that, more than Tales 1, 3, or 4, Tale 2 spotlights the fundamental nature of Kant's enterprise, which is built upon the idea (see *CPrR* AK 5:63) that a critique of practical reason – which can only take the form of agential self-understanding — can only start with the question of its own existence (which presupposes, at least to begin with, the non-impossibility of its own existence); so cannot deny its own existence, but must affirm it. In doing so, it emphasizes that the question of what understanding the concept of a categorical imperative requires only arises relevantly within the context of the strict requirements of human agential self-understanding, which is to say that the relevance of *SII* depends on *SI* being in place (or presupposed), its cogency depending on *SIII*. In consequence, what might be thought to constitute a weakness in Tale 2, the fact that it requires rather more rational engagement (or active 'thinking along with') on the part of the reader than Tales 1, 3 or 4, is revealed to be a strength. This is because, as we have tried our best to show, according to Kant, the categorical imperative is nothing other than the maxim:

> Think and act in accord with the strict requirements of human agential self-understanding.

This being the case, it is impossible to question the existence of the categorical imperative without presupposing it. Thus, it is impossible for Kant to set up what is needed to justify the categorical imperative without presupposing it. Therefore, Kant must be presupposing *SI* and the quasi-ontological inference of *SII* in order to put them in place. The only reason why this cannot be enough to establish the existence of the categorical imperative is if human agential self-understanding itself turns out to presuppose contradictory things. If so, its products are phantoms, which leaves us with no basis on which we can proceed that has any genuine significance for us. And this shows clearly why the task to establish its reality is to show that human agential self-understanding can survive its own self-reflection, which is what Kant (by *SIII*) claims to establish. But, in the final analysis, even the sceptical thought that agential self-understanding cannot survive its own self-reflection cannot be thought without presupposing agential self-reflection.[18] And it is this that Kant is really telling us when he concludes *GMM* by saying:

---

18 There are comparisons to be drawn between Descartes' fear that an evil daemon (a great deceiver) might exist to undermine the validity of his *cogito ergo sum* and Kant's raising of the possibility that human agential self-understanding may be self- may be self-deceiving. But the contrast between the two approaches is sharp in that Kant's approach neither needs nor permits an appeal

> [W]e do not indeed comprehend the practical unconditional necessity of the moral imperative, but we nevertheless comprehend its incomprehensibility. (*GMM* AK 4:463)[19]

The fourth reason is that Tale 2 more closely follows the order of presentation of *SI*, *SII* and *SIII* in *CPrR*.

This said, from the point of view of the logical structure of Kant's argument in *GMM*, it does not matter which of our four tales depicts the *presentational* structure of the argument. All four narratives tell us that Kant puts *SI*, *SII*, and *SIII* together on the basis of human agential self-understanding, conceived of as constituted by the three maxims of the *sensus communis*, to justify the existence of the categorical imperative.[20]

---

to the existence of something beyond reason to secure its claims to certainty, simply because it limits its claims to certainty to facts of pure reason, which are facts within pure reason.

19 Noting that, according to Kant, 'it is requisite to reason's lawgiving that it should need to presuppose only *itself*' (*CPrR* AK 5:21), we can now see that his argument for the moral law is precisely that the categorical imperative does presuppose itself and need only presuppose itself, though he should have added a qualification. This is that it must also presuppose 'the principle of contradiction'contradiction'contradiction', which Kant formulates as, 'Anything is either A or not A' (see *CPoJ* AK 5:197 fn), which governs formal logic, whereas agential self-understanding governs transcendental logic. Whereas the principle of contradiction is the basic rule for meaning, of *any* thinking at all, a rule that is presupposed in forming any concept, thus in any intention to ask a question, make or deny a statement in any domain (formal or non-formal), human agential self-understanding is presupposed in asking any question, making or denying any statement in any non-formal domain (i.e., any activity directed at cognition of objects). Perhaps Kant should have said that the categorical imperative needs to presuppose, and can presuppose, no synthetic propositions other than itself. This qualification does not imply a contradiction because it might also be said that the categorical imperative as the principle of human agential self-understanding incorporates the principle of contradiction in order to be a principle of understanding, so that the principle of contradiction is not a principle independent of the principle of human agential self-understanding in human agential self-understanding. In effect, the ability to think in accord with the principle of contradiction is an a priori capacity implicated in possessing the powers of the *sensus communis*.

20 A difference that does exist between what Kant says in *GMM* and *CPrR* is that, in *GMM*, he refers to its activity as a critique of pure practical reason (*GMM* AK 4:392), but in *CPrR* he says that *CPrR* is entitled *Critique of Practical Reason* not *Critique of Pure Practical Reason*, about which he says that its aim is 'to show *that there is pure practical reason*, and for this purpose it criticizes reason's entire *practical faculty*' (*CPrR* AK 5:3). Does this mean that the two works have different aims? Yes, in so far as Book Two of *CPrR* goes into matters barely hinted at in *GMM*. But we do not think this means that *GMM* and *CPrR* differ in their aim of showing that there is pure practical reason in a human agent. Both involve a critique of practical reason's entire faculty to do this. Indeed, at the end of *GMM* I, Kant declares that in order to resolve the threatened dialectic between practical and theoretical reason, 'rest' cannot be found 'except in a complete critique of our reason' (*GMM* AK 4:405).

This completes our interpretation of Kant's argument for the categorical imperative. We think that we have done enough to defend the three pillars on which it stands, which are:

A. Our default assumption that the logical structure of Kant's argument is the same in *GMM* and *CPrR*, and that the argument is an argument in which the moral law is the *ratio cognoscendi* of free will, free will the *ratio essendi* of the moral law;
B. Our claim that this argument is one from and within human agential self-understanding; and
C. Our claim that this argument is intended to show that, what we will call 'an aggressive sceptic' (who holds that it is incoherent to hold that there is a categorical imperative), and 'an active sceptic' (who denies being bound by the categorical imperative or merely doubts its existence), both adopt unconditionally untenable positions about practical reason.

We now need to say how our construction relates to the interpretations of the two commentators whose interpretations are most in line with our own – Klaus Steigleder and Michael Wolff.

Chapter Seven
Klaus Steigleder and Michael Wolff

In this chapter, we present the constructions of Klaus Steigleder and Michael Wolff, which we consider are the closest to our own. Their views on Kant's justification of the existence of a categorical imperative are essential reading, but neither has received the attention it deserves.

Steigleder's Construction

This section has three subsections.

The first subsection outlines Steigleder's construction, which he presents in Steigleder 2002, a monograph on Kant's moral theory, and in a series of subsequent articles. All these publications, except Steigleder 2006 (which is a detailed analysis of the role of the first section of *GMM* III), are published in German. We derive Steigleder's account of *GMM* largely from Steigleder 2006 supplemented by statements in Steigleder 2002. We obtain his views about the argument for the categorical imperative in *CPrR* and about the fact of reason from Steigleder 2002. Translations of passages from Steigleder 2002 are our own.

The second subsection compares Steigleder's construction to our own.

The third subsection presents our view *vs* Steigleder's of Kant's understanding of maxims. Kant makes statements about maxims that, on the surface, do not appear to be consistent with each other. However, we argue that it is possible to interpret these statements in a way that makes them mutually consistent, which Steigleder's account does not do.

Steigleder's construction outlined

This outline has three parts. The first part presents Steigleder's view of Kant's justificatory methodology. The second part outlines his view of Kant's argument in *GMM*. The third part outlines his view of the fact of reason and of how *CPrR* relates to *GMM*.

Steigleder 2002 has two parts, one on the foundations of Kant's moral philosophy (with emphasis on *GMM*), and one on Kant's doctrines of law and virtue. We focus on the first part, which has three chapters. The first chapter deals with Kant's concept of agency and practical reason and discusses different dimensions of freedom and the relationship between freedom and happiness. The second chapter discusses Kant's concept of a hypothetical imperative and defends Steigleder's view against some other constructions. The third chapter introduces the concept of an unconditional ought, discusses the justification of the moral principle in *GMM III* and *CPrR,* and presents Steigleder's view of Kant's concept of a maxim.

The subtitle of Steigleder 2002 is *'The Self-Referentiality of Pure Practical Reason'* ('Die Selbstbezüglichkeit reiner praktischer Vernunft'). This, by itself, indicates that Steigleder considers that Kant grounds normativity in human agential self-understanding.[1] As his introduction to Steigleder 2002 explains, he considers that the key to interpreting Kant's practical philosophy is to regard it as a 'theory of practical judgments' ('Theorie praktischer Urteile') (2002, xiii). According to this theory, to understand Kant's practical philosophy it is necessary to appreciate that its focus on practical judgments is not on their semantic content but on the relationship between contents of consciousness. Practical judgments are 'reflexive', judgments that an agent makes about himself or herself. Thus, the fundamental premise of Kant's justificatory methodology is that human agents cannot intelligibly make claims about what they do, can do, may do, or ought to do that imply that they do not have the properties and powers necessary for them to be able to make any practical judgments. Regarding this, Kant thinks that practical reason (practical judging) is not only involved when human agents reflect morally. It is also involved whenever they choose ends to pursue, means to achieve these ends, and in understanding themselves as subjects who act for reasons (2002, 9). The point is that, although human behaviour is always influenced by inclinations, human agents possess the ability to form interests and, when they exercise this ability, a judgment of value is involved (2002, 15). Indeed, according to Steigleder (and we agree), Kant thinks that evaluation is implicit in finding an inclination agreeable, i.e., in taking an interest in something. Thinking something agreeable does not necessarily involve a moral or aesthetic judgment, but an evaluation, not mere instinct, is necessarily involved in forming interests, simply because this involves choosing ends and it makes no sense to think of an agent choosing to pursue an end without attaching an action-motivating value to it.

---

[1] Steigleder does not use the term 'agential self-understanding', but what he means is precisely what we mean by this, which, *inter alia,* is demonstrated by the connection he makes between the methodology of Kant's argument and Alan Gewirth's 'dialectically necessary' argumentation (2002, 69 fn 13), and we will use this terminology whenever appropriate.

With this understood, Steigleder considers that Kant's argument for the existence of the categorical imperative in *GMM* may be said to begin with a human agent making a judgment of the form, 'I do A for E (voluntarily)'. Having the capacity to make a judgment of the form 'I do A for E' defines being an agent simply because a being without this capacity is not an intelligible addressee or addressor of any practical judgments and what Kant is ultimately interested in in his moral epistemology is what practical judgments agents rationally may/ought to accept.

According to Steigleder, Kant claims that a rational human agent (one who understands the judgments that make up this judgment,[2] and thus understands what it is for the human agent to be an agent), will accept (where A is necessary for E) that the agent ought to pursue A or give up E.

> Since we do not automatically want [choose] to do what is necessary for us to want to do on the basis of our actual ends... the practical necessity of wanting to do something, arising out of our actual ends, confronts us a demand, a necessitation, an ought.
> (2006, 226)

that is conditional on us retaining our actual ends.

In other words, any rational human agent necessarily adopts hypothetical imperatives by virtue of which the agent ought to accept 'If A is necessary for my chosen purpose E then I ought to pursue A or give up E'.[3]

However,

> Kant differentiates two types of conditional norms of action [hypothetical imperatives], namely, *technical norms* and *prudential norms*. Technical norms are dependent on norms that we *can* have; prudential norms, in contrast, are dependent on ends that all those beings that are under the influence of feelings of pleasure and displeasure *inevitably* have, to wit, the end of one's personal well-being, or, as Kant says, one's own happiness.
> (2006, 226)

The end of happiness is indeterminate 'because we continually interpret and reinterpret it through more specific ends' (2006, 227). Nevertheless,

> [u]ltimately, all conditional norms of action derive from the comprehensive end of 'one's own happiness', since this underlies the choice of ends on which conditional norms of action are dependent.
> (2006, 227)

---

2 We think that three judgments are involved here: the judgment that it is worthwhile for me to pursue E; the judgment that doing A will contribute to my achieving E; and the judgment that doing A is something to which I do not have a negative attitude strong enough to render me unwilling to pursue E.

3 This is one way of stating what we refer to as the 'Principle of Hypothetical Imperatives' (PHI) (about which we will have more to say in Chapter Nine).

Importantly, Steigleder claims that Kant considers that

> being knowledgeable of conditional demands, we can attain a conception of an unconditional ought by negating the essential characteristics of a conditional ought... that must necessarily lie in the faculty of pure practical reason. (2006. 227)

In other words, human agential self-understanding requires human agents to understand the concept of a categorical imperative, in consequence of which they must understand that

> [a] being that possesses the faculty of pure practical reason must understand himself or herself, on the basis of this faculty, as an unconditionally necessary end and, accordingly, attribute an absolute worth to himself. (2006, 227–228)

Consequently, *such* a being must regard the existence of every other being capable of *such* action as an end in itself in all action (2006, 228).

In short, Steigleder claims that, in *GMM* II, Kant considers

(i) that human agential self-understanding requires a human agent to have and understand the concept of a categorical imperative,
(ii) which requires the agent to have and understand the concept of pure practical reason,
(iii) which requires the agent to consider that *if pure reason is capable of being practical in human agents,* then the agent must think that all human agents exist as ends in themselves.

Thus, Steigleder considers that, by the end of *GMM* II, Kant has established that human agents can and must have the concept of a categorical imperative in the form of the FoH, in consequence of which they will be bound to adopt the FoH *only if* pure reason is capable of being practical in them.

Unless pure reason is capable of being practical in human agents, the categorical imperative is a mere thought entity, and

> [t]o establish that the moral principle is not only a thought-entity but that it possesses validity for us is the task of the Third Section of the *Groundwork*. (2006, 230)

Indeed, until it is established that pure reason is capable of being practical in us (which is what is needed to establish that the categorical imperative is a synthetic a priori practical proposition)

> [i]t could even be the case that for us all norms of action must be reducible to norms of prudence. This would be the case if all determining motivations of our action were to arise from our sensible structure of impulse. Our reason would not then be capable of determining original ends but only capable of administering the interests of inclinations.

> Consequently, it would be unfounded to dictate that we take into account the unconditionally necessary end [the existence of agents as agents] in our action.... Neither could we take such an absolute worth *as such* into account, should it exist. (2006, 229–230)

As Steigleder 2002 describes the task of *GMM* III, it is to establish that the necessary thought of the categorical imperative is not 'a chimera', a phantom, a delusion. However, he claims that Kant thinks that it might be alleged to be a delusion on two different grounds. The first potential allegation is that those who can form the idea of an unconditional ought do not possess the capacity for pure reason to be practical. The second potential allegation is that,

> for those who form the idea of an unconditional ought, this idea is not necessarily practically relevant (2002, 68)

concerning which Steigleder says that

> [t]he idea of an unconditional ought is at least necessarily practically relevant if a being capable of forming this idea must assume that it always can and must act according to this idea when acting. (2002, 68)

To understand what Steigleder is getting at here, we need to attend to a distinction he draws between a judgment of the form 'p' and a judgment of the form 'x is logically required to assume that p'. Regarding the former judgment,

> if the judging subject knows that p is wrong, he cannot be logically required to assume p. But the opposite is not true. If someone is logically required to assume p, it does not follow that p is true. (2002, 69)

He applies this distinction to the first potential allegation that morality is a delusion. If the question it poses were a question according to the first judgment (p), the question would be the *theoretical* question whether there *is* practical reason. But, according to *CPuR*, it is impossible in principle to answer this question. 'Accordingly, in *GMM* III, Kant does not even attempt to answer *this* question' (2002, 69). In effect, the first potential allegation is that the concept of a categorical imperative is a delusion because only hypothetical imperatives can exist. However, Kant considers this allegation to be incomprehensible for reasons he has already given in *CPuR*, upon which his defence of his deduction of the categorical imperative at the end of *GMM* III relies. Thus, only the second allegation needs to be addressed.

In any event, in both his monograph (2002, 101) and his article (2006, 233), Steigleder considers that *GMM* concludes that the existence of the categorical imperative has been established, which implies that Kant thinks that the second threat has been overcome by the end of *GMM* III.[4]

According to Steigleder, the first section of *GMM* III tells us what needs to be established in order to show that the categorical imperative really exists. He claims that it is particularly important to note two things:

(a) that, while Kant considers that human agents cannot know that they have free will (because it is not something that can be given in experience, but only as an idea of pure reason), given that pure practical reason and free will are reciprocal concepts, establishing that human agents must think that they have the capacity to act freely (that they can only act under the idea of freedom) is sufficient to establish the existence of the categorical imperative (2006, 232);

(b) that Kant claims that to establish this it is necessary to establish only that human agents must think that they have the capacity to act freely, not that they must think that their wills are free. If we conceive of free will in the strict sense of a freedom that can be a causality of the will independent of alien causes then we must not think of it as practical reason, i.e., we must not

> equate free choice with pure practical reason but must think of it as being *endowed* with the faculty of pure practical reason.... If free choice were equatable with pure practical reason, a being endowed with such a faculty would necessarily determine itself to activity through pure practical reason (would necessarily do what is morally good).... [But if] our capacity of choice possesses the faculty of pure practical reason, then we are always capable of determining ourselves to activity 'independently of alien... determining causes.
> (2006, 235)

Steigleder (2002, 87–88) explains how he thinks Kant argues that human agents must and can coherently think that they can act only under the idea of freedom. He presents Kant's argument in seven steps.

---

4 In our construction, we claim that showing that agential self-understanding requires Agnes to understand the concept of a categorical imperative (*SI* of our construction) is what makes *SII* of our construction practically relevant. Thus, the threat of practical irrelevance that Steigleder discusses is not quite the same as that to which we refer in our construction. However, there is no material disagreement with us here. Steigleder, in effect, makes our *SI* together with our *SIII* necessary for practical relevance, whereas we distinguish a threat of practical irrelevance from a threat of incoherence. We concur, though that Kant thinks that, to establish the authority of the idea of a categorical imperative and the existence of the categorical imperative, it is necessary to show both that understanding the concept of a categorical imperative is a strict requirement of human agential self-understanding and that this concept is coherent.

(i) With regard to our sensible experience, we distinguish between appearances and things in themselves.
(ii) A thing in itself exists independently of our capacity for sense-perception and is not knowable by us.
(iii) We must distinguish between the sensible world and the intelligible world.
(iv) We must apply this distinction to our own existence. My self as a thinking self (my essential self, that aspect of myself that enables me to think of myself in any form) must be distinguished from my self insofar as my self is accessible to me only through sense-experience.
(v) This essential self, the self as a thing in itself, is something of which we can have no sensory cognition. But we must regard ourselves as having a rational or intelligible self on account of our capacity to think and form ideas, which means that we must think of ourselves as having a capacity for activity independent of sensible determination.
(vi) As such, we must regard ourselves as taking another standpoint, one in which we see ourselves as able to act only under the idea of freedom.
(vii) However, we experience ourselves at the same time as beings with sensible impulses and needs, and in doing so we take a standpoint in which we see ourselves not only as part of the intelligible world but also as part of the sensible world.

One might ask why, even if this shows that we must think that pure reason has the capacity to be practical in us, how this shows that we can coherently think that pure reason can be practical in us. Steigleder's response is developed in a critical discussion of Henry E. Allison 1990. He maintains that Kant is not – as Allison alleges – taking a step from a negative to a positive characterization of the noumenal world because Kant does not claim that we can have positive cognition of the intelligible world.

> [T]he argument is that (necessary) ideas are sufficient for the justification of the validity of the moral law. Therefore, the reality of positive determined noumena or insights into them does not matter as against which ideas are necessary for us to develop and whether these ideas must guide us to the insight that we must assume that the moral law is necessary for us. Kant claims now that we not only make a distinction between the sensible and the intelligible world in general and that we must apply this distinction to ourselves, but that it is also necessary for us, due to the activity of reason in us, which among other things shows itself in the capacity to distinguish between the sensible and the intelligible world and to form ideas, to interpret a self that is distinct from the sensible world in the sense of a positive determination, without being able to get insight into this experience-independent self and without being able to have certainty about the reality of the objects of those ideas that we thereby make use of. (2002, 91)

In short, it is the ability to act upon the idea of a free being bound by the moral law that is important here and not any ability to have independent knowledge of its reality (2002, 92 fn 63, where Steigleder references *GMM* 4:455–463). This is because being able to form this idea and seeing himself or herself bound by it is necessary for a human agent to have a consistent self-understanding.

According to Steigleder, Allison (1990, 228) also misinterprets Kant's step (vi) above because he does not distinguish between knowledge claims and ideas when he criticizes Kant for not distinguishing between *arbitrium brutum* (choice determined by impulses) and *arbitrium liberum* (transcendental freedom) when speaking about practical freedom. According to Steigleder, the issue is what it is to have a will.

> But this can in no way be a question *whether* we see ourselves as having the capacity of agency, or, as Kant says, whether we have to assume that we have a 'will'. This is because [failing the presumption that we have a will] it is altogether unintelligible for us to address the question as to how we ought to act or whether we must regard a specific law of action as valid for us. The basic question is: 'But why, then, ought I to subject myself to this principle and do so simply as a rational being, thus also subjecting to it all other beings endowed with reason?' (*GMM* 4:449). But if we must understand ourselves as rational beings, as beings with the capacity of agency, as beings with a 'will', then, and this is Kant's argument, we must understand our 'will' in a certain way. Since we understand our will as *our* will, thus must understand ourselves as subjects of our actions, we must see ourselves in our authentic selves as rational (capable of rationality), thus must see our wills as not determined by sensibility, therefore must see ourselves in a meaningful sense as free, namely in the sense of the capacity of 'pure practical reason'. (2002, 92–93)

Steigleder also refers to Allison's claim (with reference to Kant's step [vii]) that the distinction between the two standpoints does not render it intelligible for us to be sensibly affected but not determined (Allison 1990, 225–226) and that only Kant's later distinction between 'Wille' and 'Willkür' is able to solve this problem. But, according to Steigleder, this criticism rests on misunderstanding the distinction between 'pure practical reason' and 'natural necessity', by seeing one's proper self as a purely rational will. But

> [i]f we must understand our proper selves as purely rational beings, the question would arise as to why we should not ascribe to ourselves what Kant calls a 'holy will'. The standpoint of the sensual world would then have nothing to do with our proper selves.
> (2002, 93)

Consequently, we could not explain any ought, because, in order to do so, we must view ourselves as belonging to two worlds.

> Accordingly, we must validly ascribe to ourselves a self that (1) has the capacity of pure practical reason; (2) is not identical with pure practical reason; (3) is not determined by

> grounds that are alien to [pure] reason;[5] (4) can follow grounds that are alien to [pure] reason as well; and (5) has freedom (which cannot simply be identified with the autonomy of pure practical reason) if it follows grounds that are alien to [pure] reason. Since we have to assume that we do not, by our nature, follow the law of pure practical reason, but are guided in our actions by grounds that are alien to pure practical reason and obviously 'want' to be guided by them, the law becomes an imperative for us. (2002, 94)

Thus, Steigleder maintains that, despite the fact that Kant holds that the capacity of pure practical reason is not fully intelligible to us (*per GMM* 4:458–459), in consequence of which we cannot fully grasp how a will is able to follow the law of pure practical reason, it is, nevertheless, necessary for us to ascribe the capacity of pure practical reason to ourselves and see ourselves as under the claim of an unconditional ought. Consequently, we can distinguish between the capacity of pure practical reason itself and a rational will that is capable of following reasons that are alien to pure reason. He suggests, therefore, that the distinction between 'Wille' and 'Willkür' is already present in *GMM*, even though Kant does not use these terms to describe it (2002, 95).

In any event, Steigleder considers that *GMM* concludes that the agential self-understanding of human agents coherently requires them to consider that the categorical imperative exists, which is sufficient to establish that it exists as an a priori synthetic proposition.

This brings us to Steigleder's account of the relationship between *CPrR* and *GMM* and his views about the fact of reason.

According to Steigleder, although *CPrR* presupposes *GMM's* identification and justification of the categorical imperative, *CPrR* goes a 'step further' than *GMM*, regarding which he says that

> what Kant is referring to and what constitutes the decisive further consideration [introduced by *CPrR*] is that the idea of an unconditional ought is not just an idea that we can form and think, it is, right from the beginning [of *CPrR*], also a claim under which we really see ourselves. (2002, 97)

In similar vein, he says that *CPrR* shows that

> the idea of transcendental freedom signifies something that we do not merely assume but that we also know.... This knowledge is, however, not theoretical insight into freedom but remains fully on the practical level. We know about the reality of the capacity of pure practical reason and the idea of transcendental freedom only insofar as this follows from the reality of the demand of moral ought. (2002, 99–100)

---

5 The German text has 'vernunftfremde Gründe' (literally 'grounds alien to reason'). But since the grounds referred to, here, are considerations of human practical reason, the 'Gründe' must be contrasted with requirements of pure reason.

At first sight, this is puzzling. For, *without more*, the statement that *CPrR* goes further than *GMM* by declaring that the idea of an unconditional ought is not a mere idea and that the idea of transcendental freedom is not something that we merely assume, implies that *CPrR* in some way completes Kant's argument for the existence of the categorical imperative. But this implication is contradicted by Steigleder saying almost immediately afterwards:

> *In the Groundwork*, Kant tried to show that the idea of the unconditional ought is not just a mere idea because each agent cannot act except 'under the idea of freedom' and, accordingly, must see himself in his action under the demand of the unconditional ought that follows from this idea. In the *Critique of Practical Reason* Kant goes, as has been said, a step further by calling our attention to the fact that we know this demand of unconditional ought. It is for [every finite agent]... a known 'fact' that we are under the demand of the unconditional ought. (2002, 101)

Since the way Steigleder presents Kant's argument in both Steigleder 2002 and Steigleder 2006 clearly has *GMM* concluding that human agential self-understanding requires human agents to consider that the categorical imperative exists, we consider that the statement at Steigleder 2002, 101 should be taken to present his view. The statements at 2002, 97 and 2002, 99–100 must then be regarded as missing some contextual elaboration, which is provided by appreciating that, when Steigleder makes these statements, he has already argued that Kant holds that the idea of freedom is one that a human agent must assume and that the idea of a categorical imperative is one that a human agent must have. Furthermore, he has already said that Kant holds that being required to act under the idea of freedom is enough to think that one is free. With this understood, the move from *GMM* to *CPrR* is not from 'can think' or 'merely assume', but from 'must and can think' and 'must assume', to 'know' (which the quote at 2002, 101 makes explicit). However, this still leaves open the question as to what this 'knowledge' is and in what sense this goes a 'step further' than *GMM*.

To address this, we need to consider how Steigleder interprets the 'fact of reason'. As we have already indicated in Chapter Three, like others before him, he insists that the fact of reason ('Faktum') is neither an empirical fact, an actual moral action, a form of 'intellectual intuition', nor any kind of theoretical knowledge (2002, 102–108). However, he also does not fully support Marcus Willascheks interpretation of a 'fact of reason' as a 'deed of reason' (2002, 104), which he sees as a reduction. Instead, he maintains that Kant views the Faktum as a deed *and* a fact at the same time.

> The specific character of the 'Faktum' as a claim of unconditional ought is, according to Kant, that it is something given that, at the same time, is not an external or internal

(special or temporally determined) object of experience but an immediate content of consciousness, a content of immediate knowledge, that is only intelligible as consciousness of a 'deed' of reason. (2002, 103)

Steigleder maintains that when Kant first refers to the 'fact of reason', he plays upon an ambiguity in the German of his time concerning the meaning of 'Faktum' between 'a given' and 'a deed'. The Faktum (the moral law), insofar as it is a product of understanding, is a deed of reason, which requires us to see ourselves under the moral law and to apply its claim to our actions. But we know that this is the case. So, because we know that this is so, and only with reference to this fact, we may speak about a non-theoretical 'insight' of the understanding (2002, 107–108). Steigleder calls this a genuine form of 'practical knowledge' that human agents ought to embrace (2002, 108).

However, this practical knowledge is not different from what *GMM* claims to be the case. To say that the moral law is given to human agents as the Faktum is to say that its acceptance is a strict requirement of human agential self-understanding, which is just what Steigleder thinks *GMM* purports to have established. So, in what sense does *CPrR* go 'a step further'?

In our opinion, Steigleder neither claims that Kant changes his argumentative strategy in *CPrR*, nor says something substantially different in *CPrR* from what he says in *GMM*. He does not claim that *CPrR* provides argumentation that is required to complete justification of the categorical imperative; he does not claim that *CPrR* is more explicit than *GMM*; and he also does not claim that the epistemic status of our 'insight' into freedom and the moral law is different in the two works. He only claims that, in *CPrR*, Kant presents the 'reality of the demand of moral ought' as a given, which Kant is entitled to do on the basis that he has shown in *GMM* that this demand is a strict requirement of human agential self-understanding and that the categorical imperative has, and can have, no existence except as a requirement of human agential self-understanding. As such, he seems to hold that the term 'fact of reason' merely expresses an implication of what has been established by *GMM*.

Steigleder's construction vs our own

On the basis of the account we have given of Steigleder's construction, he agrees with us that:
1. Kant's methodology is that of an argument from and within human agential self-understanding.

2. Kant neither abandons nor reverses his *GMM* position in *CPrR*. (Although Steigleder does not explicitly say that *GMM* derives the capacity for free will as the *ratio essendi* of the capacity for pure practical reason, this is implicit in his view that Kant holds that it is a strict requirement of human agential self-understanding that a human agent understand the concept of a categorical imperative already in *GMM* II).
3. Kant's argument employs *SI* of our construction (at least in its general outline and conclusion).
4. Kant holds that, from within a human agent's self-understanding (from within Agnes's agential self-understanding), because Agnes is strictly required to understand the concept of the categorical imperative, there is no gap between the idea that it is coherent for her to be required to have the concept of the categorical imperative and the idea that she is strictly required to think that the categorical imperative exists.
5. Kant holds that the role of *GMM* III is specifically to establish the existence of the categorical imperative by establishing that it is coherent for agents to think that they can be governed by the law of pure practical reason as a categorical imperative, thereby establishing that the categorical imperative exists (on which basis Steigleder agrees that Kant's argument involves *SIII* of our construction).
6. Kant holds that what it means to say that the moral law is given to agents as the fact of (pure) reason is that its acceptance is a strict requirement of human agential self-understanding.

Beyond this, there are some differences in the way in which he and we think Kant presents his argument in *GMM* III. One thing, in particular, that we are unsure about, is just why (rather than that) Steigleder thinks that Kant holds (or shows) that there is no gap between on the one hand, it not being incoherent for Agnes to think that she must have the concept of the categorical imperative, and on the other hand, Agnes being required to think that she is necessarily bound by the categorical imperative.[6]

---

[6] It should also be noted that, unlike us, Steigleder 2002 does not discuss the further argumentation of *CPrR* concerning God and human immortality and is only concerned to demonstrate that there is continuity between *GMM* and *CPrR*. The reason he gives for this restriction is that he sees an examination of Kant's doctrine of the *summum bonum* as being too demanding for the methodological scope of his book (2002, xv). This is acceptable because Kant's rational theology rests on his moral epistemology. However, we consider that things that Kant says about this grounding illuminate and clarify the cognitive status Kant assigns to the categorical imperative as the sole fact of pure reason. So, it is not insignificant that, unlike us, Steigleder does not

One possibility, which we think should be discounted because it involves a misconstruction of what Steigleder is getting at by insisting that the existence of a categorical imperative rests on having a will that has the capacity to be free, not a will that is free, is that he attributes the following reasoning to Kant.

Agnes must consider that the categorical imperative exists if she is required to think that she has the capacity for pure reason to be practical in her (has the capacity for free will), which is to say, if she is required to think that it is possible (not impossible) for her practical thoughts and actions to be governed by the law of free will as an imperative. The idea that she has such a capacity cannot be shown to be incoherent. Therefore, she must think that it is possible (not impossible) for her practical thoughts and actions to be governed by the law of free will as an imperative, and so think that the categorical imperative exists.

But, without more, such reasoning involves an equivocation. This is because the reasoning of *SIII* of our construction on the back of *SI* of our construction (both of which are part of Steigleder's construction), does not show that Agnes must think that she *has* the capacity for free will, only that it is not incoherent for her to think that she has this capacity. In other words, without more, *SI* coupled with *SIII* does not show that Agnes must consider that she is bound by the categorical imperative. This coupling only shows that Agnes must consider that it is not impossible for her to be bound by the categorical imperative, which is to say that it is not irrational for her to consider that she is bound by the categorical imperative. To think otherwise is to equivocate between ontological and epistemic concepts of possibility.

In our construction, of course, the something more that Kant relies on is the quasi-ontological reasoning of *SII* of our construction, which (ultimately) is justified on the basis of the claim that to act in accord with the strict requirements of human agential self-understanding is an end in itself (this requirement, itself, being the sole categorical imperative). And we connected this to various other claims, such as: the claim that Kant makes in *GMM* II that rational nature exists as an end in itself; his claim that this claim is a postulate (an

---

make an issue of the fact that Kant refers to moral consciousness as a fact of reason, but to the moral law as the (sole) fact of pure reason, which implies (or so we claim) that there is more than one 'Faktum' at work in the way in which *CPrR* describes the argument for the categorical imperative. And, perhaps most significantly, Steigleder does not link the categorical imperative explicitly to the maxim of reason of the *sensus communis* of *CPoJ* or the *sensus communis* to Kant's common human reason/understanding of *GMM* and *CPrR*. We do not think it necessary at this point to rehearse how attending to these things helps to elucidate Kant's argument systemically. However, we will give some further illustration of the importance of seeing the maxim of reason as the categorical imperative when we discuss Steigleder's discussion of Kant's concept of a maxim.

immediately certain proposition); his claim that the categorical imperative can and need not presuppose anything other than itself; his claim that it is incomprehensible to ground the existence of the categorical imperative by means of some interest laid down as its basis; his claim that the moral law (categorical imperative) is the fact of pure reason; and our claim that Kant regards the categorical imperative as the maxim of reason of the *sensus communis* of *CPoJ*. The general implication of all this is that Kant thinks that the criterion for a possible categorical imperative is itself the categorical imperative, which entails that the categorical imperative exists and can only exist in being a required concept of human agential self-understanding.

Now, while Steigleder does not make all of these connections in either Steigleder 2006 or Steigleder 2002, he does make some of them. Of particular significance is his claim that 'the argument is that (necessary) ideas are sufficient for the justification of the validity of the moral law' (2002, 91) (which connects directly to the way in which he characterizes the Faktum) in combination with the fact that he sees Kant's methodology of eliciting the fundamental requirements of human agential self-understanding in being grounded in the possibility of any judgments as resting on possession of the powers of human agential self-understanding (which links to the reason why he considers that, for Kant, the first allegation that the idea of a categorical imperative is a delusion does not properly arise – which links, in turn, to Kant's claim that it is incomprehensible to try to justify the categorical imperative by an interest laid at its base). Furthermore, the way in which he describes (at 2002, 87–88) how Kant argues for the existence of the categorical imperative in *GMM III* is at least not incompatible with the way in which we presented this in our Tales 1 and 4 in Chapter Six. In addition, if we take seriously his claim that the categorical imperative exists in being a necessary idea (concept) of human agential self-understanding, then we can make further sense of his claim that *GMM* shows no more than that the categorical imperative is a mere idea yet shows that acceptance the categorical imperative is a necessary requirement of human agential self-understanding. This is because, if the categorical imperative can only exist in being a necessary idea of human agential self-understanding, then showing that it is *merely* a necessary concept of human agential self-understanding is sufficient to show that acceptance of its existence is a strict requirement of human agential self-understanding.

So, if we have understood Steigleder correctly, his construction is essentially compatible with our own, and differs from our own mainly in not making any explicit link between the *sensus communis* of *CPoJ* and common human reasoning/understanding in *GMM* and *CPrR*, and in not making (at least explicitly) some of the other links we make to the idea that the categorical imperative really (undeniably) exists in being a necessary concept of human agential self-understanding.

Steigleder's construction also differs from our own in the way in which he thinks Kant presents his argument in *GMM*. Whereas we favour our Tale 2 of the way in which Kant presents his argument, we think that Steigleder's is closest to our Tale 4. This is because, while Steigleder can be read as putting *SI* in place in *GMM* II, he is very clear that he does not consider that Kant thinks that the requirement for human agents to think that they are bound by the categorical imperative is something that follows from analysis of the concept of an absolutely good will or of the categorical imperative (2006, 238–239).

Related to this, it is possible that we do not agree with everything that Steigleder has to say about the proposition that rational nature exists as an end in itself. Steigleder can be interpreted as suggesting that Kant's claim in *GMM* II that the proposition, 'All rational agents consider that their own existence to is an end in itself on the same ground', is a postulate, is the assertion that the proposition that rational nature exists as an end in itself is yet to be established (i.e., that the claim is merely a hypothesis), whereas we contend that Kant means that it is an immediately certain proposition (which is what Kant generally means by calling something a postulate). This is because Steigleder tells us that *GMM* III

> affirms what Kant could only present as a postulate in *Groundwork* II, namely, that every rational being must so conceive his or her existence that he or she exists as an end in himself or herself. (2006, 240–241)

But, as we argued in our Tale 2, Kant says that the proposition that rational nature exists as an end in itself is the ground of the categorical imperative (because it is nothing other than the immediately certain proposition that acceptance of the strict requirements of human agential self-understanding is an end in itself), and a Kantian postulate can have no *ratio cognoscendi* other than itself. Consequently, any concern Kant has for the ground of a postulate can only be a concern for its *ratio essendi*. What *GMM* III addresses in this regard is the coherence of thinking that free will, the *ratio essendi* for the moral law *as such* (the law of *pure* agential self-understanding), is a *ratio essendi* for the categorical imperative (the fundamental principle of *human* agential self-understanding), which is necessary for it to be *coherent* for Agnes to think that the existence of all agents (thus all human agents, including herself) is an end in itself. That Agnes is required to consider that the existence of all human agents is an end in itself is already established, and it is merely the coherence of this requirement that *GMM* III addresses. While it is possible that it is just this that Steigleder has in mind, it is not clear to us that this is so.

Steigleder on Kant's view of maxims vs our own

There are difficulties with the way in which Kant describes a maxim in *GMM* when he explains the FUL at AK 4:421, some of which we drew attention to at the beginning of Chapter One, and what Steigleder says about Kant's understanding of maxims raises a number of issues that provide an opening for us to contribute to what Kant generally understands a maxim to be. It is worth noting, however, that we are not entirely in agreement between ourselves as to what Steigleder's view about a Kantian maxim is.

We will first list some statements Kant makes about maxims. We will then discuss Steigleder's depiction of Kant's view and, make a proposal about how to render Kant's statements about maxims parts of a consistent comprehensive characterization of what a maxim is.

GMM AK 4:421 is not the only place where Kant makes statements about the nature of a maxim. We will not attempt to provide a comprehensive list; but an adequate account of what Kant thinks a maxim is needs to deal with claims like the following.

(1) The principles of the *sensus communis* are 'maxims', which are the most fundamental principles governing how Agnes *may and ought to think* (*CPoJ* AK 5:293–294).

(2) A maxim is a *subjective principle* and must be distinguished from the practical law. This is because the practical law is an *objective* principle (one valid for all agents, a principle according to which *every* agent *ought to act*), whereas a maxim is a *principle* in accordance with which *an agent acts* (*GMM* AK 4:421 fn).[7]

(3) According to the FUL, Agnes may only act according to a maxim if she can at the same time will the maxim to be a universal law, i.e., *to be* an objectively valid principle (*GMM* AK 4:421).

(4) Within Agnes's agential self-understanding, the principle that Agnes ought to consider her existence to be an end in itself follows from the principle that rational nature exists as an end in itself. As such, it is a subjective principle.[8] But the fact that Brian (representing every other agent) must also consider his existence to be an end in itself *on the same ground* as Agnes means that this subjective principle is also an objective one (*GMM* AK 4:428–430).

---

[7] Here, Kant says that a maxim is a subjective principle in the sense that it is one that an agent adopts.

[8] Here, Kant says that the principle that *Agnes's* existence is an end in itself is subjective, not in being a principle that she adopts, but in being a principle that she unconditionally ought to adopt, even if it is not the case that Brian unconditionally ought to adopt it.

(5) 'Practical *principles* are propositions that contain a general determination of the will... They are subjective, or *maxims*, when the condition [that which determines the will] is regarded by the subject as holding only for his will; but they are objective, or practical *laws*, when the condition is cognized as objective, that is, as holding for the will of every rational being.' (*CPrR* AK 5:19.)

(6) 'Maxims are indeed *principles* but not *imperatives*' because imperatives are rules 'indicated by an "ought".' (*CPrR* AK 5:20.)

(7) 'Imperatives... hold objectively[9] and are quite distinct from maxims.' (*CPrR* AK 5:20.)

(8) Unless an imperative is categorical, it is not a practical law. 'Hypothetical imperatives are practical *precepts* but not *laws*.' (*CPrR* AK 5:20.)

(9) '[A] *principle* [our emphasis] that is based only on the subjective condition of receptivity to a pleasure or displeasure [i.e., a hypothetical imperative]... can indeed serve as his *maxim* for the subject who possesses this receptivity but not as a *law* even for him.' (*CPrR* AK 5: 21–22.)[10]

(10) 'If a rational being is to think of his maxims as practical universal laws, he can only think of them as principles that contain the determining ground of the will not by their matter but only by their form.' (*CPrR* AK 5:27.)

(11) Maxims are '*intentions of the will* of the individual'. (*CPrR* AK 5:66.)

(12) The concept of a maxim, like that of an interest or an incentive, can only be applied to finite beings (*CPrR* AK 5:79).

(13) In applying the categorical imperative, human agents must consider whether it is possible to make it their maxim to always do something in a particular way (e.g., *GMM* AK 4:422–424).

---

9 Here, Kant uses 'holding objectively' to mean holding in a way that even hypothetical imperatives hold for Agnes even if she does not act in accord with them. This is to say that a hypothetical imperative is something that Agnes ought to adopt because there are means (M) that are necessary for her to achieve her chosen end (E), whether or not she realizes this. This is different from the sense in which Kant says that holding objectively is a feature of a practical law. However, it should be noted that a hypothetical imperative will only function as one for Agnes if she recognizes that M are necessary for E, which is to say that a hypothetical imperative only binds *Agnes* on the basis of *her capacity to understand that* M are necessary for E, not because of *the fact* that M *are* necessary for E.

10 This implies that a hypothetical imperative is a principle, which implies that a practical precept (*qua* [7]) is a principle. It is also worth noting here that the examples of maxims Kant gives at *GMM* AK 4: 422–423 depict them as hypothetical, as what Agnes may or ought to do on the basis of what she ought to do in order to achieve some contingent purpose that she has.

(14) Agnes can become conscious of the moral law as soon as she draws up maxims for herself by attention to what reason necessitates and abstraction from all empirical conditions 'to which reason directs us' (*CPrR* AK 5:29–30).

(15) '[F]or us human beings it is quite impossible to explain how and why the *universality of a maxim as law* and hence morality interests us.' (*GMM* AK 4:460.)

(16) '[E]very rational being must act as if he were *by* his maxims at all times a lawgiving member of the universal kingdom of ends.' (*GMM* AK 4:438.)

Are these statements consistent with each other? We have already noted some (but only some) apparent inconsistencies, and it is, of course, *possible* that Kant does not have a consistent concept of a maxim, or that he employs different concepts of a maxim (at different points in time and in different writings). We will not attempt a complete analysis of how he conceives of a maxim, but we will offer some strategic thoughts about this that are prompted by some things that Steigleder says about maxims.

Steigleder says that,

> [a]ccording to Kant, three kinds of practical judgments are conceivable for us as finite beings capable of action: 1. Maxims. These have the two following basic forms: (a) 'I want to achieve end E through my action'; and (b) 'I wish to carry out action A in order to achieve E'. The reality of maxims is indisputable. 2. Hypothetical Imperatives. These take the following basic forms: (a) 'I ought to do A, because I want to achieve E'; (b) 'I ought (to attempt) to achieve E_2 because I want to achieve E_1', that is, hypothetical imperatives demand the adoption of certain maxims because the agent has certain other maxims from which the necessity arises to adopt the maxims being demanded. Since the reality of maxims is indisputable, the reality of hypothetical imperatives is equally indisputable. 3. Categorical imperatives. Their basic form consists of the unconditional demand to do something or not to do something. Since practical judgments are practical judgments precisely because they express the volition of a subject capable of action, we can more fully comprehend the categorical imperative as a practical judgment if we realize that moral oughts articulate a practical necessity for an agent, which materializes as a demand for him or her (a necessitation). (2006, 231)

By saying that (according to Kant) there are only three types of practical judgments (implied by saying that three types are conceivable), not three types of maxims, and that only the first type are maxims, Steigleder implies that Kant holds that hypothetical imperative and categorical imperatives are, *in themselves,* not maxims and that the *only* practical judgments that Kant considers to be maxims are those constituted by a human agent's choice (intention) to achieve a purpose or by a human agent's choice to pursue a means to achieve a purpose. This raises the question as to how Kant thinks imperatives are related to maxims, and the implication of what Steigleder says is that Kant thinks that imperatives can constitute the content of a maxim, but only by virtue of an agent's choice to comply with the commands of a hypothetical or categorical imperative (i.e., only by an agent choosing to make compliance with such commands the agent's purpose).

An obvious problem with this is that, while Kant does, in various places, say that a maxim is a principle according to which an agent acts and also that hypothetical imperatives and categorical imperatives are not maxims, Kant also says, most dramatically, that the fundamental principles of the *sensus communis* are maxims (the maxim of reason being the categorical imperative) when none of these principles expresses the volition of a human agent as against a volition that a human agent unconditionally ought to have.

There are also other questions that can be raised by what Steigleder says here. For example, if the essence of a practical judgment for Kant is that it expresses 'the volition of a subject capable of action', how can a categorical imperative be a practical judgment?[11] Also, is it true that Kant thinks that only these three kinds of practical judgments are conceivable for human agents?[12] Furthermore, given Steigleder's view that, for Kant, the formation of an interest involves a practical judgment regardless of whether or not this implicates normative considerations, his statement that there are, for Kant, three kinds of practical judgments, suggests that the content of a maxim need not express any practical precept (rule or principle) as it might merely express a human agent's willingness to pursue a purpose regardless of what the agent thinks about the legitimacy of pursuing this purpose. Yet we are not aware that Kant ever says that maxims can have such a content, about which we will have more to say when we defend our own depiction of Kant's view of maxims.

---

[11] The last sentence of the quoted passage would, however, make sense if it is read as 'Since acts of judging are practical judgments precisely because they express the volition of a subject capable of action, we can more fully comprehend the categorical imperative as a practical judgment by viewing it not as expressing the volition of a subject capable of action, but as a proposition that prescribes what the volition of a subject capable of action ought to be'. Just as it can be said that to make a statement (to state) is to assert something (a statement) that exists (has meaning, has a propositional content) independently of being asserted, so making a practical judgment (to judge) can be said to be adoption of something (a practical judgment) that exists (has meaning, a propositional content) independent of being adopted. So, perhaps this is what Steigleder means to say. Indeed, as we will argue, recognition of such ambiguity in what constitutes a maxim as a practical judgment is important for our account of Kant's view of maxims.

[12] This problem is less acute, because it is arguable that Kant regards other normative judgments ('may' judgments) and judgments of non-impermissibility as analyzable in relation to ought judgments.

However, Steigleder 2002 has a lot more to say about Kant's view of maxims, which might clarify his view on these matters. The focus of the discussion of maxims in Steigleder 2002 (118–128) is the question whether the categorical imperative bears only on the 'moral quality of the acting person' or also on the 'moral rightness of actions' (2002, 119). Steigleder's view is that, according to Kant, the categorical imperative bears on both desiderata, and that they are interrelated because the categorical imperative specifies the criterion for right actions and understanding it provides the motive of morally good action. In *MoM*, Kant draws a distinction that structures his doctrine of right in relation to his doctrine of virtue, which Steigleder quotes.

> One can think of the relation of end to duty in two ways: one can begin with the end and seek out the maxim of actions in conformity with duty or, on the other hand, one can begin with the maxim of actions in conformity with duty and seek out the end that is also a duty.
> (AK 6:382)

Thus, the concept of a maxim must be applicable in both doctrines and must eschew any idea that human agential self-understanding can be free of normative considerations.

This said, Steigleder maintains that Kant uses the term 'maxim' in multiple ways and warns us not to treat one of these uses as providing the entirety of Kant's understanding (2002, 120). Furthermore, he claims that maxims can have different levels of generality, by which we understand him to say that they can have different kinds of judgments as their content, of which general maxims (principles) are particularly important for a number of reasons. Nevertheless,

> for Kant, ... *any* subjective determination of the will is a maxim. In Kant's theory of action, 'maxim' and 'subjective determination of the will' are exchangeable concepts.
> (2002, 122)

To like effect, he says that when imperatives are the content of maxims, the maxims are *my* practical principles, 'the subjective realisations of imperatives. But, similarly, a decision against the claim of an imperative can [also] produce a maxim' (2002, 125).

However, while maxims always result from particular-occurrent (individual) decisions of an agent, Steigleder stresses that Kant holds that agents necessarily operate within the framework of a 'network of maxims', that are made up of 'super-ordinate and sub-ordinate' 'determinations of the will of different levels of generality and different kinds' such as technical, prudential, and categorical imperatives (2002, 125). which is what enables agents to evaluate their actions normatively (2002, 128).

All of this makes it clear that Steigleder's overall aim, here, is to show that Kant holds that 'every concrete determination of the will' is a maxim, while maxims, by their very nature, are part of a reflexive orientation of agents in which they evaluate their purposes of action in the light of normative considerations.

We are, however, unable to agree between ourselves as to whether what Steigleder holds to be 'concrete determinations of the will' are confined to decisions based on normative considerations (thus, express only practical precepts) (Düwell) or whether (as Steigleder 2006 seems to imply, and Steigleder 2002, 122, 125 arguably does too) they include judgments that simply reflect something being found agreeable (Beyleveld). Nevertheless, whatever the truth about this, both Steigleder 2002 and Steigleder 2006 follow Kant in his insistence in (6) and (7) of our list that maxims *as such* are not imperatives, while the way in which Steigleder 2002 makes the concept of a maxim integral to Kant's moral project, merely serves to make it all the more pressing that Kant have a concept of a maxim that enables him to say that both subjective and objective determinations of the will are maxims. In any event, as we see it, the most fundamental problem posed by Kant's statements about maxims is that it cannot be true that maxims *as such* are principles that include the maxims of the *sensus communis* and that imperatives are not maxims, for all the maxims of the *sensus communis* are unconditionally binding principles and the maxim of reason is the categorical imperative. This means that either Kant is inconsistent, or he has two different concepts of a maxim that he uses in different contexts, or there is something about the different contexts in which he refers to maxims that reveals that he has one concept of a maxim and only appears to have two concepts.

In our opinion, Kant thinks that a maxim is a *practical precept* (though he generally refers to a principle, [9] in our list being an exception)[13] that Agnes *might* choose to adopt (i.e., can *possibly* as against can *permissibly* choose to adopt), not a practical precept (let alone *any* purpose) that she *does* choose to adopt. And the apparent inconsistencies between Kant's statements that

---

13 We take a practical precept to be a practical judgment with a normative content, conditional or unconditional. So (as a category) it includes technical and prudential imperatives as well as unconditional ones, judgments of permissibility, impermissibility, and non-impermissibility, and judgments about the rationality of any such judgments. Only some of these are, for Kant, principles (which he uses generally to refer to unconditional imperatives). So, there is a case for saying that Kant's view is that a maxim is a principle that Agnes might choose to adopt. The case for this is strongest when applying the concept of a maxim in Kant's specification of the FUL. However, the FUL can be restated as requiring Agnes not to adopt any practical precept not consistent with the categorical imperative, not merely as requiring her to adopt only principles that she can also regard as objective principles, and we think that there are good reasons for doing so on Kant's own terms. However, there are complexities here that require attention to the way in which Kant applies the categorical imperative that are beyond the scope of this book.

Agnes's maxim is a principle/practical precept that she adopts and imperatives not being maxims are removed by attending to the context in which Kant makes these statements. In other words, that Agnes chooses to adopt a practical precept makes it *her* maxim, but it does not make it *a* maxim, and the contexts in which Kant says that a maxim is the principle/practical precept in accord with which Agnes acts, are those in which she is considering whether a principle/practical precept is one in accordance with which she may choose to act (i.e., can legitimately make *a* maxim *her* maxim).[14]

This view is driven by the following considerations.

First, the principles of the *sensus communis* are the fundamental principles of Kant's entire transcendental philosophy. Are we to believe that calling the fundamental a priori synthetic principle of human agential self-understanding the 'maxim' of reason is a slip of the pen? If Kant attaches any importance to the terms he uses, then it is not unreasonable to expect him to take the greatest care with the way in which he characterizes his most fundamental concepts and propositions.

Secondly, the idea that Kant holds that maxims are an agent's chosen purposes *whatever their content* does not comply with his claim that Agnes can become aware of the moral law as soon as she draws up maxims for herself (*CPrR* AK 5:29) ([14] in our list). As we have depicted the process involved, which is the process described by *SI* of our construction, Agnes's moral consciousness is not given to her merely by the fact that she, by virtue of being an agent, chooses purposes to pursue or adopts means to her chosen purposes, but by her being required to have the concept of a practical precept, and most specifically, the concept of a hypothetical imperative, as a strict requirement of her agential self-understanding. The process of abstraction by which Kant says that Agnes can have moral consciousness (have the concept of the moral law) is not one performed on the concept of a particular occurrent purpose *per se,* but on the concept of a hypothetical imperative.[15] But this implies that Agnes's chosen

---

[14] With reference to our remarks Chapter One note 3, we consider a maxim to be a judgment in the sense of a proposition with the content of a practical precept, not a judgment in the sense of an act of judging (by which Agnes makes a maxim her maxim). To say this is not to deny that maxims can only exist if human agents are capable of judging. It merely presupposes that formation of a concept does not entail application of the concept to oneself, and that propositions (with notable exceptions, paramountly, the proposition that to act in accord with the strict requirements of human agential self-understanding is an end in itself) do not have to be accepted just because they can be conceived.

[15] It is also at least odd to refer to the process of choosing a purpose for the mere reason that one desires to achieve it as a matter of drawing it up. Choosing to pursue something because one desires it involves a direct form of practical judgment. The judgment is constituted by the choosing and involves no process other than the choosing.

purposes are not maxims simply in being her chosen purposes. (i.e., maxims are not produced simply by choosing purposes to pursue).

Thirdly, that the content of a maxim is always a *practical precept* is further supported by Kant's claim that maxims are intentions of the will (see [11] in our list). This is because Kant claims that 'the will is nothing other than practical reason' (*GMM* AK 4:412). Thus, he holds that maxims are intentions of practical reason, ends *set by* Agnes's *practical reason,* not by Agnes in any other way. Furthermore, it must be borne in mind that *the reason why* he holds that the will is nothing other than practical reason is because he holds that Agnes possesses a will *only* by virtue of having 'the capacity to act *in accordance with the representation* of laws, that is, in accordance with principles' (*GMM* AK 4:412).[16] This implies that Kant thinks that to act in accordance with a maxim is *not* to act in accord with one's chosen purpose simply *qua* this purpose being a purpose, but to act in accord with a purpose that one presents to oneself as a matter of *legitimacy* in some way. This amounts to saying that Agnes, by virtue of possessing practical reason, necessarily adopts a view on practical reasonableness (i.e., she necessarily thinks that there are rational *vs* irrational thoughts and actions and has some view about this). At the most general level, the content of such a personal view (which we will refer to as a 'subjective viewpoint on practical reasonableness' or *'SPR'*) will be a second order view about the permissibility of applying the idea of permissibility to the adoption of purposes. The view that there is a categorical imperative is such a second order view. So is the view that there is no categorical imperative, the view that there cannot be a categorical imperative, the view that there are ends in themselves, the view that there are no ends in themselves, and the view that the only kind of rationality is instrumental rationality in terms of hypothetical imperatives. Under a second order *SPR* there might also, depending on the nature of the *SPR*, be practical precepts (first order *SPRs*) that specify the content or form of practically reasonable practical precepts.

However, on the basis of the reasons we have given so far, it might be conceded that we have made a good case for holding that Kant's maxims have the content of practical precepts, yet claim that we have not yet shown that he does not hold (inconsistently with his claim that fundamental principles of the *sensus communis* are maxims) that maxims are *chosen* practical precepts.

---

[16] Note, too, that while Kant is concerned to judge the legitimacy of actions, he does not do so directly, but via judgment of the rationality of the maxim of an agent's action (the content of which, *per* [13], is to act always in a certain way, i.e., to act in a particular way as a matter of principle in some sense). This sits uneasily with Steigleder's (2006, 231) view of the two basic forms of a maxim because the forms characterize human actions as such.

Our response to this is that it not actually clear that Kant ever says that maxims *are* chosen practical precepts. This is because his statements to the effect that a maxim is a principle or practical precept according to which Agnes acts (see, e.g., [2] in our list) are made in the context of Agnes considering whether an action that satisfies a practical precept *she adopts or is contemplating adopting,* or a practical precept that she adopts or is contemplating adopting, is consistent with a practical precept she unconditionally ought to adopt. In other words, they are made in the context of applying a formula of the categorical imperative to assess the rational permissibility of *her* actions or *chosen* practical precepts (i.e., of *her chosen* maxims). On the other hand, when (for example) Kant describes the categorical imperative as the maxim of reason, he is not viewing the categorical imperative as a practical precept that Agnes has chosen to be assessed, but as the supreme standard for the assessment of the rational permissibility of all her actions and practical precepts. And, once this is appreciated, his two apparently inconsistent characterizations of a maxim are revealed not to be inconsistent at all.

This, however, still leaves open the possibility that Kant has two concepts of a maxim that are not inconsistent simply because of their use in different contexts.

This is acceptable *only if* it is not claimed that the two concepts are independent. This is because (as Steigleder also insists), for Kant, all Agnes's decisions must be deeply integrated in Agnes's agential self-understanding. Because maxims are practical precepts set by Agnes's practical reason, there are two kinds of maxims. The first kind comprises practical precepts that Agnes might contingently choose to treat as *rationally acceptable* reasons for her to act (i.e., as what she might choose to regard as rationally acceptable reasons by her exercise of Willkür), while the second kind comprises practical precepts set by *pure* practical reason to Agnes by itself (which presupposes her possession of Wille).

This generates two specific concepts within the general concept of a maxim as an intention of Agnes's will.

Concept I   A maxim is a *practical precept* (any 'ought' or 'may' statement, including any statement about such statements) that Agnes *might* choose to adopt, a precept that she *might* adopt as her personal standard (or under her personal standard) for assessing the rational permissibility of her actions.

Concept II   A maxim is an apodictic imperative for Agnes.[17]

---

[17] The imperative for Agnes to adopt the principle that her existence is an end in itself (the maxim of understanding) and the imperative for Agnes to act in accord with the moral law *as such* (the maxim of the power of judgment), the bi-conditional relation between which constitutes the imperative for Agnes and all other agents to act in accord with the FoH (the maxim of reason), are both such maxims.

Given that an apodictic imperative is a practical precept, a Concept II maxim is a sub-category of a Concept I maxim. However, by its very concept, a categorical imperative is both a Concept I maxim and a Concept II maxim. Because it is a principle that *can* apply only to an agent who can and must reason in terms of hypothetical imperatives, it is a principle that is capable of being chosen or not chosen (i.e., one that *might* be chosen). Because it is, *at the same time, the form of application of* the law of pure practical reason to human agents, conformity with it by human agents is an end in itself. Consequently, the possibility (coherence) of this simultaneity entails that Agnes must accept that it unconditionally ought to be chosen if it *can* be chosen. Correlatively, Agnes *may* only think that it *may* be chosen by accepting that it unconditionally ought to be chosen. Because actions, purposes, or precepts that Agnes thinks good or evil independently of validation or rejection by the moral law are merely expressions of her choice, this touches the heart of Kant's claim

> *that the concept of good and evil must not be determined before the moral law... but only... after it and by means of it* (CPrR AK 5:63)

which he calls 'the paradox of method in a *Critique of Practical Reason*' (AK 5: 62–63).[18]

Further elaboration is needed to complete this account, which requires commentary on at least all of Kant's statements in our list.[19] We cannot attend to this here, but what we have said is sufficient for the purpose of this chapter. We are aware that our proposal goes beyond the scope of what Kant explicitly says. Nevertheless, we consider that it offers a way to render Kant's various statements about maxims consistent with each other without requiring the

---

18 This reflects our contention that, at its simplest, Kant's argument for the existence of the categorical imperative is as follows. The concept of a categorical imperative is such that it (in the form of the FUL, FoH, etc.) exists, and can only exist, in its acceptance being a strict requirement of human agential self-understanding. This is because (by its concept) it is, and can only be, the strict requirement to act in accord with the strict requirements of human agential self-understanding. As such, its existence cannot intelligibly be thought to rest, or be thought to need to rest, on anything external to the strict requirements of human agential self-understanding. Consequently, all that is needed to establish that the categorical imperative exists is to establish that the concept of a strict requirement of human agential self-understanding cannot be shown to be an incoherent concept. This is established by the fact that possession of the a priori powers required for human agential self-understanding is necessary for any human agent to assert, deny, doubt, or question, any synthetic statement, which is established by what it means to assert, deny, doubt, or question, any synthetic statement.
19 There are several other commentaries on what Kant takes a maxim to be. Any complete exposition of Kant's idea of a maxim must also take account of these.

introduction of propositions that Kant would not find acceptable. Furthermore, given Steigleder's own view of Kant's critical methodology, we consider that it is a way in which he could and should have proceeded in his aim of coherently linking Kant's uses of the term 'a maxim' to the role of the concept of a maxim in Kant's moral theory as a whole. If we are correct in this, it further illustrates just how important it is to have the maxims of the *sensus communis* in mind when trying to interpret Kant.

Michael Wolff

Michael Wolff's construction is presented in a very scholarly and technical examination of Kant's justification of the categorical imperative in *GMM* III (Wolff 2015) and of the role that the fact of reason performs in justification of the categorical imperative in *CPrR* (Wolff 2009). Translations from these publications are our own.

Wolff's analyses are meticulous, involving almost line by line commentaries on Kant's texts. This makes it very challenging to summarize his construction and to relate it to our own without going into all of its details. Indeed, it makes it very difficult to evidence our interpretation of his analysis without giving as much attention to it as we have given to *CPrR* and *GMM* themselves. There is also very little published commentary on Wolff's analysis, and what little we have come across is very brief and not very helpful.[20] Consequently, what we say about Wolff is very much a schematic presentation of our understanding of his construction that is rather short of detailed references. Our justification for this is that our intention is not to provide a detailed critique of his construction but merely to indicate what we take his position to be and how we think it relates to our own. We recommend that our readers study Wolff's two articles carefully in any event.

This said, we have no doubt that Wolff's analysis shares the following contentions with our construction.

---

20 For example, Owen Ware (2017) says nothing about Wolff's analysis apart from telling us that he agrees with it that *GMM* and *CPrR* are consistent with each other and that Kant reasons from pure practical reason to free will in both works, and that he disagrees with Wolff's claim that Kant justifies the existence of the categorical imperative on the basis of the disanalogy that Kant claims between the moral law as a postulate and the postulates of geometry (137 fn 5). Jochen Bojanowski (2017), tells us that Wolff's analysis is exceptionally enlightening, but provides very little detail apart from agreeing with Wolff that Kant argues that the moral law is given to human agents by exposition of its concept (2017, 76–77, fns 38, 39 and 41).

Michael Wolff — 167

A. The argument for the existence of the categorical imperative in *CPrR* does not merely presuppose the argument given in *GMM*. *CPrR* presents the argument of *GMM* in a 'more systematic and methodologically perfected manner' for *CPrR's* distinctive purpose of justifying faith in the existence of God and human immortality (2009, 546).

B. The moral law is the *ratio essendi* of free will in *GMM* as well as in *CPrR*. According to Wolff, Kant (at *GMM* III AK 4:447) announces that it is possible

> to make comprehensible the possibility of the categorical imperative as a synthetic proposition a priori, which constitutes a 'deduction of the concept of freedom from pure practical reason' (2009, 546, fn 64)

regarding which, Wolff emphasizes that this deduction is equivalent to the deduction in *CPrR*

> of the 'capacity' of freedom, the 'principle' of which is the fundamental principle of pure practical reason. (2009, 546, fn 64)[21]

The categorical imperative is established by its acceptance being a strict requirement of human agential self-understanding. As Wolff puts it, Kant holds that,

> because agents find the necessary criterion to judge their maxims in their own thinking and their own pure (i.e., non-empirical) will, they cannot deny the fact of reason.
> (2009, 539)

C. The existence of the categorical imperative is posited in its exposition, and consequently is established by the coherence of its concept. Nothing else is needed because the moral law is a postulate, indeed, the sole postulate, of pure reason as a whole (2009, 542–548).[22]

---

[21] It should be noted, however, that Wolff insists on distinguishing the law of pure practical reason from the moral law *as such* and from the categorical imperative in a way that does not obviously square with the way in which we relate these things. We discuss this below.

[22] In arguing for this, Wolff focusses, as we do, on the disanalogy that Kant draws between the law of pure practical reason and the postulates of geometry at *CPrR* AK 5:31. It is in Kant's invocation of this disanalogy that Wolff portrays Kant as arguing that the existence of the categorical imperative is a genuine fact, indeed, an apodictic truth. It is also on this basis that Wolff, in effect, introduces *SII* of our construction into his depiction of Kant's argument in *CPrR*, by linking this, as we do, to the distinction Kant draws between the epistemic status of this postulate from that of God and human immortality (2015, 542–548). Wolff is also one of the very few commentators who, like us, stresses the importance of Kant's designation of the

That Wolff holds that Kant propounds C and D means that he, in effect (while not engaging in any such structuring), agrees that Kant's justification of the existence of the categorical imperative amounts to combining *SI*, *SII* and *SIII* of our construction. But just how he thinks Kant does this cannot be easily summarized. And we are far from certain what Wolff's view is about where in *GMM* Kant puts *SI*, *SII*, and *SIII* in place, which is to say that we are unsure which (if any) of the four tales we offered he would prefer, and we will not speculate about this.

In any event, what is more important, is that we think that his analysis of how *GMM III* deals with the charge of possible vicious circularity in deriving free will from pure practical reason from pure practical reason is illuminating in relation to Kant's reasoning about both *SII* and *SIII*, about the moral law being held to be the sole fact of pure reason in *GMM*, and about the way in which Kant thinks that pure practical reason has primacy over pure theoretical reasoning.

As we understand Wolff, he considers that the reason why Kant thinks that there is no *petitio* involved in Agnes holding that she *has* free will on the basis of having the concept of pure practical reason, and thus that pure reason is practical in her (which is to say that the categorical imperative exists) is that, in being able to have the concept of pure practical reason, Agnes must accept that she inhabits the intelligible world as well as the world of sense. Insofar as she inhabits the intelligible world, she must accept that she is bound by the law of pure practical reason. This is simply because, as an idea of pure reason, the existence of the law of pure practical reason is something that neither requires, nor can have, any support from considerations that apply to her as belonging to the world of sense. But, because she does inhabit the world of sense, she must accept the law of pure practical reason as a categorical imperative for her. In this way, the categorical imperative is presented to Agnes as the fact of pure reason. In effect, Wolff is saying that Kant views the categorical imperative as the fact of pure reason in seeing it as being presented to her by its exposition (2015, 515).[23] This, in effect, ties the idea of the fact of pure reason to the

---

moral law as the *sole* principle of *pure* practical reason, e.g. 2009, 535–536. Regarding this, he says that, for Kant, the fact of reason designates that determination of the will is 'the *sole* fact of *pure* reason that is not subject to "censorship" or "critique" by theoretical reason' (2009, 548). Since 'determination of the will' is determination of it by free will as the *ratio essendi* of pure practical reason, Wolff's view is at least compatible with our own on this. However, there are other things he says about the fact of reason that do not seem to be compatible with our view, which we discuss below.

23 Wolff discusses the relationship between the idea of 'exposition' in *CPrR* and that articulated in the 'doctrine of method' in *CPuR* (2009, 515–517). He contends that 'the first part of the analytic of the second critique does not contain an exposition of *given concepts*', but only an 'exposition' and 'supreme principle' (2009, 517). He argues that an explication of the basis

quasi-ontological character of the reasoning of our *SII* even though Wolff does not describe it in these terms.

As for *SIII*, Wolff maintains that, when envisaging a sceptic who claims that it is not coherent for Agnes to think that she has free will, Kant, in effect, claims that the sceptic must rely on the arguments of the antithesis of the Third Antinomy. However, these can be countered by the arguments supporting the thesis of the Third Antinomy, and (crucially) Kant regards these arguments, in themselves, as equally strong. But the fact remains that, in order for Agnes to think of herself as an agent, she must consider that she has free will. Consequently, *for all practical purposes* (*but only for these purposes*), Agnes must consider herself to have free will (2015, 50–57). In this way, Wolff links Kant's reasoning in relation to *SIII* (on the back of *SII*, itself on the back of *SI*) to Kant's thesis that pure practical reason has priority over pure theoretical reasoning, but only for practical purposes.

This reasoning is basically consistent with our construction. So, what are the differences between our constructions?

One difference is that Wolff does not identify many of the links we highlight between human agential self-understanding and the maxims of the *sensus communis* of *CPoJ*. This has two downsides: (1) that the nature of Kant's argument as one from and within human agential self-understanding is not as explicitly articulated as it could and should be; (2) that, while Wolff explicitly refers to the supreme practical principle being present in the judgment of common human reason, and explains that Kant holds it to be accessible to all rational beings because it has its origin in pure reason, the link we make between 'common human reason' and 'human agential self-understanding' as the *sensus communis* of *CPoJ* is not made explicitly, though materially implied.[24]

Another difference is that, while Wolff links Kant's claim about the moral law being the *sole* fact of pure reason to the distinction Kant draws between the epistemic status of free will *vs* the epistemic status of the existence of God and human immortality (2015, 524, fn 24),[25] he does not explicitly link this distinction to what we depict as Kant's quasi-analogy between Anselm's ontological argument for the existence of God and his own claim that the existence of the

---

of such an exposition is possible in the practical realm in a way that is fully compatible with the 'doctrine of method' of *CPuR* (518–521).

24 And this is also true of Steigleder's analysis.

25 Here Wolff discusses statements Kant makes 'on the postulates of pure practical reason in general' (*CPrR* 5:132–33) and observes that Kant is not altogether clear here about the status of the postulates. However, he stresses that there is a clear distinction between the status of the practical law and that of the postulates of God and immortality of the soul.

categorical imperative is posited in its exposition. In our opinion, while this does not affect the cogency of Wolff's analysis, it does make it more difficult to comprehend the role that Kant's claim that the categorical imperative is a postulate plays in his argument for the existence of the categorical imperative. It is significant in this regard that, while Wolff does link the distinction between the epistemic status of God and human immortality *vs* that of free will to the moral law as the sole fact of pure reason, other things he says about the fact of reason are more difficult to reconcile with our view.

In our construction, Kant holds that consciousness of the moral law (engagement with the concept of morality) is a fact of reason, that the moral law is given to Agnes as a strict requirement of her agential self-understanding is a/the fact of pure reason (so, because the moral law as the categorical imperative is the strict requirement to act in accord with the strict requirements of human agential self-understanding, the existence of the moral law/categorical imperative is also a/the fact of pure reason), and to say that the moral law-free will is the *sole* fact of *pure* reason is to say that it is the only fact of pure practical reason that is a fact of pure reason as a whole. But, while Wolff's view concerning the sole fact of pure reason seems (at least implicitly) to be compatible with our own, he does not distinguish between a fact of reason and the fact of pure reason as we do.

According to Wolff

> Consciousness that the content of the practical fundamental law objectively determines the will is what Kant calls 'consciousness of this fundamental law'. Kant does not assume that this consciousness is something that we can simply attribute to all rational beings. But he does assume that we, as human beings, will be 'immediately conscious' of the fundamental law 'as soon as we form maxims of the will' (5: 29). (Wolff 2009, 530)

Furthermore

> The effect of determination of the will by pure reason that Kant calls a 'Factum' is... exactly analogous to what Kant calls the construction of mathematical concepts in pure intuition. Both cases are the result of an act of synthesis. Just as the construction of a concept in pure intuition can be understood as the result of an act of synthesis of the understanding (the activity of a pure capacity of imagination), so can the consciousness of the practical fundamental law that Kant calls a fact of reason be seen as the result of an act of synthesis of pure reason that is entailed in the determination of the will by pure reason. This act is seemingly precisely what, according to Kant, makes pure reason *practical* reason. Why, therefore, does Kant call... the fact of reason a fact? My concluding answer is that he does so, not because he, thereby, wants to *justify* in any way the validity of the moral fundamental law, but because he wants to explain its givenness and the extent to which this depends on an activity of reason. Actually, saying this in the form or a mere *explanatory remark* to a postulate (which Kant makes explicit at 5:31.1) already leads us to expect that that this does not go beyond such an explanation (2009, 533–534)

Two things here call for comment. First, Wolff does not say much about his concept of justification (rechtfertigen) in Wolff 2009. But, in our terminology, to show that something is necessarily given in our agential self-understanding is enough to justify it provided only that the idea of a strict requirement of human agential self-understanding is coherent, and we are sure that Wolff considers that Kant holds this to be the case. Hence, we consider that the apparent incompatibility on this is merely terminological. However, secondly, Wolff does not seem to distinguish between the idea that having the concept of the moral law is a fact of reason and the idea that the existence of the moral law is a/the fact of *pure* reason, and the impression we get is that he thinks of both consciousness of the moral law and the existence of the moral law as being facts of *pure* reason, which definitely does not accord with Kant's terminology.

A third difference, about which we are even more uncertain (which might link to our uncertainty about the second difference), concerns the question of how we and Wolff, respectively, view the relationship between pure practical reason, the moral law *as such, as such*, and the categorical imperative. For it is in relation to this that we consider that the most important *substantive* differences (as against mere differences of presentation and/or detail or scope), *if they exist*, are likely to lie between our accounts.

Our view, as we have tried to make clear throughout, is that Kant thinks of the moral law *as such* as the law of pure practical reason, which is a law of nature for any purely rational agent unaffected by heteronomous incentives, and the categorical imperative is the moral law *as such* in the form it must take in its possible application to agents who are not purely rational in being affected by heteronomous incentives.

Wolff, on the other hand, says that Kant's Principle of Autonomy

> [C]hoose only in such a way that the maxims of your choice are also included as universal law in the same volition (*GMM* AK 4:440)

which Kant says is the supreme principle of morality, and which Wolff identifies with the Fundamental Law of Pure Practical Reason

> So act that the maxim of your will could always hold at the same time as a principle in a giving of universal law (*CPrR* AK 5:30)

is the only principle that Kant calls the supreme principle of morality (2009, 526). The moral law *as such* is a law of nature for a purely rational agent, and the categorical imperative, which is the application of the moral law *as such* to human agents, is the supreme principle of morals (the principle from which all moral duties are to be derived) (2009, 525). Furthermore, he claims that Kant derives the moral law and the categorical imperative from the Principle of

Autonomy (Fundamental Law of Pure Practical Reason), and so does not consider the Principle of Autonomy to be a formula for either the moral law *as such* or the categorical imperative (2009, 547–548), which further implies that he considers it wrong to identify the Fundamental Law of Pure Practical Reason with the FUL, which we and most other commentators do.[26]

Now, if (and to the extent that) what Wolff means, when he says that the moral law *as such* and the categorical imperative are derived from the Fundamental Law of Pure Practical Reason, is that the concept of the moral law *as such* is derived from the concept of pure practical reason (which gives Agnes the concept of free will as a postulate of pure reason as a whole), which requires her to accept that the moral law as the categorical imperative exists provided only that the concept of a categorical imperative is coherent, then we agree with him.

However, in claiming that the Principle of Autonomy is not a formula for the moral law *as such*/the categorical imperative, Wolff implies that Agnes's having the concept of pure practical reason is prior to her having the concept of a categorical imperative.

But this is not in line with our construction. For, in our construction, the concepts of a categorical imperative, an unconditional imperative or law, and pure practical reason are posited by understanding the concept of a hypothetical imperative in seeing that the concept of a categorical imperative is the mere inverse of the concept of a hypothetical imperative, and that it is a strict requirement of Agnes's agential self-understanding that she have the concept of a hypothetical imperative. It is only through being a human agent that *Agnes* can have any comprehension of what a purely rational agent must think. And it is for this reason that, in our construction, the bi-conditional relation between the maxim of understanding and the maxim of the power of judgment postulates that *Agnes* cannot coherently think of herself as the particular heteronomously affected agent

---

26 According to Wolff,

> the moral law is not, as is often assumed, the fundamental principle of pure practical reason itself, but only a specification of this law. It applies as a duty only to human beings, while the fundamental practical law must be understood to apply to all possible rational beings, including the 'supreme' and 'entirely sufficient intelligence' (if there is one) (§7, Anm. 2, 5: 32.17 and 31). The expression 'So act that...' in the proposition that in §7 articulates the fundamental law that is superior to the moral law, therefore does not articulate (as might be, and frequently has been, thought) an imperative. The grammatical form of this proposition can be explained solely by its function as a practical postulate. As a general practical postulate, 'so act' is not addressed to specific rational beings. Rather, the way the to understand the postulate is that [it articulates that] pure practical reason addresses itself and in so doing addresses all rational beings as such a proposition. (2009, 525)

that she is unless she accepts that she has the *a priori* powers of agential self-understanding that all agents must have, *yet (at the same time)* cannot coherently think that *she* can have these a priori powers without being the particular heteronomously affected agent that she is. In our construction, the true postulate of pure reason (the immediately certain proposition that grounds everything synthetic that agents can think) is the command to act in accord with the strict requirements of human agential self-understanding understood in terms of the structure of the *sensus communis*. Consequently, in our construction, no epistemic priority can be given to pure practical reason over the categorical imperative. Granted, Kant *does* say that pure reason is practical and gives the categorical imperative to human agents (*CPrR* AK 5:31), which might seem to suggest otherwise. But this, which we have argued is equivalent to saying that the achievement of human agential understanding is the sole end in itself (which means that the categorical imperative is the strict and unconditional requirement to strive to achieve this end), does not permit such an interpretation. Indeed, in terms of the genesis of ideas, bearing in mind the nature of the bi-conditionality of the maxim of understanding and the maxim of the power of judgment that Kant says constitutes the maxim of reason, if anything, it is the idea of a categorical imperative (as the inverse of the idea of a hypothetical imperative) that grounds the idea of the moral law *as such* and that of pure practical reason.

All of this is very theoretical. But there is a straightforward textual reason for questioning Wolff's claim that the Principle of Autonomy is not a formula for, or characterization of, the categorical imperative. And this is that Kant says:

> [T]hat the above principle of autonomy [which he has just designated 'the supreme principle of morality'] is the sole principle of morals [Prinzip der Moral] can well be shown by mere analysis of the concepts of morality. For, by this analysis we find that its [morality's] principle must be a categorical imperative, while this commands neither more nor less than just this autonomy. (*GMM* AK 4:440)

And this is reiterated when Kant says that

> [a]n absolutely good will, whose principle must be a categorical imperative, will therefore... contain merely the form of volition as such and indeed as autonomy; that is, the fitness of the maxims of every good will to make themselves into universal law. (*GMM* AK 4:444)

However, according to Wolff (2015, 3–4), commenting on this latter passage, it is ambiguous what Kant means when he says that the principle of autonomy must be a categorical imperative. This is because the principle of autonomy is a rule that must be valid for all rational beings with a will, including God, who (as an infinite being) cannot be subject to any obligation thus to any imperative (as Kant insists in *GMM* AK 4:389). Consequently, in reading Kant's claim that the Principle of Autonomy is the supreme principle of morality, we must read in that it is so only in its application to finite rational beings not in itself.

However, while this is true, it does not account for the fact that Kant holds that only finite rational beings can have maxims (*CPrR* AK 5:79), and we do not see why this requires us to modify our reading of Kant's text, according to which describing the categorical imperative as the sole principle of morals merely signifies that the Principle of Autonomy (the supreme principle of morality), in being the categorical imperative, is the sole criterion for assessing the validity of all maxims, *including itself*.

This said, because of the very technical nature of Wolff's analysis, and the fact that we are sure that Wolff analysis is very much in line with our own, we are not confident that we have correctly interpreted what he says about the Principle of Autonomy. If so, we apologise to him. But if we have not misunderstood him on this then what we take to be Wolff's mistaken view on this point illustrates once more the importance we attach to linking Kant's argument and its methodology to his claims about the maxims of the *sensus communis*.

Chapter Eight
Owen Ware

Owen Ware holds several propositions of our construction. He rejects the *WAV* because Kant says that *CPrR* presupposes *GMM's* account of the justification of the categorical imperative, and that what the *WAV* claims to be Kant's derivation of the moral law in *GMM* from free will Kant says is preliminary to rendering comprehensible the deduction of free will from pure practical reason from pure practical reason in a human agent, and with it the categorical imperative (Ware 2017, 119). Furthermore, he points out that those passages in *CPrR* that the *WAV* takes to be Kant's denial that the categorical imperative can be justified as an apodictic a priori synthetic practical proposition by a deduction, only amount to a denial that it can be justified as such by a *theoretical* deduction; and, in any event, Kant makes entirely compatible denials in *GMM* (Ware 2017, 124–126). The arguments for the categorical imperative that Kant offers in *GMM* and *CPrR*, while presented in different ways, have the same logical (i.e., justificatory) structure.

Despite this, Ware's account is seriously at odds with our own. Whereas we claim that Kant aims to refute those whom we have designated as 'active sceptics' as well as those whom we have designated as 'aggressive sceptics', Ware claims that Kant believes that it is neither possible nor necessary to rebut our active sceptics, and only believes that he can rebut our aggressive sceptics. As Ware puts it,

> Kant did not regard refuting the skeptic to be the measure of success for his moral philosophy. He was very much speaking to those of us who are committed to morality, but who lack the self-understanding necessary to make this commitment intelligible.
> (Ware 2017, 135)

How, then, can Ware say that Kant thinks that the categorical imperative is an *apodictic* a priori synthetic practical proposition?

According to Ware, Kant believes that his argument cannot succeed if addressed to *any* human agent, an agent like our Agnes, whom we characterize as being able to hold, as a matter of her actual (as against rationally required) commitments, *any* position on or about the rationality of practical precepts (thus including aggressive and active scepticism), and that he does not need to do so. Kant believes that *any* argument for a categorical imperative can only succeed, and therefore need only succeed, when addressed to that subset of human agents who happen to hold that there is a categorical imperative, human agents represented by someone we will call 'McAgnes', a morally committed human agent.

Given the concept of morality, McAgnes must, *relative to his contingent acceptance of morality*, consider that the categorical imperative is the FUL, that he has free will, and that the FUL is an apodictic a priori synthetic practical proposition. That Kant holds that McAgnes's commitment to morality is rationally optional, not unintelligible, i.e., defensible, is due to the fact that there are no grounds in theoretical reason that can prove that McAgnes cannot have free will, and that all agents, morally committed or not, must (by virtue of possessing reason) at least recognize the rational possibility of a categorical imperative. Thus, Kant thinks that McAgnes can justify, and needs to justify, his commitment only against an aggressive sceptic, a sceptic who claims that it is unintelligible for McAgnes to even entertain the possibility of a categorical imperative.

The reasons that Ware gives for his interpretation are, essentially, as follows.

First, and foremost, he contends that what Kant thinks is beyond our comprehension at the end of *GMM* III is 'precisely' 'to justify the necessity of the moral law' (Ware 2017, 135). However, this interpretation rests on Ware's contention that, in deriving the moral law from pure practical reason, and disavowing the possibility of a theoretical deduction of pure practical reason, Kant denies the possibility of a deduction that is capable of refuting the active sceptic (Ware 2017, 135). Ware holds four other positions that are linked to this and help to illuminate it, though three of them are expressed in earlier publications. These are:

1   Although Kant operates from the internal viewpoint of an agent, the account of this procedure suggested by, e.g., Pauline Kleingeld (2010) for *CPrR* (according to which the moral law is justified as a product of human agential self-understanding) is untenable. This is because it rests on the idea that the kind of freedom that is the *ratio essendi* of the moral law (Wille) is the same as that which characterizes the idea of a hypothetical imperative (the kind involved in thinking that that one can choose between incentives – Willkür) and it is not. Anyway, Kant cannot be reasoning like this because *CPrR* would then be offering a morally neutral deduction, which he disavows by claiming that the moral law/pure practical reason is the *ratio cognoscendi* of free will (Ware 2014, 9 fn 25).

2   The only kind of sceptic that Kant addresses is internal to someone like McAgnes, not a third party engaged in an adversarial debate with him. The relevant sceptic is someone like McAgnes, who is worried that his moral commitment might not be intelligible and is seeking assurance that it is rationally acceptable (Ware 2016).

3   Kant is adamant that the critique of practical reason can only begin from principles. The idea of freedom

is valid only as a necessary presupposition of reason in a being that believes itself to be conscious of a will, that is, of a capacity distinct from a mere faculty of desire (namely to determine itself to action as an intelligence, hence according to laws of reason independently of natural instincts) (*GMM* AK 4:459)

i.e., 'valid only for a being conscious of a capacity to act according to laws of reason, that is, according to moral laws'. (Ware 2017, 141–142 fn 38)

4 The reason why Kant claims that McAgnes is able to defend his moral commitment against himself as an aggressive sceptic is that Kant derives his a priori synthetic practical propositions by a procedure modelled on the experimental method of chemistry (Ware 2014, esp. 10–14).

We will comment on each of these claims in turn.

Ware on What Kant Thinks is Incomprehensible

Ware's claim that, when Kant says that it is impossible to comprehend 'the practical unconditional necessity of the moral imperative' (*GMM* AK 4:463), he means that it is impossible to refute the active sceptic, is mistaken for at least the following four reasons.

(1) It conflates seeing the practical unconditional necessity of the categorical imperative (establishing that pure reason is necessarily practical in a human agent) with comprehending the practical unconditional necessity of the categorical imperative (giving a morally neutral reason why pure reason is practical). Like us, Ware recognizes that Kant considers that it is impossible and unnecessary to give a morally neutral explanation of the categorically binding nature of a categorical imperative. However, he interprets this to mean that Kant thinks that only those agents who accept that pure reason is practical are rationally required to accept the categorical imperative. This is because he does not view Kant's claim that pure reason is practical as the claim that pure agential self-understanding is an end in itself, that the categorical imperative is the command to act only in accordance with the strict requirements of human agential self-understanding, and that it can have and needs no *proof* (*external justification*), simply because any human demand for justification necessarily presupposes human agential self-understanding. But it is for this reason that Kant says,

> It is therefore no censure of our deduction of the supreme principle of morality, but a reproach that must be brought against human reason in general, that it cannot make

> comprehensible as regards its absolute necessity an unconditional practical law (such as the categorical imperative must be). (*GMM* AK 4:463)

In other words, Ware errs by not recognizing that Kant claims that the normative necessity of the categorical imperative must be accepted in order to even question its normative necessity, in consequence of which the very idea of human agential self-understanding cannot be morally neutral, without this affecting the fact that the categorical imperative is absolutely (unconditionally) binding on all human agents, whether or not they actually recognize this. Kant's denial of the possibility of making the absolute necessity of the categorical imperative comprehensible is the claim that acceptance of the categorical imperative cannot be presuppositionless because acceptance of *any* claim presupposes human reason (the possession of the powers of human agential self-understanding). Despite this, because the categorical imperative is the law of human agential self-understanding, its acceptance is rationally necessary without qualification.

(2) To hold that Kant is only addressing human agents like McAgnes flies in the face of the fact that he claims that the moral law is the supreme law of practical reason, not the supreme law of moral reason alone. Time and again, Kant insists that the very idea of the moral law is that of a law for all agents, and only a law for any human agent because it is a law for all agents.

(3) Ware's interpretation cannot account for the fact that Kant uses his justification of the categorical imperative to justify his claim that faith and immortality is rationally necessary for all agents, not merely for those who believe in the moral law.

(4) Given the fact that the concept of a categorical imperative is the concept of an imperative that all practical precepts of all human agents must be consistent with, the very idea that Kant can be addressing only human agents like McAgnes is incoherent. This is because, given Kant's analysis of the concept of a categorical imperative, unless McAgnes believes that all human agents are bound by the categorical imperative, he is not morally committed. In other words, McAgnes, in being morally committed, must believe that any form of moral scepticism is unintelligible (unless the very idea of a categorical imperative is incoherent). It is precisely this that is the sting in the tail of Kant's quasi-ontological reasoning. The idea of a categorical imperative cannot be shown to be intelligible (thus refuting the aggressive sceptic) without refuting the active sceptic as well, because its acceptance cannot be shown to be intelligible without showing its conscious non-acceptance to be unintelligible.

Ware on Agential Self-understanding

Ware conjoins the views of, e.g., Thomas E. Hill (1998) and Christine Korsgaard (1996b), who argue that the moral law as a categorical imperative is implicit in the inescapability of deliberation (Ware 2017, 129), with Pauline Kleingelds (2010) characterization of Kant's argument in *CPrR* in terms of human agential self-understanding (Ware 2014, 9 fn 25). We are not concerned here with whether or not Hill and/or Korsgaard deploy Kant's methodology of human agential self-understanding for his critical philosophy. But insofar as we have aligned ourselves with Kleingeld, we do not accept the way in which Ware characterizes her view of derivation of the categorical imperative as a strict requirement of human agential self-understanding. If he is right in his characterization of Kleingelds position, then we have misunderstood Kleingelds position.

Ware depicts Kleingelds view of Kant's derivation as being grounded in identifying the free will that is the *ratio essendi* of a *categorical* imperative (Wille) with the capacity for voluntariness that Agnes must acknowledge if she is to recognize an imperative as *hypothetical* (Willkür). But it is not. Kleingeld views Kant's derivation as being grounded in Agnes being required to engage with the concept of a categorical imperative by understanding how a *hypothetical* imperative can be thought of as an *imperative* for Agnes by Agnes. Kleingeld does not think that Kant treats a categorical imperative as *analytically* derived (deduced) from a hypothetical one, which would be a theoretical deduction. She thinks that Kant holds that the idea of an imperative *as such* (thus the concept of a categorical *imperative* and that of a hypothetical *imperative*) is a construct of human agential self-understanding, not a construct of the concept of being a heteronomously affected agent. As we have already said, Ware's failure to understand Kant's concept of pure practical reason is at the heart of his failure to see that Kant considers that the question 'Why ought I to act in accord with the strict requirements of human agential self-understanding?' is sufficiently and necessarily answered by 'Because I necessarily presuppose that I ought to do so in asking this question!'; and his misunderstanding of what Kleingeld claims shows that this is so.

Ware's Claim that Kant does not Treat Refuting any Sceptic on an Adversarial Model

Ware is right about this, but it does not support his position.

Given that Kant's argument is a construction from and within human agential *self*-understanding, it should go without saying that he does not treat the relevant sceptic as a third party whom he is trying to persuade to be morally committed.¹ But it does not follow from this that the only relevant sceptic is someone like McAgnes, who needs no persuasion to be morally committed, so whose scepticism does not extend beyond worrying, because he does not understand how a categorical imperative is possible, that his moral commitment might be indefensible because it is incoherent. The relevant sceptic is any human agent, someone represented by our Agnes, who can (as a matter of contingent commitment) present herself as an active sceptic or an aggressive one, but is presumed for *critical* purposes to begin as someone who doubts that there is a categorical imperative because this is the only stance she can adopt without begging the question (*CPrR* AK 5:63). In thinking of the rules of human agential self-understanding as the principles of the *sensus communis*, Kant thinks of Agnes as reaching agential self-understanding through a dialogue with herself, constituted as a dialogue between *her*self (first person Agnes) and her*self* (second person Agnes), which is a dialogue between her idea of herself as her particular (heteronomous) self and her idea of herself as a universal self (someone possessing the universal powers of a priori reason/understanding necessary for her or any other heteronomously affected being to have any idea of itself at all). Conceiving of human agential self-understanding in terms of such a dialogue does not imply solipsism of any kind. This is because of the bi-conditional relationship that exists between Agnes as the particular agent that she is and Agnes as an agent at all. There is nothing imaginary about Agnes's existence as an agent *per se*, as Agnes being an agent *per se* is a presupposition of Agnes being the particular agent that she is even though *she* cannot be *an* agent without being the particular agent that she is. Given Kant's claim that the maxim of reason is a synthesis between the maxim of understanding and the maxim of the power of judgment (*CPoJ* AK 5:295), Kant's idea of what it is to be a real agent must be conceived in these terms from the internal viewpoint of a human agent.²

---

1 David Enoch (2006) also portrays 'constructivist' attempts to defeat the active sceptic as adversarial in which McAgnes is trying to persuade a sceptical Agnes.

2 The point is that, while Kant would agree with Stephen Darwall 2006 that adopting the moral point of view *involves* adopting the second person standpoint, unlike Darwall, he does not *identify* the moral point of view with the second person standpoint. It also follows from this that discourse theorists (like Micha Werner 2002) (who claim that philosophers like Kant and Gewirth, who reason from the internal viewpoint of an individual agent, employ a monological strategy that cannot show why Agnes ought to treat other agents as ends in themselves) fail to comprehend the concept of agency with which Kant and Gewirth operate. The significance of viewing human agential self-understanding in terms of the *sensus communis* is that the second person standpoint cannot be viewed as a factual given (a brute fact) because it is only intelligible to Agnes as internally linked to consistent thinking about herself. By the same token, the first person standpoint of Kant's reasoning is not adopted as a brute fact either, but

Ware's Claim that Kant Begins from Principles

Kant's argument does begin from principles. But these are the principles of the *sensus communis*, the principles of the sub-faculties (powers) of human agential self-understanding. As such, Kant's argument does not only address human agents like McAgnes, because the powers of human agential self-understanding are powers known a priori to be necessarily possessed by any human agent because their possession is necessary to be an intelligible addressee or addressor of any practical precepts. Furthermore, Kant holds that only by being aware of morality can Agnes be aware of free will. So, he holds that only on the basis that Agnes ought to be morally committed will she be rationally required to think that she has free will. But this is all that Kant means by the passage that Ware cites from *GMM* AK 4:459. This passage does not address the question as to why McAgnes (or Agnes for that matter) ought to believe himself (or herself) to have the capacity to think morally. This becomes clear if we place the passage in its context.

To begin with, Kant declares free will to hold as a necessary presupposition for anyone who is conscious that they have a will, and this is anyone capable of guiding their behaviour by practical precepts (anyone like Agnes, not only that subset of agents represented by McAgnes).

> [T]he principle of morality . . . is declared by reason to be . . . a law for all rational beings insofar as they have a will, that is, the ability to determine their causality by the representation of rules [which include hypothetical imperatives]. It is, therefore, not limited to human beings only but applies to all finite beings that have reason and will.
> (*CPrR* AK 5:32)

So, given that Ware agrees that *GMM* is consistent with *CPrR*, when Kant says that the moral law

> is valid only as a necessary presupposition of reason in a being that believes itself to be conscious of a will, that is, of a capacity distinct from a mere faculty of desire (namely to determine itself to action as an intelligence, hence according to laws of reason independently of natural instincts). (*GMM* AK 4:459)

Ware does not legitimately interpret Kant as saying that the moral law is

> valid only for a being conscious of a capacity to act according to laws of reason, that is, according to moral laws. (Ware 2017, 141–142 fn 38)

---

as something necessary to make the idea of a *common* sense intelligible *to Agnes*. (See further Beyleveld 2017 and Düwell 2017; and compare the similar position of Kenneth Westphal 2016).

if he restricts beings conscious of an ability to act according to the moral law to human agents *like McAgnes*. A being conscious of having a will is any agent. And human agents necessarily have the powers of human agential self-understanding *and* are conscious of having such powers (even if they are unable to specify what they are or how they operate), because the powers of human agential self-understanding are self-reflecting and confer the *capacity* to act according to the moral law.

This is confirmed directly by what Kant says in *GMM*. The passage that Ware relies on (*GMM* AK 4:459) comes after the section where Kant claims (through his 'three worlds' analysis) that

> the human being claims for himself a will which lets nothing be put to his account that belongs merely to his desires and inclinations, and on the contrary thinks as possible by means of it – indeed as necessary – actions that can be done only by disregarding all desires and sensible incitements. (*GMM* AK 4:457)

This means that Kant is referring to human agents who understand what it is for them to be agents. So, when Kant says that

> a human being really finds in himself a capacity by which he distinguishes himself from all other things, even from himself insofar as he is affected by objects, and that is *reason* (*GMM* AK 4:452)

and that '[a]ll human beings think of themselves as having free will' (*GMM* AK 4:455), it really is all human agents *within the frame of their agential self-understanding*,[3] not just all human agents *like McAgnes*, to whom he is referring.

So the consciousness that Kant is talking about in the passage Ware quotes (from *GMM* AK 4:459) is not a contingent commitment to act in accord with moral laws, but awareness of possessing powers of common human reason that confer an ability to act according to the moral law, which is nothing other than the ability to act according to the powers of human agential self-understanding. And, of this, Kant says:

> By *thinking* itself into a world of understanding practical reason does not at all overstep its boundaries, but would certainly do so if it wanted to *intuit* or *feel* itself into it.
> (*GMM* AK 4:458)

---

3 Reading this in context requires us to read 'all human beings' as all 'reflective human beings', of whom Kant says that they 'must come to a conclusion of this kind' (*GMM* AK 4:451). Kant is not to be read as saying all human beings actually think of themselves as having free will.

But overstepping pure reason's bounds (which one does by failing to comprehend pure reason's ground, which is itself, and trying to substitute it by others) is exactly what McAgnes does if he thinks it is coherent for him to ground his commitment to morality on any basis other than as a strict requirement of reflection by the powers of common human reason (meaning, to repeat, the a priori powers of the mind that constitute the *sensus communis* of *CPoJ*) upon themselves.

In effect, Ware is asking us to believe that Kant regards fundamental principles as what R. G. Collingwood (1940) designates as 'absolute presuppositions'. Like Kant, Collingwood holds that there is no presuppositionless knowledge. According to Collingwood, every 'statement' is logically an answer to a question, and (generally) a question only arises on the presupposition of a statement. There are, however, some presuppositions of questions (hence of the answers to them) that are not statements.

These are absolute presuppositions (*vs.* 'relative presuppositions', which are 'statements') from which the holder thinks legitimate questions arise, but which have no truth value and for which no reasons can be given as they do not rest on any presuppositions themselves.

Up to a point, Kant's fundamental principles[4] are like Collingwood's absolute presuppositions, for he tells us that

> [i]mmediately certain judgments [or 'elementary propositions'] *a priori* can be called principles, insofar as other judgments are proved from them, but they themselves cannot be subordinated to any other [hence are 'unprovable', i.e., 'indemonstrable'].[5] On this account they are also called *principles* (beginnings). (Jäsche Logic AK 9:110)

But Kant says that fundamental principles are immediately certain judgments a priori. He can only agree to fundamental principles being Collingwoodian absolute presuppositions if he holds that what makes judgments immediately 'certain' judgments a priori is that they are commitments of a human agent the immediate

---

4 Kant tends not to qualify principles as fundamental *vs* non-fundamental, though he is not always consistent about this (at least by implication).
5 Because Kant is very insistent that we cannot prove or demonstrate (fundamental) principles, thus cannot demonstrate or prove the categorical imperative, we have scrupulously tried to avoid such locutions in favour of 'justifying' or 'establishing' the existence of the categorical imperative (to which Kant has no objection). This said, it is central to our interpretation that Kant has no objection to the claim that to justify/establish the existence of the categorical imperative is to demonstrate/prove that human agential self-understanding strictly requires human agents to accept that the categorical imperative exists. In fact, Kant often refers to 'proving' the reality of free will or of pure reason being practical, etc. When he does so, he is not contradicting himself. What he is claiming to prove is that human agential self-understanding strictly requires acceptance of free will, pure practical reason, etc.

certainty of which is constituted by the fact that the human agent is committed to them and refuses to accept any statements that do not presuppose them. In other words, their certainty is constituted by being held as absolutely dogmatic commitments. But this renders their certainty an empirical psychological construct, and the categorical imperative a heteronomous principle, which Kant holds to be a self-contradictory idea. Unlike Collingwood, Kant thinks that fundamental principles are certain in the sense of being rationally indubitable, because the fundamental principles of human agential self-understanding (the maxims of the *sensus communis*) are rationally necessary due to being presuppositions of the very possibility of querying the rational status of any practical precepts (and even of any synthetic statements). As such, they establish themselves in human agential self-understanding, which is a frame beyond which it is unintelligible for agents to think they can step. It is this that Kant means when he says that it is

> no censure of our deduction of the supreme principle of morality, but a reproach that must be brought against human reason in general that it cannot make comprehensible as regards its absolute necessity an unconditional practical law . . . through a condition.
> (*GMM* AK 4:463)

It is not the fact that the categorical imperative is absolutely rationally necessary that cannot be comprehended. What is incomprehensible is that it can be thought to be absolutely necessary on the basis of a condition external to itself. Ware misses the irony in Kant's statement. He takes Kant to be saying that it is a reproach to be brought against the powers of human reason that they cannot establish that the categorical imperative is absolutely necessary. In fact, Kant is saying that the categorical imperative is absolutely rationally necessary because it is incomprehensible to reproach the powers of human reason in relation to the question of the existence of the categorical imperative (because the categorical imperative is the principle of the powers of human reason, and these powers must be presupposed and employed in order to bring any reproach against themselves). And, do we really need to add that it is just this that makes the categorical imperative the (sole) fact of pure reason?

From Kant's point of view, Collingwood's theory escapes the indefinite regress horn of the Pyrrhonian Dilemma of the Criterion only to be impaled on the question-begging horn. This is because there can be no rational debate between two persons who are committed to different absolute presuppositions. From the point of view of each person who does not adopt the same absolute presuppositions, the other necessarily begs the question, and that is the end of the matter. Collingwood will respond that, because absolute presuppositions are neither true nor false, different absolute presuppositions do not even contradict, even when they say incompatible things. Thus, their proponents do not beg any questions against the other, as different absolute presuppositions regulate entirely incommensurable world views.

But this raises the question as to how adherents of different absolute presuppositions can possibly know that they adopt different absolute presuppositions. And Kant's view is that they cannot without presupposing some common principles, and that (if the purported absolute presuppositions are not purely formal and take an object) the common principles necessarily are the three maxims of human agential self-understanding.[6]

Ware on Kant's use of the Experimental Method in Chemistry

According to Ware (2014), the focus of Kant's generation of a priori synthetic propositions is examples like the gallows scenario presented to the lustful man (*CPrR* AK 5:30), in relation to which Kant exhorts us to conduct thought experiments analogous to experiments in chemistry.

> In my understanding, the aim of Kant's thought experiment is to elicit this fact [the fact that people can come to deliberate without letting empirical motives enter into their maxims] from the reader, so that he or she may see how people separate duty from self-interest as if the two were unmixable chemical compounds.[7] In this respect, when we work through the steps of the experiment, we take up a deliberative perspective available to all rational beings. And that is why Kant thinks we have grounds to treat moral consciousness 'as a fact that precedes all subtle reasoning about its possibility' (AK 5:91), deciding that it must spring from a pure faculty within us. Beyond this, we do not need a

---

6 See Beyleveld 1975, for a critique of Collingwood's theory along these lines. We also consider that Kant would not accept that contradictions presuppose statements capable of being true or false. He regards them as functions of incompatible meanings/understandings. Thus, he would not regard the principles of truth-functional logical calculi as fundamental principles of understanding. As Kant views the principle of contradiction, insofar as it is a *fundamental* principle, it specifies what it means to affirm, deny, and conjoin anything in thought. So, he would regard the propositional calculus, because it operates with a specific concept of valid inference (material implication) that is truth functional, as against the concept of conceptual entailment (which is not truth functional), as a calculus with limited application. In other words, he considers the semantic principle of contradiction to be a law of all thought and would consider the principle of contradiction of the propositional calculus and other truth-functional calculi to be only a law of truth-functional thought.

7 This is far from clear. Unmixable compounds cannot be separated, because they can only be separated if they can be mixed in the first place.

> long, complex strategy of proof. The *Tatsache* of moral consciousness shows that reason can be practical of itself, and 'all subtle reasoning against its possibility being practical is futile' (AK 5:3). (Ware 2014, 12–13)

On this account, the fact of reason is the fact that agents are necessarily able to think of themselves as possessing pure practical reason. This is true, if we add 'by virtue of exercising their a priori powers of human agential self-understanding'. But, in any event, Kant believes that it is not only possible for pure reason to be practical. He claims that pure reason necessarily is practical. The moral law, by being the sole fact of pure reason, does not announce itself as something that agents *are permitted to* recognize; it announces itself as something that all agents *unconditionally ought to* adopt. As we pointed out in Chapter Five, the fact that agents have reason, the fact that moral consciousness is a fact of this fact (a fact of reason), and the fact that the moral law is the sole fact of pure reason (sole fact of the fact of reason) are three distinct a priori facts related a priori in and by human agential self-understanding and none of them is an empirical fact. Ware's account fails to recognize this dynamic and locates the fact of reason/sole fact of pure reason in the wrong fact in the wrong way.

If there is one thing that explains Ware's failure to comprehend Kant's argument, it is this. By not understanding that Kant's argument is one from and within human agential self-understanding in the way in which we have explained it, he fails to recognize that the base upon which the intelligibility claim (*SIII*) works is the conjunction of *SI* with *SII*. Insofar as Ware does perhaps recognize *SI*, he still fails to appreciate the central role that the quasi-ontological inference of *SII* plays in Kant's justification, or even that it plays any role. But Kant is explicit in his use of this inference; it is needed to explain the use he makes of his derivation of free will; and he is adamant that the categorical imperative governs the wills of all human agents. As we have shown, Kant's attachment to all these features is persistent. There is also no basis for thinking that Kant thinks that they are not consistent with each other, or that Kant does not take them all seriously. So why does Ware's analysis ignore or downplay them? We do not know. Perhaps it is because he considers some of them to involve invalid reasoning and wants to read Kant as charitably as he thinks is possible. But, as we have insisted throughout, even if they do involve invalid reasoning, they are still essential components of Kant's justification of the categorical imperative. To be charitable to Kant it is necessary to interpret him according to commitments that he firmly and clearly holds. And this is what we have attempted to do.

Chapter Nine
How Valid is Kant's Argument?

We have tried to avoid our personal views about the validity of Kant's argument affecting our interpretation. When Kant is not explicit about things, or there is some ambiguity in his text, we have felt free to attribute views to him on the basis of what we think he ought to be saying *on his own terms*. But there is a big difference between charitable construction and attributing views that, no matter how well they are rationally supported, are alien to Kant's philosophy. The difference, however, is not always easy for the interpreter to see. So, to assist the reader to see where our predilections lie, and how they might have influenced our reading, we will conclude with a brief and schematic sketch of our own critical evaluation of Kant's argument. These comments should be taken to do no more than orientate our own thinking to what we have portrayed as Kant's. We make no attempt to justify them fully. We assert some without offering any justification; and some of our comments are mere suggestions, involving issues over which we ourselves are not wholly agreed.

Our Agreements with Kant

We have argued that, at the heart of Kant's argument is the idea that there are a priori rules rooted in the agential self-understanding of any heteronomously affected agent that are not only the key to what human beings can claim to hold practically, but also to what they can claim to know/judge theoretically and aesthetically. All human thought and knowledge about objects is limited by a priori rules that are constructions or presuppositions of human agential self-understanding.[1] We agree, and we also agree with Kant's response to those who question this on either Humean internalist or moral realist externalist grounds. This is to say that we also think that holding oneself bound by hypothetical imperatives or a priori moral intuitions can be rendered intelligible only on the presupposition that one is capable of understanding the concept of a categorical imperative. In order to understand what it is to be a human agent, an agent who necessarily is subject to hypothetical imperatives, Agnes must understand what an imperative is, and to understand this requires her to understand what a categorical imperative is.

---

[1] For an excellent analysis of this, see Wayne Waxman 2014.

https://doi.org/10.1515/9783110691344-009

Given this, we also have no difficulty with the claim that, if Agnes understands the concept of a categorical imperative, then she must think that it is categorically imperative for her to eschew all practical precepts that are contrary to any imperative that has the character of a categorical imperative. We also accept that Kant's FUL describes the formal character of a categorical imperative, that it is identifiable as such simply by understanding the concept of a categorical imperative, and (on the sole proviso that the idea of a categorical imperative is not incoherent) that it can be applied to the conditions of human life to distinguish what is permissible from what is not.[2] In short, we consider that Kant has established that the FUL is the supreme principle of morality/pure practical reason and the categorical imperative for human agents, provided only that the concept of a categorical imperative is coherent, which it must be if the concept of human agential self-understanding is coherent. Furthermore, we agree that it is coherent because its coherence cannot be questioned without employing the powers of human agential self-understanding.

Our Disagreements with Kant

It is from this point on that we begin to have difficulties with Kant's argument, and these difficulties have implications for the further specification of the categorical imperative, for Kant's theses about God and human immortality, and for his philosophical anthropology. The simplest way to describe what our difficulties are is to say what mistakes we think Kant makes, on which basis we will be able to indicate very briefly and schematically why we think Kant errs on his own basic terms, which we consider coincide with our own.

We think that Kant is wrong when he says that:

(A) The FoH is a formula for the categorical imperative *if* it is interpreted as categorically prohibiting suicide unless to save one's own life or the life of another, which Kant does at, e.g., *GMM* AK 4:429.

(B) Free will (conceived to be a noumenal property linked to human immortality) (*Wille*) is reciprocal to the moral law and a/the *ratio essendi* of the moral law as the categorical imperative.

(C) The existence of God and human immortality are postulates of pure practical reason, meaning that belief (faith) in God and human immortality is a strict requirement of human agential self-understanding for practical purposes.

---

2 Which is not to say that we agree with the way in which he thinks it is to be applied.

Instead, on Kant's own fundamental premises, the sound exposition of the requirements of human agential self-understanding strictly requires human agents to hold the following.

(a) They may do anything to themselves *unless* so doing (i) would endanger the abilities of others to act in accord with the requirements of their own agential self-understanding, and/or (ii) implicates failure to respect a need to preserve and develop their own capacities for agential self-understanding within the context of any actions they might engage in. These conditions underpin a complex set of duties, perfect and imperfect, to oneself and others. However, they do not support an unconditional perfect duty to oneself to defend one's own life *when* one's life is understood in terms of the conditions for one's continued physical existence. Agnes's agential self-understanding imposes a duty on her to respect her life only in the sense of requiring her to recognize that she (and all other finite embodied agents) have inalienable rights of control over the necessary material conditions for their lives under the will conception of rights, which is to say that it empowers Agnes to release Brian from the duties Agnes must think Brian has to Agnes that are reciprocal to Agnes's rights to the necessary material conditions for her life. So, it does not impose a perfect duty on Agnes to protect her bodily existence and the conditions for it *except* (as Kant has it) when this is necessary to respect the rights of other agents. Agnes's agential self-understanding, her *intelligible* existence as a human agent, not her physical existence as a finite embodied being, is what must be regarded wholly unconditionally by Agnes to be an end in itself.

(b) Having the powers of human agential self-understanding (soundly using which requires Agnes to entertain the *possibility* of free willl as a noumenal property *together with* the *possibility* of determinism, hence to refrain from either believing or disbelieving the existence of either) is the *ratio essendi* of the moral law as the categorical imperative.

(c) *If* human agential self-understanding postulates the possibility of the *summum bonum*, then, at most, it strictly requires Agnes to hope that God and human immortality exist. As such, it not only reveals that knowledge of God and human immortality is impossible, but requires (contrary to Kant) both faith (belief) and disbelief in God and human immortality to be eschewed practically as well as theoretically. In other words, it requires radical agnosticism as against either theism or atheism. *If,* on the other hand, it is not clear that the categorical imperatives postulates the possibility of the *summum bonum*, or if the postulation of the *summum bonum* does not even require hope that God and human immortality exist, then there is no justification for assigning the ideas of God and human immortality any significant role in explaining the status of the categorical imperative.

The problem with Kant's Formula of Humanity as a formula for the categorical imperative

We agree with Kant that, as a finite embodied agent, Agnes (by understanding what it is for her to act) necessarily has the idea of a hypothetical imperative. Consequently, she cannot understand what it is for her to be an agent unless she understands the concept of a hypothetical imperative. However, the idea of a hypothetical imperative is that of an imperative governed by the 'Principle of Hypothetical Imperatives' (PHI):

> If doing X (or having Y) is necessary for Agnes to pursue or achieve her chosen purpose E (or for her to act under her chosen practical precept P) then Agnes ought to do X (or defend/pursue having Y), *unless and only unless* she is willing to give up E (or P).

But the idea that Agnes ought to do S *unless and only unless* something else Z, is the idea that it is *unconditionally* true that she *categorically* ought to do S *unless* Z. It is the idea that if Z does not apply then Agnes unconditionally must do S. She cannot understand what it is for something to be conditional if she does not understand what it is for something to be unconditional. So, understanding the idea of a hypothetical imperative requires Agnes to have and understand the concept of a categorical imperative, and (because understanding the concept of a hypothetical imperative is a strict requirement of her agential self-understanding) so too is understanding the concept of a categorical imperative and acceptance of the PHI. Given that acceptance of a strict requirement of her agential self-understanding is categorically imperative for her, and that there can be only one categorical imperative for her, anything that Agnes must accept by virtue of understanding the concept of a categorical imperative (e.g., the FUL) must be structured in terms of the PHI. Now, because there are means (conditions), such as her life, that Agnes must possess that are necessary for her to act at all or to act successfully regardless of her chosen purposes or practical precepts, it follows that it is a strict requirement of Agnes's agential self-understanding that she categorically must accept (e.g.)

> I (Agnes) categorically ought to act consistently with preservation of my life, *unless* I am willing to forfeit my ability to act.

But, because Agnes cannot understand the concept of a categorical imperative without accepting the FUL, she must accept

> I (Agnes) categorically ought to act consistently with the preservation of the life of every agent who is not willing to forfeit his/her/its ability to act.

However, because life is only one (albeit the most fundamental) example of an unconditionally necessary instrumental condition of finite embodied action, and Agnes represents any finite embodied agent, the categorical imperative is more properly expressed as

All finite embodied agents categorically ought to act consistently with the preservation of the unconditionally necessary instrumental conditions of action (conditions the absence of which has some negative impact on one's ability to act or act successfully, regardless of one's purposes) of all finite embodied agents, unless the agents affected by their actions are willing to forfeit their ability to act to the extent that not possessing these conditions will (regardless of their purposes) negatively affect their ability to act or act successfully.[3]

Kant's FoH states that Agnes must always treat humanity in her own person and in the person of all other agents never merely as a means but always at the same time as an end (i.e., always as an end in itself). This is fine *only if* the command to treat humanity in a person as an end in itself is the command to treat the strict requirements of the agential self-understanding of all human agents as ends in themselves and never to subordinate these requirements to ends that are not strict requirements of human agential self-understanding. In so doing, however, it must be recognized that the strict requirements of human agential self-understanding must be in accord with the PHI, as human agential self-understanding reveals this to be the only form in which a categorically binding 'ought' can coherently be thought to be binding on a human agent.

Whether or not Kant recognizes the PHI, as we have defined it, is a matter of conjecture. He claims that

> Whoever wills the end also wills (insofar as reason has decisive influence on his actions) the indispensably necessary means to it that are within his power. (*GMM* AK 4:417)

is analytic, and some commentators refer to this proposition as 'the principle of hypothetical imperatives'. But that does not make it the PHI, for the PHI itself is not analytic. Acceptance of the PHI is a strict requirement of human agential self-understanding, and what is analytic is that acceptance of the PHI is a strict requirement of human agential self-understanding. In other words, what is contained in the concept of agency is that human agential self-understanding strictly requires agents to accept that all their practical precepts must be structured in accord with the PHI.[4] We will not go into this further here. Nor will we engage with

---

[3] This is, in our opinion, the most accurate way of stating Alan Gewirth's (1978) Principle of Generic Consistency.
[4] On which see, e.g., Beyleveld and Bos 2009, Beyleveld 2017.

discussions in the literature about just what Kant himself recognizes. What we do suggest, however, is that, if Kant does accept that acceptance of the PHI is a strict requirement of human agential self-understanding (and we think that he ought to), then he does not fully comprehend what human agential self-understanding strictly requires, for it is through the PHI that he must interpret the FoH.

Putting this in the frame of Kant's three maxims of the *sensus communis*, and specifying what it is for Agnes to regard her existence as an end in itself in the way in which we think it ought to be depicted, Kant's maxim of understanding is 'Agnes must regard her existence as the particular agent that she is as an end in itself'. The maxim of the power of judgment is 'Agnes ought to regard the existence of all other agents as an end in itself', and the maxim of reason is 'Agnes ought to regard the existence of every agent, including herself, as an end in itself', this entailing that all finite embodied agents categorically ought to act consistently with the preservation of the unconditionally necessary instrumental conditions of action of all finite embodied agents, unless the agents affected by their actions are willing to forfeit their ability to act (in the way that we have elaborated this above).

The reason why Agnes must accept the maxim of understanding is that, as a finite embodied agent, she necessarily imposes hypothetical imperatives on herself, and defines her own normative existence by the hypothetical imperatives she is prepared to accept. However, understanding this, which is necessary for her to understand what it is for her to be the particular agent that she is, strictly requires her to accept the PHI. So, given that, as a finite embodied agent, Agnes has instrumental needs that affect all her actions, understanding this strictly requires her to consider her existence as the particular agent that she is to be an end in itself.

The reason why she must accept the maxim of the power of judgment is as follows. The powers of agential self-understanding, exercise of which strictly requires Agnes to accept the maxim of understanding, are possessed by all agents (thus, also by Brian). It follows from this that the maxim of understanding strictly requires Brian to consider his existence as the particular agent that he is to be an end in itself, and also strictly requires Agnes to recognize that Brian is strictly required to consider this to be the case. However, in thinking that her existence *is* an end in itself, Agnes must think that *Brian* ought to regard *her* existence as an end in itself. At the same time, being required to strictly recognize that Brian must think that his existence is an end in itself, means that Agnes is strictly required to recognize that she cannot coherently think that Brian ought to regard her existence as an end in itself if doing so would require him to act contrary to regarding his own existence as an end in itself. Thus, Agnes must also regard

Brian's existence as an end in itself, which is to say that the maxim of understanding presupposes the maxim of the power of judgment.

From this the maxim of reason follows directly.

In this way, Agnes's understanding of herself as the particular agent that she is strictly requires her to reason in terms of the strict requirements of the agential self-understanding of all agents, which strictly requires her to accept the categorical imperative as the FoH) as we depict what it is to regard one's existence as an end in itself.[5]

Our problem with Kant's view of free will as a ratio essendi of the categorical imperative

We agree with Kant that Agnes cannot coherently think that she is bound by a categorical imperative and also believe that all her actions are by their nature the product of mechanistic causal forces that are totally beyond her control. But Kant thinks that, because there must be unity between theoretical and practical reason, even though the existence of a categorical imperative presupposes that Agnes has (the capacity for) free will yet is also subject to the universal law of mechanism, the fact that it is not possible to show that Agnes does not have free will in the sense that not having free will implies that all her actions are mechanistically determined strictly requires Agnes to believe that all her actions are (with regard to her being an intelligible being) not mechanistically determined and that she has noumenal free will and is immortal.

However, we do not consider that belief in noumenal free will is the only way to effect the unity between theoretical and practical reason that Kant rightly demands. Agnes can reconcile the presuppositions of pure practical reason with those of pure theoretical reason by neither believing nor disbelieving that she has noumenal free will, by doubting both the existence and the nonexistence of noumenal free will.

Agnes must believe that her will is free only in the sense of not believing that it is necessarily mechanistically determined (not to be confused with believing that her will is necessarily not mechanistically determined), which we can designate as believing that it is not impossible that she has noumenal free will. This, of course, raises the question as to whether merely doubting whether or not she has noumenal free will is adequate to constitute the *ratio essendi* of a categorical imperative. We do not see why it is inadequate unless one considers the existence of

---

5 See further Beyleveld 2013.

a categorical imperative to be a construct of being an agent rather than a matter of understanding, cognition of a categorical imperative being a matter of cognition of what exists external to understanding rather than of cognition of what is constituted by and in understanding. In other words, we consider that the proper way to think the *metaphysical* possibility of things being otherwise that is required by '"ought" implies "can"' is in terms of necessarily certain uncertainty about the noumenal nature of things.

As such, the maxim of reason, which is a synthesis of the maxim of the understanding with the maxim of the power of judgment, unifies theoretical and practical reason by rendering the maxims of understanding and the power of judgment consistent *with each other,* whereas Kant (in effect) views this synthesis as being arrived at by subordination of the maxim of understanding to the maxim of the power of judgment.[6]

Our thoughts in this direction are, but rather more tentatively, also driven by reflecting on the ideas of freedom/autonomy implicit in acceptance of the PHI as a strict requirement of human agential self-understanding. The kind of freedom that the PHI itself presupposes, the ability to choose between means and ends when they are in conflict, is an ability to act voluntarily (the possession of Willkür). The kind of freedom presupposed by the ability to act in accord with the PHI is the ability to act on the strict requirements of human agential self-understanding. Now, as Kant himself appreciates, to act voluntarily is to act with the feeling that one is in control of one's actions, but that one can have this feeling even if it is entirely the result of mechanistic causes. At the same time, when one acts in accord with the strict requirements of human agential self-understanding, one might not be acting on the basis of human agential self-understanding, but as the result of mechanistic causal forces. But the two cases differ in that voluntary decisions can be mechanistically caused whereas actions *for the sake of* human agential self-understanding cannot coherently be thought to be so. Because there must be unity between theoretical and practical reason, it seems to us that the idea of freedom that characterizes action under the categorical imperative must be consistent with both the idea of voluntariness (which enables a categorical imperative to be an imperative) and the idea of autonomy connected to the idea of a categorical imperative as categorical. In our opinion, this idea can only be instantiated ontologically as reference to a state of irresolvable doubt about whether or not one has noumenal free will.[7]

---

[6] Evidenced by his holding that *'homo noumenon'* (Agnes as an *'intelligible being'*) gives the law to *'homo phaenomenon'* (Agnes as a *'natural'* or *'sensible being'*) (*MoM* AK 6:417–418).

[7] According to Jochen Bojanowski (2017, 63 fn 15), Kant operates with negative and positive concepts of free will both theoretically and practically, and it is an error to see the spontaneity

Another way of putting all of this is as follows. In our opinion, given that the *ratio cognoscendi* of the categorical imperative is human agential self-understanding, the *ratio essendi* of the categorical imperative is being a human agent. But being a human agent is not constituted by having noumenal free will, for this ignores that a categorical imperative only applies to heteronomously affected agents. It is also not constituted by having noumenal free will *and* being mechanistically determined either, for this idea is a contradiction in terms. According to Kant, it is constituted by having noumenal free will and appearing (and only appearing) to be mechanistically determined. But (because Kant links heteronomy to mechanistic causation) does this not imply that human agents only appear to be bound by a categorical imperative as it seems to imply that they only appear to be heteronomously affected? Consequently, for human agents to be genuinely bound by the categorical imperative, their heteronomy and autonomy must be thought of as equally real. The only way we think this can be done is to conceive of their autonomy (viewed in terms of noumenal free will), not as denial of genuine heteronomy (viewed as mechanistically determined), but merely as the non-affirmability of autonomy (viewed in terms of noumenal free will), and heteronomy, not as denial of autonomy (viewed in terms of noumenal free will), but as the non-affirmability of heteronomy (viewed as mechanistically determined). In other words, the *ratio essendi* of the categorical imperative must be constituted by human agential existence being constituted by the possession of powers that render *both* noumenal free willnoumenal free will and mechanistically determined heteronomy no more, *and no less*, than possibilities in human agential self-understanding.

Our problems with the existence of God and human immortality as practical postulates

It follows from what we have just said that *if* Kant is right that the existence of a categorical imperative postulates the possibility of the *summum bonum*, then the

---

he associates with theoretical reason as purely negative, with the free will he associates with morality being purely positive. Negative theoretical freedom is freedom from mechanistic causes. Positive theoretical freedom is being the first self-cause in a series of mechanistic causes. Negative free will is independence from heteronomous sources. Positive free will (Wille) is the capacity to act from pure practical reason. This is correct and helpful. In these terms, our view is that the possibility of negative free will is a *ratio essendi* of the categorical imperative when coupled with the mere possibility of positive free will (the latter necessarily being coupled with the mere possibility of determination by mechanistic causes).

categorical imperative as the law of human agential self-understanding strictly requires noumenal free will, human immortality, the existence of God and the *summum bonum* all to be accorded the same status. If to hope that X is to desire that X but to be uncertain about the existence of X (in the sense of neither believing nor disbelieving that X is the case), then being strictly required to desire that X be the case, whilst being strictly required to be uncertain as to whether or not X is the case, means being strictly required to hope that X is the case. Thus, if the possibility of the *summum* bonum is postulated, then it is arguable that human agential self-understanding, in strictly requiring all agents to accept that there is a categorical imperative, strictly requires them to hope (and do no more than hope) that they have noumenal free will, are immortal, that God exists, and that the *summum bonum* will be brought about. On this basis, agents ought to be neither theists nor atheists but radical agnostics (i.e., both theoretical and practical agnostics) about *all* noumenal matters. To use Kant's terminology, only on this basis can thinking in accord with oneself be thought distinctly.

When Kant says that Agnes must have faith that, e.g., God exists, he means that she must take the proposition 'God exists' to be true for practical purposes, by which he means that Agnes must take it to be true for the sake of having a coherent practical viewpoint governed by the categorical imperative. What then, for practical purposes, is the difference between having faith that God exists and distinctly hoping that God exists? What action, in relation to the idea of God, does distinctly hoping that God exists require? It does not require acting as though God exists. This is what having faith in God requires. It also does not merely require acting in accord with the categorical imperative, for that does not require any belief *about* God. Instead, it requires acting on the supposition that God *might* exist. To do so is to act on the supposition that action to bring about the *summum bonum* is not hopeless, and this is equivalent to acting on the supposition that one's existence does ultimately have a meaning, a value (that one can never comprehend fully), for the whole Kantian project, as we see it, rests on the idea that human beings can only have and construct any meaning within the frame governed by human agential self-understanding.[8]

But if the existence of a categorical imperative does not postulate the possibility of the *summum bonum*, then it seems to us that no cognitive value in relation to moral theory, indeed in relation to philosophical anthropology, must be assigned to ideas of God or human immortality at all. Kant's claim (e.g., *CPuR* A817–819; B 845–847) that it is only on the basis of having moral consciousness

---

[8] For further thoughts in this direction see especially Beyleveld 2012, Beyleveld and Ziche 2015, and Beyleveld 2016.

that the ideas of God and human immortality can arise must then be recognized as false or at least unjustified, with the consequence that engagement with the ideas of God and human immortality are unnecessary for human agential self-understanding. Because such an eventuality negates the rational necessity of agnosticism, it rescues both atheism and theism from a charge of irrationality and categorizes both as matters of non-rational commitment. However, this raises questions about the role these commitments can play in the life of a rational agent, and this is a question that certainly goes beyond the scope of this book, and upon which we do not fully agree.

In any event, whichever line on the *summum bonum* is correct, we contend that Kant cannot be right that faith in God is a rationally necessary commitment as a strict requirement of human agential self-understanding.

Our general thought is this. There is a clear tension between Kant's claims (on the one hand) that agents can become aware of the idea of a categorical imperative as soon as they draw up maxims for themselves (by abstraction from the idea of a hypothetical imperative) and the idea of free will as built into the idea of a categorical imperative, and his claims (on the other hand) that the moral law *as such* (the law of a free will) gives the categorical imperative to human agents and that acting in accordance with the law of free will represents the true nature of human agents. In our opinion, the latter view underpins his view that faith in God and human immortality is unconditionally rationally necessary, whereas the former view permits (at most) only the view that hope that God exists and human agents are immortal is rationally necessary, and we consider that the logic of his argument for the categorical imperative relies on the former view.

Bibliography

Allison, Henry E. (1990). *Kant's Theory of Freedom*, Cambridge: Cambridge University Press.
Ameriks, Karl. (1981). 'Kant's Deduction of Freedom and Morality'. *Journal of the History of Philosophy*, 19(1): 53–79.
Beck, Lewis White. (1960a). A Commentary on Kant's *Critique of Practical Reason*. Chicago: University of Chicago Press.
Beck, Lewis White. (1960b). 'The Fact of Reason: An Essay in Justification in Ethics.' Translated from 'Das Faktum der Vernunft: Zur Rechtfertigungsproblematik in der Ethik' *Kant-Studien* 52: 271–282. In Lewis White Beck: *Studies in the Philosophy of Kant*, 200–214. Indianapolis: Bobbs-Merrill.
Bell, David. (1987). 'The Art of Judgement'. *Mind* 96 (382): 221–244.
Berger, Peter L., and Luckmann, Thomas. (1966). *The Social Construction of Reality. A Treatise in the Sociology of Knowledge*. Garden City, New York: Doubleday.
Beyleveld, Deryck. (1975). *Epistemological Foundations of Sociological Theory*. Unpublished PhD Dissertation, University of East Anglia.
Beyleveld, Deryck. (1991). *The Dialectical Necessity of Morality: An Analysis and Defense of Alan Gewirth's Argument to the Principle of Generic Consistency*. Chicago: University of Chicago Press.
Beyleveld, Deryck. (1999). 'Gewirth and Kant on Justifying the Supreme Principle of Morality.' In Michael Boylan (ed.): *Gewirth: Critical Essays on Action, Rationality, and Community*, 97–117. New York and London: Rowman and Littlefield.
Beyleveld, Deryck. (2012). 'Hope and Belief.' In R. J. Jenkins and E. Sullivan (eds.): *Philosophy of Mind*, 1–36. New York: Nova Science Publishers.
Beyleveld, Deryck. (2013). 'Williams' False Dilemma: How to Give Categorically Binding Impartial Reasons to Real Agents.' *Journal of Moral Philosophy* 10(2): 204–226.
Beyleveld, Deryck. (2015). 'Korsgaard v. Gewirth on Universalization: Why Gewirthians are Kantians and Kantians Ought to be Gewirthians.' *Journal of Moral Philosophy* 12(5): 573–597.
Beyleveld, Deryck. (2016). 'Gewirth vs Kant on Kant's Maxim of Reason: Towards a Gewirthian Philosophical Anthropology.' In Per Bauhn (ed.): *Gewirthian Perspectives on Human Rights*, 13–29. Abingdon, Oxford: Routledge.
Beyleveld, Deryck. (2017). 'Transcendental Arguments for a Categorical Imperative as Arguments from Agential Self-Understanding.' In Jens Peter Brune, Robert Stern, and Micha Werner (eds.) *Transcendental Arguments in Moral Theory*, 141–159. Berlin: De Gruyter.
Beyleveld, Deryck, and Bos, Gerhard. (2009). 'The Foundational Role of the Principle of Instrumental Reason in Alan Gewirth's Argument to the Principle of Generic Consistency: A Response to Andrew Chitty.' *King's Law Journal* 20(1): 1–20.
Beyleveld Deryck, and Brownsword, Roger. (2001). *Human Dignity in Bioethics and Biolaw*. Oxford: Oxford University Press.
Beyleveld Deryck, and Ziche, Paul. (2015). 'Towards a Kantian Phenomenology of Hope.' *Ethical Theory and Moral Practice*. 18(5): 927–942.
Bojanowski, Jochen. (2006). *Kant's Theorie der Freiheit: Rekonstruktion und Rehabilitierung. (Kant's Theory of Freedom: Reconstruction and Rehabilitation.)* Berlin/New York: De Gruyter.

Bojanowski, Jochen. (2017). 'Kant on the Justification of Moral Principles.' *Kant-Studien*. 108(1): 55–88.
Chung, Kenneth K.H. (2010). Kant and the Fact of Reason. https://ir.lib.uwo.ca/etd/5.
Collingwood, Robin George. (1940). *An Essay on Metaphysics*. Oxford: Clarendon Press.
Darwall, Stephen. (2006). *The Second-Person Standpoint: Morality, Respect and Accountability*. Cambridge, MA: Harvard University Press.
Dilthey, Wilhelm. (1989). *Introduction to the Human Sciences. Selected Works Vol. I*. Rudolf A. Makkreel and Frithjof Rodi, (eds.). Princeton NJ: Princeton University Press.
Düring, Dascha, and Düwell, Marcus. (2017). 'Hope, Agency, and Aesthetic Sensibility: A Response to Beyleveld's Account of Kantian Hope.' In Patrick Capps and Shaun D. Pattinson (eds.): *Ethical Rationalism and the Law*, 55–71. Oxford: Hart Publishing.
Düwell, Marcus. (2017). 'Transcendental Arguments and Practical Self-Understanding: Gewirthian Perspectives.' In Jens Peter Brune, Robert Stern, and Micha Werner (eds.) *Transcendental Arguments in Moral Theory*, 161–178. Berlin: De Gruyter.
Enoch, David. (2006). 'Agency, Shmagency: Why Normativity Won't Come from What is Constitutive of Action.' *Philosophical Review*, 115(2): 169–198.
Enoch, David. (2011). 'Shmagency Revisited.' In Michael Brady (ed.): *New Waves in Metaethics*, 208–233. Palgrave Macmillan.
Gadamer, Hans-Georg. (2013). *Truth and Method*. Trans. Joel Weinsheimer and Donald G. Marshall. London: Bloomsbury Academic.
Gewirth, Alan. (1978). *Reason and Morality*. Chicago: University of Chicago Press.
Gewirth, Alan. (1999). 'Replies to My Colleagues.' In Michael Boylan (ed.): *Gewirth: Critical Essays on Action, Rationality and Community*. Lanham: Rowman and Littlefield, 191–213.
Grenberg, Jeanine. (2013). *Kant's Defense of Common Human Experience: A Phenomenological Account*. Cambridge: Cambridge University Press.
Guyer, Paul. (2007). *Kant's Groundwork for the Metaphysics of Morals: A Reader's Guide*. London: Routledge.
Heidegger, Martin. (2010). *Being and Time*. Trans. Joan Stambaugh. Revised and with a Foreword by Dennis J. Schmidt. Albany, New York: The State University of New York Press.
Henrich, Dieter. (1960). 'Der Begriff der sittlichen Einsicht und Kants Lehre vom Faktum der Vernunft.' In Dieter Henrich, W. Schulz and K-H Volkmann-Schluck (eds.): *Die Gegenwart der Griechen im neueren Denken. Festschrift für Hans-Georg Gadamer zum 60. Geburtstag*, 130–172. Tübingen: Mohr Siebeck.
Henrich, Dieter. (1975). 'Die Deduktion des Sittengesetzes. Über die Gründe der Dunkelheit des letzten Abschnittes von Kants 'Grundlegung zur Metaphysik der Sitten.' In Alexander Schwaan (ed.): *Denken im Schatten des Nihilismus*. Festschrift für Wilhelm Weischedel, Darmstadt: Wissenschaftliche Buchgesellschaft, 55–112.
Henrich, Diether. (1989). 'Kant's Notion of a Deduction and the Methodological Background of the First Critique.' In Eckhart Forster (ed.): *Kant's Transcendental Deductions*. Stanford: Stanford University Press, 29–46.
Hill, Thomas E. Jr. (1998). Kant's Argument for the Rationality of Moral Conduct.' In Paul Guyer (ed.): *Kant's Groundwork of the Metaphysics of Morals: Critical Essays*, 249–272. New York, NY: Rowman & Littlefield.
Kant, Immanuel. (1777). *Blomberg Logic*. In Paul Guyer and Allen W. Wood (eds). *Lectures on Logic*. The Cambridge Edition of the Works of Immanuel Kant. 2009.
Kant, Immanuel. (1781). *Critique of Pure Reason*. First edition. Second edition 1787. Edited and translated by Norman Kemp-Smith. London: Macmillan. 1933.

Kant, Immanuel. (1785). *Groundwork of the Metaphysics of Morals*. Edited and translated by Mary Gregor. Cambridge Texts in the History of Philosophy. 1998. Edited and translated by Mary Gregor and Jens Timmermann 2012. Cambridge: Cambridge University Press.
Kant, Immanuel. (1786). 'What Does It Mean to Orient Oneself in Thinking?' In A. Wood and G. Di Giovanni (eds.): *Religion and Rational Theology*. The Cambridge Edition of the Works of Immanuel Kant. Cambridge: Cambridge University Press, 1–18. 1996.
Kant, Immanuel. (1788). *Critique of Practical Reason*. Edited and translated by Mary Gregor. Cambridge Texts in the History of Philosophy. Cambridge: Cambridge University Press. 1997.
Kant, Immanuel. (1790). *Critique of the Power of Judgment*. 1st edition. 2nd Edition 1793. 2nd edition together with the first Introduction, edited by Paul Guyer, and translated by Paul Guyer and Eric Matthews. Cambridge Edition of the Works of Immanuel Kant. Cambridge: Cambridge University Press. 2000.
Kant, Immanuel. (1793). *Religion within the Boundaries of Mere Reason*. In Allen Wood and George di Giovanni (eds,) *Kant: Religion Within the Boundaries of Mere Reason and Other Writings*. Cambridge Texts in the History of Philosophy. 1998.
Kant, Immanuel. (1797). *Metaphysics of Morals*. Edited and translated by Mary Gregor. Cambridge Texts in the History of Philosophy. Cambridge: Cambridge University Press. 1996.
Kant, Immanuel. (1798). *Anthropology from a Practical Point of View*. Robert B. Louden (ed). Cambridge Texts in the History of Philosophy. Cambridge: Cambridge University Press. 2006.
Kant, Immanuel. (1800). *Jäsche Logic*. In Paul Guyer and Allen W. Wood (eds). *Lectures on Logic*. The Cambridge Edition of the Works of Immanuel Kant. 2009.
Kleingeld, Pauline. (2010). 'Moral Consciousness and the "Fact of Reason."' In Andrews Reath and Jens Timmermann (eds.): *Kant's Critique of Practical Reason. A Critical Guide*. Cambridge: Cambridge University Press, 55–72.
Kleingeld, Pauline, and Willaschek, Marcus. (2019). 'Autonomy without Paradox: Kant, Self-Legislation and the Moral Law'. *Philosophers' Imprint* 19:(6) 1–18.
Korsgaard, Christine M. (1989). 'Morality as Freedom.' In Yirmiyahu Yovel (ed.): *Kant's Practical Philosophy Reconsidered*. Dordrecht: Kluwer Academic, 23–48.
Korsgaard, Christine M. (1996a). *Sources of Normativity*. Cambridge: Cambridge University Press.
Korsgaard, Christine M. (1996b). *Creating the Kingdom of Ends*. Cambridge: Cambridge University Press.
Korsgaard, Christine M. (2002). 'Self-Constitution: Agency, Identity and Integrity.' *The Locke Lectures at Oxford University* May and June 2002. www.people.fas.harvard.edu/-korsgaard.
Longuenesse, Beatrice. (1998). *Kant and the Capacity to Judge: Sensibility and Discursivity in the Transcendental Analytic of the* 'Critique of Pure Reason.' Princeton: Princeton University Press.
Łuków, Paweł. (1993). 'The Fact of Reason: Kant's Passage to Ordinary Moral Knowledge.' *Kant-Studien* 84: 204–221.
McCarthy, Michael H. (1982). 'Kant's Rejection of the Argument of Groundwork III.' *Kant-Studien* 73: 169–190.
Makkreel, Rudolf. (1990). *Imagination and Interpretation in Kant: The Hermeneutical Import of the* Critique of Judgment. Chicago: University of Chicago Press.

Makkreel, Rudolf. (1992). *Dilthey, Philosopher of the Human Studies*. Princeton NJ: Princeton University Press.
Makkreel, Rudolf. (2015). *Orientation and Judgment in Hermeneutics*. Chicago: University of Chicago Press.
O'Neill, Onora. (1989). *Constructions of Reason: Explorations of Kant's Practical Philosophy*. Cambridge: Cambridge University Press.
O'Neill, Onora. (1992).'Vindicating Reason.' In P. Guyer (ed): *The Cambridge Companion to Kant*, Cambridge: Cambridge University Press.
O'Neill, Onora. (2002). 'Autonomy and the Fact of Reason in the Kritik der praktischen Vernunft (§§ 7–8, 30–41).' In Otfried Höffe (ed.): *Kritik der praktischen Vernunft. Klassiker Auslagen Bd. 26*, Berlin: Akademie Verlag, 81–98.
Paton, H. J. (2000). *The Categorical Imperative. A Study in Kant's Moral Philosophy*, London (originally 1947).
Proops, Ian. (2003). 'Kant's Legal Metaphor and the Nature of a Deduction.' *Journal of the History of Philosophy*. 41: 209–229.
Puls, Heiko. (2011). 'Freiheit als Unabhängigkeit von bioß subjektiv bestimmenden Ursachen – Kants Auflösuvvng des Zirkelverdachts im dritten Abschnitt der *Grundlegung zur Metaphysik der Sitten.*' (Freedom as Independence from Purely Subjective Determining Causes: Kant's Resolution of the Suspected Circle in the Third Section of *Groundwork of the Metaphysics of Morals'*). In *Zeitschrift für Philosophische Forschung* 65: 534–562.
Puls, Heiko. (2014). '*Quo errat demonstrator* – warum es in der Grundlegung eine Faktum-These gibt. Drei Argumente gegen Dieter Schöneker's Interpretation.' *(Quo errat demonstratur* – Why There is a Fact Thesis in the Groundwork: Three Arguments against Dieter Schöneker's Interpretation.') In Heiko Puls (ed.): *Kants Rechtfertigung des Sittengesetzes in Grundlegung* III: *Deducktion oder Faktum?* 15–32. Berlin: Walter de Gruyter.
Quine, Willard Von Orman. (1951).'Two Dogmas of Empiricism.' *The Philosophical Review* 60(1): 20–43.
Rawls, John. (2000). *Lectures on the History of Moral Philosophy*, edited by Barbara Herman. Cambridge/Mass, London.
Reath, Andrews. (1997). 'Introduction.' In *Critique of Pure Reason*, by Immanuel Kant, edited by Mary Gregor, vii–xxxi. Cambridge: Cambridge University Press.
Reath Andrews. (2012). 'Kant's Moral Philosophy.' In Roger Crisp (ed.): *The Oxford Handbook on the History of Ethics*, 443–464. Oxford: Oxford University Press.
Rosati, Connie. (2003). 'Agency and the Open Question Argument.' Ethics 113: 490–527.
Ross, William David. (1954). 'Kant's Ethical Theory: A Commentary on the *Grundlegung Zur Metaphysik Der Sitten.*' Oxford: Oxford University Press.
Schleiermacher, Friedrich Daniel Ernst. (1978). *Hermeneutics: The Handwritten Manuscripts*, Trans. James Duke and Jack Forstman. Oxford: Oxford University Press. Reprinted Atlanta: Scholars Press, 1986.
Schönecker, Dieter. (1999). *Kant Grundlegung III. Die Deduktion des kategorischen Imperativs. (Kant's Groundwork III. The Deduction of the Categorical Imperative)*, Freiburg, Münche: Karl Alber-Verlag.
Schönecker, Dieter. (2006). 'How Is a Categorical Imperative Possible?' In Christopher Horn and Dieter Schönecker (eds.): *Groundwork for the Metaphysics of Morals*, 301–323. Berlin: De Gruyter.

Schönecker, Dieter. (2013). 'Kant's Moral Intuitionism: The Fact of Reason and Moral Dispositions.' *Kant Studies Online* 1: 1–38.

Schönecker, Dieter. (2014). 'Warum es in der Grundlegung keine Faktum-These gibt. Drei Argumente.' ('Why There is No Fact-Thesis in the *Groundwork*. Three Arguments.') In Heiko Puls (ed.): *Kants Rechtfetigung des Sittengetzes in Grundlegung* III: *Deduction Oder Faktum?* 1–15. Berlin Walter de Gruyter.

Sextus Empiricus. (1934), *Outlines of Pyrrhonism*. Trans. Rev. R. G. Bury. Cambridge, MA: Harvard University Press.

Stagneth, Bettina. (2001). 'Das "Faktum der Vernunft". Versuch einer Ortsbestimmung.' ('The "Fact of Reason": Trying to Get One's Bearings.'). In *Akten des IX. Internationalen Kant-Kongresses, Bd. 3*. Berlin: De Gruyter, 104–122.

Steigleder, Klaus. (2002). *Kants Moralphilosophie. Die Selbstbezüglichkeit reiner praktischer Vernunft*. (*Kant's Moral Philosophy: The Self-Referential Nature of Pure Practical Reason*.) Weimar: Metzler.

Steigleder, Klaus. (2006). 'The Analytic Relationship of Freedom and Morality (GMS III, 1)'. In Christoph Horn and Dieter Schönecker (eds.): *Groundwork for the Metaphysics of Morals*. Berlin/New York: De Gruyter, 225–246.

Sussman, David. (2008). 'From Deduction to Deed: Kant's Grounding of the Moral Law.' *Kantian Review*. 13: 52–81.

Timmermann, Jens. (2010). 'Reversal or Retreat? Kant's Deductions of Freedom and Morality.' In Jens Timmermann and Andrews Reath (eds.): *Kant's Critique of Practical Reason: A Critical Guide*, 73–89. Cambridge: Cambridge University Press.

Velleman, David. (1989). *Practical Reflection*. Princeton: Princeton University Press.

Velleman, David. (2004a). 'Precis of *The Possibility of Practical Reason*.' *Philosophical Studies* 121: 225–238.

Velleman, David. (2004b). 'Replies to Discussion on *The Possibility of Practical Reason*.' *Philosophical Studies* 121: 277–298.

Ware, Owen. (2014). 'Rethinking Kant's Fact of Reason'. *Philosopher's Imprint*. 32: 1–21.

Ware, Owen. (2016). 'Skepticism in Kant's groundwork.' *European Journal of Philosophy*. 24: 375–396.

Ware, Owen. (2017). 'Kant's Deduction of Morality and Freedom.' *Canadian Journal of Philosophy*, 47(1): 116–147.

Waxman, Wayne. (2014). *Kant's Anatomy of the Intelligent Mind*. Oxford: Oxford University Press.

Waxman, Wayne. (2019). *A Guide to Kant's Psychologism: via Locke, Berkeley, Hume, and Wittgenstein*. New York/ Abingdon,Oxon: Routledge.

Weber, Max. (1997). *Sociological Writings*. Wolf Heydebrandt (ed.): London: Bloomsbury Academic.

Werner, Micha. (2002). 'Minimalistische Handlungstheorie – gescheiterte Letztbegründung: Ein Blick auf Alan Gewirth.' In Holger Burckhart and Horst Gronke (eds.): *Philosophieren aus dem Diskurs. Beiträge zur Diskurspragmatik*, 308–328.Würzburg: Königshausen & Neuman.

Westphal, Kenneth R. (2002). 'Kantian Justification of Possession.' In Mark Timmons (ed.): *Kant's Metaphysics of Morals: Interpretative Essays*. Oxford: Oxford University Press.

Westphal, Kenneth R. (2012). 'Norm Acquisition, Rational Judgment and Moral Particularism.' *Theory and Research in Education*. 10(1): 3–25.

Westphal, Kenneth R. (2016). *How Hume and Kant Reconstruct Natural Law: Justifying Strict Objectivity without Debating Moral Realism*. Oxford: Carendon Press.

Willaschek, Marcus. (1991). 'Die Tat der Vernunft. Zur Bedeutung der Kantischen These vom "Factum der Vernunft."' ('The Deed of Reason: Concerning the Meaning of Kant's Thesis of "The Fact of Reason."') In Gerhard Funke (ed.): *Akten des VII. Internationalen Kant-Kongresses Mainz 1990, Bd. II.*, 455–466. Bonn/Berlin: Bouvier.

Willaschek, Marcus. (1992). *Praktische Vernunft. Handlungstheorie und Moralbegründung bei Kant. (Practical Reason: Action Theory and the Foundations of Morality in Kant.)* Weimar: Metzler.

Williams, Terence Charles. (1968). *The Concept of the Categorical Imperative: A Study of the Place of the Categorical Imperative in Kant's Ethical Theory*. Oxford: Oxford University Press.

Wood, Allen W. (2008). *Kantian Ethics*. Cambridge: Cambridge University Press.

Wolff, Michael. (2009). 'Warum das Faktum der Vernunft ein Faktum ist. Auflösung einiger Verständnisschwierigkeiten in Kants Grundlegung der Moral.' ('The Reason Why the Fact of Reason is a Fact. Resolving Some Difficulties with Understanding Kant's Foundations of Morality.') *Deutsche Zeitschrift für Philosophie*, 57(4): 511–549.

Wolff, Michael. (2015).'Warum der kategorische Imperativ nach Kants Ansicht gültig ist. Beschreibung der Argumentationsstruktur in Dritten Abschnitt seiner Grundlegung zur Metaphysik der Sitten.' In D. Schönecker (ed.): *Kants Begründung von Freiheit und Moral in 'Grundlegung III'. Neue Interpretationen*. Paderborn: Mentis Verlag 257–320.

Subject Index

a priori concepts VI, 1, 3, 6, 7, 8, 10, 11, 13, 14, 15, 16, 18, 20, 21, 23, 25, 28, 30, 35, 36, 40, 41, 42, 48, 49, 51, 57, 58, 59, 60, 61, 63, 64, 66, 72, 74, 75, 76, 77, 78, 79, 80, 81, 83, 86, 87, 88, 89, 90, 91, 92, 93, 94, 97, 100, 101, 108, 109, 165, 172, 173, 180, 181, 183, 186
– as ground of the moral law 20, 94, 97, 102
a priori synthetic 6, 7, 8, 9, 21, 24, 29, 30, 32, 47, 52, 57, 58, 63, 65, 69, 71, 82, 101, 162, 177, 185
absolute presupposition 41, 183, 184, 185
active scepticism 175
agency 5, 12, 41, 73, 105, 106, 107, 141, 148
agential self-understanding V, VI, 1, 2, 3, 4, 5, 6, 7, 8, 9, 10, 11, 12, 14, 15, 16, 17, 18, 19, 20, 21, 22, 23, 24, 25, 27, 28, 29, 30, 32, 37, 40, 41, 43, 44, 45, 46, 50, 51, 52, 54, 55, 57, 60, 61, 62, 63, 65, 68, 69, 71, 77, 79, 81, 82, 83, 84, 90, 92, 97, 100, 105, 109, 110, 142, 151, 153, 154, 156, 160, 162, 164, 169, 170, 171, 172, 173, 178, 179, 180, 181, 182, 184, 185, 186
– and categorical imperative V, VI, 2, 3, 4, 5, 7, 8, 9, 10, 11, 14, 15, 16, 17, 18, 19, 26, 27, 28, 31, 32, 35, 37, 38, 39, 40, 41, 43, 44, 48, 49, 50, 53, 54, 64, 67, 68, 82, 85, 90, 98, 100, 103, 105, 144, 149, 150, 151, 152, 154, 155, 170, 177, 178, 179
– and rational nature 37, 44, 50, 105, 109
– as ground of the moral law 5, 7, 18, 22, 62, 90, 93, 97, 99, 109, 151, 152, 176
– as *ratio cognoscendi* of the moral law 9, 37, 91
– *and categorical imperative* 103
agnosticism 3, 10, 11
aim of *CPrR* 19, 71, 73, 84, 85
– vs *GMM* 33, 167
aim of *GMM* 2, 25, 26, 145, 152
analytic 1, 2, 5, 6, 12, 20, 41, 42, 57, 58, 59, 88, 105, 106, 179
anthropology 72
– philosophical anthropology 2, 10, 24
– practical 49

antinomy 2, 10, 14, 22, 47, 64, 89
atheism 3, 10, 11
autonomy 6, 8, 9, 20, 30, 58, 60, 61, 149, 173
– identical to free will 13
– principle of 171, 172, 173, 174

beauty 81
bi-conditional relationship between being a particular agent and being an agent at all 24, 25, 180
bon sens 77

categorical imperative V, VI, 1, 2, 3, 4, 5, 6, 7, 8, 9, 10, 11, 12, 13, 14, 15, 16, 17, 18, 19, 20, 21, 22, 23, 24, 25, 26, 27, 28, 29, 30, 31, 32, 36, 39, 41, 42, 43, 44, 46, 47, 48, 49, 50, 51, 52, 53, 54, 55, 57, 58, 59, 60, 61, 63, 64, 65, 66, 67, 68, 73, 74, 76, 77, 81, 85, 87, 88, 89, 90, 92, 93, 94, 95, 98, 101, 103, 104, 105, 106, 107, 108, 109, 110, 141, 143, 144, 145, 146, 149, 150, 151, 152, 153, 154, 155, 157, 158, 159, 160, 161, 163, 164, 165, 166, 167, 168, 169, 170, 171, 172, 173, 174, 175, 176, 177, 178, 179, 180, 183, 184, 186
– a priori synthetic proposition V, 1, 2, 6, 14, 20, 23, 26, 28, 32, 37, 43, 44, 57, 59, 65, 71, 83, 85, 101, 102, 103, 144, 149, 167, 175, 176
  – vs categorical imperative 158
– and maxim of reason 78, 81, 153, 154, 159, 161, 164, 173
– and principle of hypothetical imperatives 7, 10, 48, 49, 88, 145, 158, 159
– applies only to heteronomously affected agents VI, 8, 13, 24, 30, 37, 41, 52, 71, 101, 171
– as objective practical law 15
– can and need presuppose nothing other than itself 9, 26, 42

– criterion for 14, 16, 37, 38, 39, 40, 44, 154, 160, 174
– does not rest on any presupposition 26
– formulae for 2, 49, 64
– law for all agents 178
– only one 2, 4, 49, 53, 54
– social nature of 43
– task of justifying 19
– *vs* moral law *as such* VI, 10, 12, 18, 26, 29, 61, 65, 72, 73, 81, 105, 171, 172, 173
circularity in justifying the moral law 65
– alleged 9, 16, 99, 168
clarity 38
coherentism 40, 41
common human understanding V, VI, 10, 22, 36, 45, 69, 75, 76, 77, 88, 105
– as common sense 36
– as *sensus communis* V, VI, 75, 76, 77, 92, 100
common reason 11, 35
common sense 36, 78, 91
– *vs sensus communis* 75
comprehension 8, 9, 14, 45, 172, 176
– and levels of understanding 8, 47
– not absolute 8, 9, 42
construction of agency 61
constructivism 61
contradiction 7, 9, 16, 19, 41, 57, 59, 64, 104, 185
– in concept of a categorical imperative 59
– principle of 28, 41, 185
critique of pure practical reason 17, 28, 82

deduction 1, 2, 3, 5, 6, 7, 8, 14, 17, 21, 24, 27, 28, 29, 30, 40, 41, 65, 67, 92, 101, 102, 103, 104, 105, 106, 145, 167, 175, 176, 177, 179, 184
deed of reason 66, 150, 151
defence 14, 17, 27, 28, 33, 35, 42, 105, 106, 145
definition 2, 15, 47
determinism 3, 104, 105
dialectical necessity 5, 9
discourse theory 180
distinctness 38, 39

entailment *vs* material implication 185
explanation 6, 7, 10, 16, 26, 45, 92, 97, 104, 170, 177
– limits of 7
exposition 1, 2, 3, 14, 15, 16, 17, 21, 25, 26, 27, 28, 38, 39, 44, 47, 58, 65, 74, 101, 102, 165, 166, 167, 168, 169
– metaphysical exposition 16, 106
– metaphysical 15, 16
– transcendental exposition 16, 17
– transcendental 16
externalism 1

fact of pure reason 5, 8, 10, 26, 29, 48, 51, 53, 65, 96, 102, 109, 110, 154, 168, 170, 171, 184, 186
– implicitly in *GMM* 19, 29, 110
fact of reason 4, 21, 29, 30, 66, 67, 68, 90, 99, 100, 107, 109, 110, 141, 149, 150, 151, 166, 167, 170, 171, 186
faith 2, 3, 10, 11, 72, 73, 74, 96, 167
Faktum 66, 150, 151, 154
first-person standpoint 11, 42, 78, 79, 180
followability 11, 79
Formula of Humanity (FOH) 2, 5, 6, 7, 16, 19, 21, 49, 85, 144, 164
Formula of the Kingdom of Ends (FKE) 16
Formula of Universal Law (FUL) 1, 2, 4, 5, 10, 11, 12, 13, 14, 17, 22, 25, 26, 35, 37, 43, 47, 48, 49, 50, 52, 53, 54, 61, 64, 78, 79, 85, 94, 95, 98, 100, 101, 156, 161, 165, 172, 176
foundationalism 40, 41, 44
foundationalist coherentism 41, 42
free will V, VI, 1, 2, 3, 4, 5, 6, 7, 8, 9, 11, 13, 14, 18, 19, 20, 21, 22, 24, 26, 28, 29, 30, 51, 52, 59, 61, 63, 74, 78, 80, 82, 83, 89, 90, 91, 93, 95, 96, 97, 98, 104, 106, 146, 153, 166, 169, 170, 172, 175, 176, 181, 182, 183, 186
– as a *ratio essendi* of the categorical imperative 9, 24, 28, 52, 101, 105, 179
– derived from pure practical reason 2, 3, 4, 17, 18, 19, 21, 22, 24, 26, 29, 30, 31, 65, 97, 100, 146, 152, 153, 168, 175

– keystone to all speculative ideas 65
– noumenal 2, 3, 7, 8, 9, 10, 51, 103
– possible VI, 6, 7, 20, 21, 31, 64, 72, 74, 102, 103, 105
– *ratio essendi* of the moral law 5, 7, 16, 18, 22, 24, 26, 27, 29, 50, 52, 91, 99, 105, 155, 167
– reciprocal to the moral law 3, 4, 5, 9, 19, 20, 21, 23, 24, 26, 28, 30, 51, 58, 64, 65, 72, 80, 83, 90, 91, 92, 94, 95, 96, 106
fundamental principle of pure practical reason 167, 172
fundamental questions for philosophy 71, 72

gallows example 91, 92, 93, 185
God VI, 2, 3, 8, 9, 10, 11, 17, 18, 19, 51, 72, 73, 83, 93, 96, 97, 103, 167, 169, 170, 173
Godfaith 10, 178
good will 11, 16, 18, 42, 44, 58, 155, 173

hardened scoundrel example 92
hermeneutics 45, 46, 47
hope 3, 10, 11, 72, 74, 101, 102
humanity VI, 5, 10, 16, 73
hypothetical imperatives 1, 4, 5, 6, 7, 10, 12, 24, 48, 58, 62, 80, 88, 89, 90, 98, 142, 143, 157, 158, 159, 162, 163, 165, 172, 173, 176, 179, 181
– vs categorical imperative 7, 10, 11, 48, 49, 54, 88, 89, 90, 98, 145

I think 7
idealism 7
imagination 20, 80, 81, 170
immediate certainty 183
immortality 2, 3, 10, 11, 17, 18, 19, 51, 72, 73, 74, 80, 83, 87, 95, 96, 103, 152, 167, 169, 170, 178
intelligible world 6, 60, 63, 81, 89, 95, 147, 168
internalism (Humean) 7, 62

justification 1, 2, 3, 4, 5, 6, 8, 9, 10, 11, 12, 14, 17, 18, 19, 21, 22, 23, 24, 27, 29, 30, 31, 32, 33, 37, 40, 41, 42, 43, 44, 47, 68, 71, 73, 74, 76, 78, 87, 91, 92, 93, 94, 98, 101, 102, 141, 142, 147, 149, 151, 154, 166, 168, 171, 175, 177, 178, 186
– vs explanation 73, 94
– vs presentation 27

law of nature 13, 19, 29, 30, 64, 65, 171
legislation 100
logic 1, 11, 12, 22, 24, 26, 28, 29, 31, 32, 33, 42, 52, 57, 72, 85, 104, 145, 175

material implication 185
maxim of reason 6, 7, 8, 18, 23, 24, 44, 75, 78, 79, 81, 82, 89, 153, 154, 159, 161, 164, 173, 180
maxim of the power of judgment 6, 8, 23, 44, 46, 78, 79, 81, 89, 164, 172, 173, 180
maxim of understanding 6, 8, 23, 44, 45, 46, 78, 81, 89, 164, 172, 173, 180
maxims of the *sensus communis* 6, 10, 11, 18, 19, 22, 23, 24, 28, 32, 39, 40, 44, 46, 76, 78, 89, 98, 161, 166, 169, 174, 184
– as precepts for reaching Wisdom 75, 77
mechanistic causality 7, 8, 13, 26, 45, 61, 73, 80
moral consciousness 4, 10, 17, 22, 30, 65, 79, 83, 88, 91, 92, 93, 105, 107, 108, 109, 110, 152, 162, 185, 186
– constituted as having the concept of morality 108, 109, 170
– fact of reason 4, 17, 22, 30, 48, 91, 107, 108, 109, 152, 170, 186
moral law V, VI, 1, 2, 3, 4, 5, 7, 8, 9, 10, 11, 12, 13, 14, 16, 17, 18, 19, 20, 21, 22, 23, 24, 25, 26, 27, 28, 29, 30, 32, 36, 38, 39, 41, 42, 48, 49, 50, 51, 57, 58, 59, 60, 62, 63, 64, 65, 66, 67, 68, 72, 73, 74, 76, 80, 81, 82, 83, 84, 85, 86, 87, 88, 90, 91, 92, 93, 94, 95, 96, 97, 98, 99, 100, 101, 102, 103, 104, 105, 106, 107, 108, 109, 110, 147, 148, 151, 152, 153, 154, 155, 158, 162, 164, 165, 166, 167, 168, 169, 170, 171, 172, 173, 175, 176, 178, 179, 181, 182, 186
– as a law of nature 13, 29, 30, 171

208 —— Subject Index

negative freedom 81
noumena 2, 3, 7, 8, 9, 10, 23, 51, 60, 63, 64, 89, 103, 147

objective principles 2, 13, 15, 16, 17, 55, 156

paradox of method 42, 165
phaenomena
philosophy V, 1, 2, 3, 6, 7, 12, 15, 17, 19, 24, 25, 32, 35, 40, 42, 69, 71, 73, 76, 84, 96, 141, 142, 162, 175, 179
postulate 1, 2, 3, 9, 10, 16, 19, 20, 30, 31, 38, 44, 51, 72, 74, 80, 83, 96, 153, 155, 166, 167, 170, 172, 173
– of pure reason as a whole 51, 74, 96, 167, 172
postulate categorical imperative 3
practical reason 7, 8, 9, 10, 14, 16, 17, 18, 25, 27, 28, 29, 30, 32, 35, 36, 39, 41, 42, 52, 59, 62, 65, 68, 73, 81, 83, 92, 100, 101, 102, 108, 109, 141, 142, 145, 146, 149, 163, 164, 170, 176, 178, 182
principles 6, 10, 12, 15, 16, 30, 32, 40, 41, 49, 65, 66, 68, 69, 75, 76, 77, 82, 88, 97, 101, 102, 106, 107, 156, 157, 159, 160, 161, 162, 163, 176, 180, 181, 183, 184, 185
principle, categorical imperative as an a priori proposition 65
principle of hypothetical imperatives (PHI) 4, 5, 6, 8
product of reason 66, 68, 98
proof 97, 177, 185
public reason 43, 79
pure practical reason VI, 1, 2, 3, 4, 5, 7, 8, 9, 10, 11, 12, 13, 17, 18, 20, 21, 22, 24, 25, 26, 29, 30, 31, 41, 50, 51, 52, 58, 59, 60, 61, 62, 65, 66, 67, 68, 71, 72, 74, 81, 82, 83, 86, 87, 90, 93, 94, 96, 97, 98, 99, 100, 101, 102, 105, 108, 109, 144, 146, 148, 149, 152, 164, 165, 166, 167, 168, 169, 170, 171, 172, 173, 175, 176, 179, 183, 186
Pyrrhonian Dilemma of the Criterion (quasi-ontological reasoning) 39, 40, 42, 44, 53, 61, 98, 109, 184

ratio cognoscendi 3, 4, 5, 9, 21, 23, 24, 26, 28, 29, 30, 31, 37, 91, 92, 93, 96, 99, 155, 176
of the moral law
– of free will 24, 28
– reciprocal to the moral law 24, 28
ratio essendi of the categorical imperative 7, 9, 18, 28, 105
ratio essendi of the moral law 2, 3, 5, 16, 21, 24, 27, 29, 50, 52, 99, 105, 176
ratio essendi of the categorical imperative
– *vs* moral law *as such* 18
rational nature 2, 15, 16, 17, 18, 19, 20, 42, 50, 55, 99, 100, 101, 153, 155, 156
rationality 17, 148, 161, 163, 175
realism 7, 63
relationship between *GMM* and *CPrR* 27, 29, 31, 152
relative presuppositions 183

scepticism 14, 98, 104, 105, 178, 180
second person standpoint 180
sensible world 13, 61, 64, 84, 89, 147
sensus communis V, VI, 3, 24, 28, 30, 45, 53, 71, 75, 76, 77, 78, 79, 80, 81, 82, 83, 88, 92, 93, 99, 100, 108, 109, 153, 154, 156, 159, 162, 163, 169, 173, 180, 181, 183
sensus vulgaris 75, 76
sole fact of pure reason 3, 4, 6, 16, 17, 18, 31, 32, 42, 50, 51, 57, 65, 67, 68, 74, 85, 96, 97, 98, 99, 102, 108, 152, 168, 169, 170, 186
– implicitly in *GMM* 19, 168
solipsism 180
subjective principles 2, 15, 54, 55, 156
sublime 81, 84
summum bonum 3, 9, 10, 11, 72, 80, 96, 152

thinking V, VI, 1, 6, 10, 12, 13, 14, 15, 16, 19, 26, 27, 38, 39, 40, 45, 46, 53, 54, 57, 61, 62, 64, 65, 75, 76, 77, 78, 82, 83, 142, 147, 155, 167, 176, 180, 182, 186
third antinomy 73, 79, 86
three worlds 5, 26, 89, 92, 182

transcendental deduction V, 4, 5, 6, 7, 8, 21, 28, 29, 30, 31, 47, 68, 101, 103, 104, 106
transcendental exposition 16
– transcendental 106
typics 64

understanding VI, 1, 2, 3, 4, 5, 6, 7, 8, 9, 10, 11, 12, 13, 14, 15, 16, 18, 19, 20, 21, 22, 23, 24, 26, 27, 28, 32, 35, 36, 37, 38, 39, 41, 43, 44, 45, 46, 47, 48, 49, 51, 52, 53, 54, 58, 60, 61, 63, 64, 66, 68, 75, 76, 77, 78, 79, 80, 82, 84, 85, 86, 88, 89, 94, 96, 97, 98, 99, 100, 101, 102, 106, 109, 141, 142, 146, 148, 151, 153, 154, 156, 160, 166, 170, 172, 179, 180, 185, 186

– broad 45, 46
unity of theoretical and practical reason 23
universal law of mechanism VI, 1, 5, 7, 20, 52, 59, 62, 64, 81, 101
universality 7, 12, 13, 15, 107, 158

Verstand 32, 35, 45, 46, 47, 79
Verstehen 32, 35, 45, 46, 47

WAV 3, 4, 5, 20, 21, 22, 23, 24, 26, 27, 28, 30, 67, 91, 105, 106, 175
world of understanding 60, 61, 62, 63, 81, 89, 182

Persons Index

Allison 3, 4, 22, 27, 105–110, 147, 148
Ameriks 3, 22
Anselm 51, 95, 169

Beck VI, 4, 28, 29, 67, 99, 100
Bell 6
Berger p 45
Beyleveld 5, 7, 8, 9, 10, 24, 62, 63, 73, 74, 161, 180, 185
Bojanowski 4, 5, 8, 24, 28, 66, 86, 101, 104, 105, 166
Bos 5, 8
Brownsword 8

Colleingwood 41, 183–185

Darwall 4, 22, 180
Descartes 27
Dilthey 45
Düwell 8, 161, 181
Düwell 63

Enoch 61, 62, 180

Gadamer 45
Gewirth 5, 8, 9, 22, 62, 142, 180
Grenberg 93
Guyer 4, 21

Hegel 5
Heidegger 45
Henrich 3, 6, 21, 22, 52, 67, 101
Hill 179
Hume 1, 7, 39, 40, 42, 57, 62

Kleingeld VI, 4, 5, 28, 66–67, 99, 100, 176, 179
Korsgaard 3, 62, 179

Longuenesse 6
Luckmann 45
Łuków 93

Makkreel 6, 45
McCarthy 4, 29, 30

O'Neill VI, 3, 4, 5, 6, 11, 30, 40–44, 67, 77, 82, 93, 94, 104

Paton 3, 6, 21
Proops 67
Puls 4, 5, 24, 30, 31, 93

Quine 41

Rawls 3, 22
Reath 3, 22, 41
Rosati 62
Ross 3

Schleiermacher 45
Schönecker 3, 21, 82
Sextus Empiricus 39
Stagneth 66
Steigleder VI, 4, 5, 6, 10, 13, 29, 31, 33, 63, 66, 141–166, 169
Sussman 4, 22, 66

Timmermann 4, 18, 19, 21, 103

Velleman 62

Ware 4, 5, 6, 14, 23, 28, 31, 33, 104, 175–186
Waxman 1, 6, 7
Weber 45
Werner 180
Westphal VI, 3, 5, 6, 7, 11, 39, 40, 42–44, 181
Willaschek 66, 100, 150
Williams, TC 3
Wolff VI, 1, 3, 4, 5, 6, 10, 24, 29, 31, 33, 66, 94, 104, 141, 166–174
Wood 4, 21

Ziche 10, 73, 74

www.ingramcontent.com/pod-product-compliance
Lightning Source LLC
Chambersburg PA
CBHW030651230426
43665CB00011B/1043